Palgrave Shakespeare Studies

General Editors: **Michael Dobson** and **Dympna Callaghan**

Co-founding Editor: **Gail Kern Paster**

Editorial Advisory Board: **Michael Neill**, University of Auckland; **David Schalkwyk**, Folger Shakespeare Library; **Lois D. Potter**, University of Delaware; **Margreta de Grazia**, University of Pennsylvania; **Peter Holland**, University of Notre Dame

Palgrave Shakespeare Studies takes Shakespeare as its focus but strives to understand the significance of his oeuvre in relation to his contemporaries, subsequent writers and historical and political contexts. By extending the scope of Shakespeare and English Renaissance Studies the series will open up the field to examinations of previously neglected aspects or sources in the period's art and thought. Titles in the *Palgrave Shakespeare Studies* series seek to understand anew both where the literary achievements of the English Renaissance came from and where they have brought us.

Titles include:

Pascale Aebischer, Edward J. Esche and Nigel Wheale (*editors*)
REMAKING SHAKESPEARE
Performance across Media, Genres and Cultures

James P. Bednarz
SHAKESPEARE AND THE TRUTH OF LOVE
The Mystery of 'The Phoenix and Turtle'

Mark Thornton Burnett
FILMING SHAKESPEARE IN THE GLOBAL MARKETPLACE

Carla Dente and Sara Soncini (*editors*)
SHAKESPEARE AND CONFLICT
A European Perspective

Cary DiPietro and Hugh Grady (*editors*)
SHAKESPEARE AND THE URGENCY OF NOW
Criticism and Theory in the 21st Century

Kate Flaherty, Penny Gay and L. E. Semler (*editors*)
TEACHING SHAKESPEARE BEYOND THE CENTRE
Australasian Perspectives

Lowell Gallagher and Shankar Raman (*editors*)
KNOWING SHAKESPEARE
Senses, Embodiment and Cognition

Stefan Herbrechter and Ivan Callus (*editors*)
POSTHUMANIST SHAKESPEARES

David Hillman
SHAKESPEARE'S ENTRAILS
Belief, Scepticism and the Interior of the Body

Anna Kamaralli
SHAKESPEARE AND THE SHREW
Performing the Defiant Female Voice

Jane Kingsley-Smith
SHAKESPEARE'S DRAMA OF EXILE

Stephen Purcell
POPULAR SHAKESPEARE
Simulation and Subversion on the Modern Stage

Erica Sheen
SHAKESPEARE AND THE INSTITUTION OF THEATRE

Paul Yachnin and Jessica Slights
SHAKESPEARE AND CHARACTER
Theory, History, Performance, and Theatrical Persons

Palgrave Shakespeare Studies
Series Standing Order ISBN 978–1–403–91164–3 (hardback)
978–1–403–91165–0 (paperback)
(*outside North America only*)

You can receive future titles in this series as they are published by placing a standing order. Please contact your bookseller or, in case of difficulty, write to us at the address below with your name and address, the title of the series and the ISBN quoted above.

Customer Services Department, Macmillan Distribution Ltd, Houndmills, Basingstoke, Hampshire RG21 6XS, England

Shakespeare and the Urgency of Now

Criticism and Theory in the 21st Century

Edited by

Cary DiPietro
University of Toronto Mississauga, Canada

and

Hugh Grady
Arcadia University, USA

palgrave
macmillan

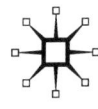

Selection, introduction and editorial matter © Cary DiPietro and
Hugh Grady 2013
Individual chapters © Contributors 2013

All rights reserved. No reproduction, copy or transmission of this
publication may be made without written permission.

No portion of this publication may be reproduced, copied or transmitted
save with written permission or in accordance with the provisions of the
Copyright, Designs and Patents Act 1988, or under the terms of any
licence permitting limited copying issued by the Copyright Licensing
Agency, Saffron House, 6–10 Kirby Street, London EC1N 8TS.

Any person who does any unauthorized act in relation to this publication
may be liable to criminal prosecution and civil claims for damages.

The authors have asserted their rights to be identified as the authors of this
work in accordance with the Copyright, Designs and Patents Act 1988.

First published 2013 by
PALGRAVE MACMILLAN

Palgrave Macmillan in the UK is an imprint of Macmillan Publishers Limited,
registered in England, company number 785998, of Houndmills, Basingstoke,
Hampshire RG21 6XS.

Palgrave Macmillan in the US is a division of St Martin's Press LLC,
175 Fifth Avenue, New York, NY 10010.

Palgrave Macmillan is the global academic imprint of the above companies
and has companies and representatives throughout the world.

Palgrave® and Macmillan® are registered trademarks in the United States,
the United Kingdom, Europe and other countries.

ISBN 978–1–137–01730–7

This book is printed on paper suitable for recycling and made from fully
managed and sustained forest sources. Logging, pulping and manufacturing
processes are expected to conform to the environmental regulations of the
country of origin.

A catalogue record for this book is available from the British Library.

A catalog record for this book is available from the Library of Congress.

Typeset by MPS Limited, Chennai, India.

Contents

List of Illustrations   vii

Foreword: "A Bigger Splash"   viii
Terence Hawkes

Acknowledgments   xix

Notes on Contributors   xx

Introduction   1
Cary DiPietro and Hugh Grady

1 Presentism, Anachronism, and *Titus Andronicus*   9
Cary DiPietro and Hugh Grady

2 The Presentist Threat to Editions of Shakespeare   38
Gabriel Egan

3 Shakespeare Dwelling: *Pericles* and the Affordances of Action   60
Julia Reinhard Lupton

4 Performing Place in *The Tempest*   83
Cary DiPietro

5 Green Economics and the English Renaissance: From Capital to the Commons   103
Charles Whitney

6 "Consuming means, soon preys upon itself": Political Expediency and Environmental Degradation in *Richard II*   126
Lynne Bruckner

7 "What light through yonder window speaks?": The Nature Theater of Oklahoma *Romeo and Juliet* and the Cult(ure) of Shakespeare   148
W. B. Worthen

8 Reification, Mourning, and the Aesthetic in
  Antony and Cleopatra and *The Winter's Tale* 172
  Hugh Grady

9 The Hour is Unknown: *Julius Caesar*, et cetera 188
  Mark Robson

Index 209

List of Illustrations

7.1 Robert M. Johanson and Anne Gridley rehearsing the Nature Theatre of Oklahoma *Romeo and Juliet.* In this photograph, both the footlights and the prompter's box are still under construction. Design by Peter Nigrini   155

Foreword: "A Bigger Splash"

Terence Hawkes

Aging offers curious pleasures and one of them involves our experience of the past. Like most people, I can remember many events that lodge in the mind with some urgency. Some are more obviously important than others: explosions, accidents, the deaths of presidents and monarchs. Some are wholly personal: births, deaths, songs, books, films, and plays. They all exist in the flurry of circumstances with which experience surrounds us. Then, as the years develop, some that seemed irretrievably personal seem to acquire a specific, nonpersonal dimension. An actor becomes extremely famous, a book gains popularity, a film begins a trend, a politician rises to eminence. Certain events seem to become underlined: they stand out, their progress can be plotted, their lifecycle is fixed, they subside, or ascend, into a quite different realm of being. We are often surprised to discover that they are not simply events that have occurred "in the past": they have become "history."

This sense, that history is made in the collective mind and not by the single percipient, is part of everyone's experience. What we call "history" is transmitted or awarded not while we experience things but much later, subsequently and after we have watched them. The idea is neatly presented in W. H. Auden's poem "Musée des Beaux Arts," as Breughel's painting of the fall of Icarus focuses on that phenomenon. It is clear that the tragedy of Icarus's flight to freedom is barely noticed by anybody as it occurs, and that the moment is only marked in the museum by a painting that depicts the event almost in its absence:

> ... how everything turns away
> Quite leisurely from the disaster; the ploughman may
> Have heard the splash, the forsaken cry,
> But for him it was not an important failure: the sun shone
> As it had to on the white legs disappearing into the green
> Water; and the expensive delicate ship that must have seen
> Something amazing, a boy falling out of the sky,
> Had somewhere to get to and sailed calmly on.

The essence of the poem proposes that, until now, we have not been able to articulate what happened then. The "Musée des Beaux Arts," acting perhaps in the way that art ought to, indicates what the people portrayed in the painting do not see. Their "now" subsequently establishes what we see as the "then." There is a quite different poem on Brueghel's painting written by William Carlos Williams, called "Landscape with the Fall of Icarus." It navigates different territory, but reaches a similar conclusion:

>   unsignificantly
>   off the coast
>   there was
>
>   a splash quite unnoticed
>   this was
>   Icarus drowning

We live in a confusing and perplexed world at the mercy of innumerable pressures, but perhaps we can be guided by the example of Icarus. With his "quite unnoticed" splash in mind, it would be foolish to erect a clear and firm notion of what any myth or fable or art can bring to or represent in our culture. In the case of Shakespeare, our sense of the role offered by his theatre and his plays seems almost literally up for grabs. Economic pressures, political processes, educational programs all want a piece of the Bard, and the evidence provided by an anthology called *Shakespeare and the Urgency of Now* will do well to respect these claims. To look for one specific symptom or set of concerns that includes all the other claimants would be impossible. However, there is one obvious issue that perhaps prevails and its spoor manifests itself quite distinctly in the current jungle. It is one that unites all the recent and powerful new discourses, all the new readings and reweaving of the work of a playwright from 400 years ago, and in the process it generates various frames of reference that demand attention. It involves the notion of history.

The sense that we *make* history, that we *have* to make it, and that we can therefore hope to choose which histories we *do* make, leads snugly into the issue of how the past and the present coexist in us and how each affects the other. When we consider the notion of Shakespeare's "urgency of now" with which the pieces in the present volume are concerned, this becomes supremely important. The surface of contemporary consciousness produces many bubbles and all kinds of surprising and apparently unconnected winds burst and whistle through them. Yet it is also true that these dissimilar institutional, economic, and environmental pressures seem to make use of Shakespeare as a distinctive cultural enterprise. Of course, we could treat each of Shakespeare's plays as an independent signifying object in its own right, with its own commitment to an early seventeenth-century process of cause and effect. However, this does not deal with the massive "Shakespeare" role that all of the plays have in our culture. As Hugh Grady and Cary DiPietro argue in the Introduction to this volume, the concern here is with the whole of the "Shakespeare" issue in our society. Given that the theoretical innovations of our world "draw from the discourses of our present historical moment," they feel quite rightly that they need to focus on a movement that most clearly emerged in the wake of the apparent triumph of historicism.[1] The essence of the "urgency of now" is quite clearly focused in what replaced it. They call it "critical Presentism."

We know, nevertheless, that the problem of history is long-dwelling and we must avoid one major Scylla and one Charybdis. The first is noted by the historian E. H. Carr and is indicated by the magic words used by three generations of historians: *Wie es eigentlich gewesen* (as it actually happened). As Carr indicates, this is "like an incantation–designed like most incantations to save them from the tiresome obligation to think for themselves."[2] The Charybdis is mentioned by Sir George Clark, in his introduction to *The Cambridge Modern History*. It claims that "since all historical judgements involve persons and points of view, one is as good as another and there is no 'objective' historical truth."[3]

Of course, certain truths seem inescapable. Still, it is the case that they do not tell us finally "what actually happened" on the one hand, or alternatively suggest that one judgment is necessarily as good as another. The events of September 3, 1939 (the date Britain and France declared war on Germany) seem to represent an evident truth in respect of European and indeed world history. However, there is also a sense in which something much less concrete or objective is also true. A different response, for instance, took place to this event in the United States (which declared war on Germany on December 11, 1941), and the response of Germany and its allies, including Russia, would also no doubt have been different.

In a different key, many at the first performance of *Hamlet* would have recognized the name of the playwright in question, but the bulk of the audience would never have read any of Shakespeare's works. Most of them could not read.[4] I always hoped to surprise some of my younger students by suggesting that Shakespeare had never read Dryden, Pope, Wordsworth, Keats, or Shelley. But the truth is that by now, in the modern world, of course he has. We cannot separate Shakespeare from the literature that came after (as well as before) him in our culture and that makes us respond to him as part and parcel of what that literature in the end involves. This will include both its principles of inclusion and exclusion: what the literary canon requires that we read and what for various reasons it forbids. These constitute the unstated but rigid principles by which what we call literature licenses how we concern ourselves with the world. The same is equally the case if we include major thinkers like Marx or Freud. Shakespeare certainly influenced both of these philosophers and the plain truth is that now they influence him. To deny that is to deny the necessary reverberation and reechoing in that continuing memory vault in which all cultures persist. To accept it helps to initiate the discussion of Presentism.

Presentism presents us with an unending dialogue between present and past, and demands interaction between what we call "facts" from both ends of that 400-year channel of time. The undeniable patterns that the present imposes on the past, its notions "of which literary figures to lionize, which to mythologize, and of what stimulates the desire to make meanings of texts from earlier historical conjectures," assume primary importance.[5] Major concerns will be with the questions of "place," and of history "in a place," whether this is concerned with space, time, or culture, and there is no doubt that the essays presented here clearly take time to deal with that question.

For instance, in Lynne Bruckner's chapter she indicates that the issue of the environment and its relation to human beings has a crucial role. Nobody is able to legislate for significant environmental change, unless that change leads to further degradation of the world in which we live. This continues a pattern that she observes in *Richard II* indicating how the king mandates the exploitation of natural resources, which shadows the human and nonhuman worlds. Only at Richard's death does he find the "human humus" from which the plant-like Bolingbroke will grow. From a similar viewpoint, Cary DiPietro's careful essay considers our attachment to "place" and to a sense of belonging to a particular place in the world. His chapter on *The Tempest* poses a crucial question: how does our ethical commitment to the preservation of places of cultural heritage or the integrity of local ecology square with the ways in which theatre functions and perhaps commit us to collapsing geographical and temporal distances in generating a worldview? Interestingly, the theatre's illusion of nearness to place may in fact motivate an "ethic of responsibility" toward ecology, which combines our felt attachment to place with the theatre's roles as a virtual network of global information.[6]

The broader issue of place also concerns Julia Reinhart Lupton. As her essay on *Pericles* observes, the past and present are linked by the play's emphasis on "a church of craft"; that is, "an environment where any and all acts of making have value to our humanness."[7] In those experiments in living constructed within her shelter—almost an academy—Marina exercises a deliberate form of craftivism designed to secure and transmit a range of knowledges, virtues, and comportments, which foster the possibility of politics. So the play uses culture to embody "the urgency of the now" with particular reference to the present place of performance, in the theatre. *Pericles* thus investigates human efforts to generate political speech out of theological and biopolitical forms of life, and seems to urge drama's commitment to transformation through theatrical making, active audition, and hermeneutic reencounter. As a result, on the stage, Marina becomes almost a priestess of culture.

However, this volume does not offer a "Presentism" that collapses past and present into a transcendent timelessness. In fact, it acknowledges the process and the practice of what dialogue with the past actually entails. Essentially, it offers a demonstration of a process rather than a theoretical manifesto, a series of gestures that allows the critic to lay his cards on the table, while at the same time showing in surprising ways how "the political unconscious" works in particular situations. Indeed, "making meaning," as I have characterized this activity elsewhere, requires the active preservation of the scholarly critic, alive to contemporary social, political, and cultural concerns and with a capacity that extends far beyond the restricted and restrictive ideological business of mobilizing "judgment."[8] In this respect, Charles Whitney's chapter adds a necessary economic gloss to the notion of place. It links the early modern assault on commons rights to today's assault on the environmental commons, juxtaposing the present historical moment to the moment of *As You Like It*. Whitney traces parallels between today's so-called New Economics, which is strongly inflected by green tendencies, and traditional, morally inflected economic attitudes and practices of the early modern period.

It is important that the realm of the aesthetic takes up two of the essays in this volume. Hugh Grady's chapter is quite specific, saying that the interpretation of Shakespeare is always closely linked to the aesthetic practices and assumptions of the interpreter's era, and it is hard to disagree with that. Approaching the subject historically, he argues that aesthetics now seems to be secular, in that it includes the political. This has an impact on such Shakespeare plays as *Antony and Cleopatra* and *The Winter's Tale*. Grady makes the point that in both of these works, Shakespeare implies a concept of the aesthetic as an aspect of an emerging secular modernity, one that uses death and mourning as resources to create tragic and tragi-comic beauty. Meanwhile, Mark Robson urges that within Shakespeare's texts an aesthetics of dissociation prevails. Characters remark on something as extraneous or outlandish and the effect is a process of formal estrangement, in which the presentation of that content is itself strange. In the case of *Julius Caesar*, this is most obviously conveyed as a relation between time and death, in which the emphasis is placed on a "trembling" between predictability and unpredictability. The frequent invocation of omens, portents, dreams, soothsaying, and so on marks a desire to master the future that is repeatedly frustrated. The oscillation between the known and the unknown—for characters and for the audience—takes on a particular political charge with the play's staging of debates over sovereignty, legitimacy, and the mechanics of power. The numerous strategies that characters and the play offer for controlling—or failing to control—the future are related back to a consideration of the structural and formal openness of Shakespearean drama itself.

Given this shifting between known and unknown, the question of what we think of as the fundamental rock of the Shakespeare experience, the text of the plays, naturally also draws considerable

Presentist attention. We know that playscripts began as handwritten authorial papers and that these, or copies of them, must have been licensed by the state censor. We know that someone must have written out single actors' parts, with each containing just the speeches spoken by one character plus the cues. Perhaps the songs were written out on further pieces of paper and taken away for setting to music, and "letters"—and other documents to be read aloud as part of the action—must have been copied out to make properties. The more we think about it, the more it seems that the artistic unity of an early modern playscript disappears before our eyes and in its place emerges a collection of mutable fragments leading semi-independent lives in the textual economy of the early modern theatre. As Gabriel Egan observes, this is disturbingly well suited to our dominant post-theoretical, post-modern, Presentist taste for the fragmentary over the coherent, the mutable over the stable, multiplicity over singularity. However, Egan's essay explores some of the consequences that develop when editors are willing to emend, finding the paradoxical effect that radical textual interventions may produce conservative readings and conservative editing may produce radical readings.

Against this background, more than one notion of "staging" is discussed in this volume. Of course, this sort of commitment has a long history. More than 40 years ago in the 1960s, John Barton and Peter Hall committed themselves to a kind of "Presentism" in the staging of their significant production of *The Wars of the Roses*. As Peter Hall put it, "There is no such thing as a perfect and enduring interpretation, or one that lets 'the play speak for itself,'" adding "what follows is therefore an expression of what we found meaningful in the 1960s in Shakespeare's view of history. Its value is ephemeral, and its judgements are inevitably... of the decade which produced it and us."[9] It is true that you cannot simply let a Shakespeare play "speak for itself." Other issues will have their say. Worse, all public discourses can find themselves recruited into the same narrative when one mode of discourse tips into another. They may seem to speak different things, but in effect they all seem to say the same thing. This is the sort of area when the aesthetics of a production, as well as the staging, becomes of great interest to the Presentist critic, particularly when the public discourses surrounding a production begin to infiltrate and even take over the production itself. For instance, when the subterranean movements of the John Profumo–Christine Keeler affair surfaced in London in 1963–4, it produced a major scandal. John Profumo was the highly respected Member of Parliament for Stratford, no less, and his activities must certainly have generated a kind of public concern with heresy and revolution to which *The Wars of the Roses* would also have felt vitally connected. Certainly, most Presentist critics, particularly those concerned with the process of "making meaning," would think that worthy of notice.

The fact that public discourses may find themselves inhabiting a similar narrative to a play also sparks W. B. Worthen's essay, which looks at a delightful literary reconstitution or even a dramatic recrudescence of *Romeo and Juliet*. In a production by The Nature Theatre of Oklahoma, two actors perform the play not simply, but rather in the form of the story of the play as it is recalled by eight participants, something that leads to what might be called a different shaping of history. In short, The Nature Theatre of Oklahoma offers a *Romeo and Juliet* that addresses the spectral status of Shakespeare as literary dramatist, and it indicates the social consequences of the principal paradigm that sustains a "literary" conception of drama in performance. In a casual, often embarrassed, even irritable discourse, it uses the performance of the play as a mode of inquiry into contemporary US culture. Like Mark Twain's comic version of *Romeo and Juliet*, it offers contemporary American speech to evidence a newly democratic, demotic Shakespeare. This newly formed Shakespeare's language is "imprecise... repetitive, slangy, cool rather than learned... and full of ums, ands, ahhs."[10] As a result, The Nature Theatre of Oklahoma explores a widespread legitimation crisis, having to do with the relationship between Shakespeare's authorial inscription, his writing, and the forms of its cultural transmission—as literature, as theatre, and in contemporary pedagogy. Worthen takes an important Presentist concern with the political sense of a "ministerial" notion of theatre, in which performance essentially restates, "edits" or "interprets," literary drama by other means. He assesses the widespread publication of "modern" or "popular" translations of Shakespeare's plays and concludes that the concept that this offers mere "interpretations" of the text must surely be untrustworthy.

Most Presentists would agree heartily with this: "All history is contemporary history," as the Italian historian Benedetto Croce said. Indeed, it is on the battleground of the present, with all of its subterfuges, its deviations, its conflicts, and its resolutions, that the future will be ultimately secured. Inherent in the activities of Presentism in this volume is a manifesto for future action that challenges both the mystifications to which literary texts have been subjected and many of those demystifications that have claimed to liberate it. Thus, it is important that we should also take up the part played in Britain by different non-English races, which have always occupied an important, sometimes even central role in the country's history and so impinge on its role in the present.

In short, we should not forget that Britain has certainly, since well before the Middle Ages, never been a simple funfair for the "English," but always a racial playground. A large number of those citizens involved in the relatively new entity called "Britain"—a massive ideological project that obsessed Tudor and Stuart politicians—either spoke odd varieties of English or were chiefly proficient in languages in addition to English. England was only one of the four civilizations that made Britain: the others were Ireland, Scotland, and Wales.

To take merely one example, Shakespeare's Henry V proudly confessed that "I am a Welshman" and later "I am Welsh, you know, good countryman" (*Henry V*, 4.1.52 and 4.7.103). The actors who performed the plays would have contained at least two players who in fact speak Welsh on stage, Owain Glyndwr and his daughter, Lady Mortimer. The text of *1 Henry IV* indicates a completed interchange with her father: as the text says, "*Glyndwr speaks to her in Welsh, and she answers him in the same*," followed by three full speeches in which "*The lady speaks in Welsh*" (3.1.192–206), culminating in her singing of a "*Welsh song*" (238). The whole passage, in a language that is completely different from English, may take about ten minutes. Indeed, there was a time when prophecies about the return of the Welsh hero-king to rule over the whole island of Britain almost seemed about to come true. Henry VII was certainly a Welshman. He packed his court with his countrymen, named his eldest son Arthur, and took care to observe St. David's day. As the lineaments of the Tudor dynasty unfolded, Welsh speakers poured into London. As Gwyn A. Williams puts it, "An integrated Britain becomes visible first in a major migration of the Welsh to the centre of power," the process reaching its climax in the reign of Elizabeth I.[11] Under Elizabeth, denounced by A. L. Rowse as "that red-headed Welsh harridan," the "remote and distinguished past" of the Welsh effectively made available—at least in influential intellectual terms—some sort of underpinning for the new "British" national identity. For English speakers, of course, that meant coming face to face with an almost unacceptable "given": it runs full tilt into a material human world that seems wholly other. Worse, shockingly, it is one that claims rights to the same island.

The current rise of nationalist sentiment throughout the world makes this issue very much a Presentist concern. However, since we began with the high-flying Icarus, then perhaps we should finish with him. Many poets have written about Icarus, and about Brueghel. However, one of the most interesting notions is contained in a disturbing painting—whose subject is not necessarily Icarus at all—by David Hockney. Deliberately pointing to the absence of any real sense of history, it suggests someone diving into a pool in California in which any semblance of an individual has been wholly removed. All we now see is a violent motion of the water. Perhaps we will rush to supply a figure, to make it indicate a person or an event. But the artist does not. The painting's title is the real clue about what Icarus seems to be representing for a world afflicted with multiple opportunities for meanings, from which, for a split second, it is required to make history. Here is history immediately before history is made: it is as if Icarus (if it is he) has only just entered the water and we know nothing about him or any of his adventures. We respond, stunned, to this "urgency of now." It is a fine example of a moment where Presentism astonishingly begins to drench us with the enormous—though brief—display of its powers. Its title seems wholly suitable for my foreword for this volume. It is called, simply, "A Bigger Splash."

Notes

1. Many people currently seem to be writing about history and Presentism with discernment and I daresay that I quote from some of them without overtly meaning to. In this paragraph, I'm quoting from DiPietro and Grady in their Introduction to this volume, p. 3, though also with reference to, amongst others, John Drakakis, "The Critical Process of Terence Hawkes," forthcoming in *Poetics Today*.
2. E. H. Carr, *What Is History* (Harmondsworth: Penguin Books, 1985), pp. 8–9.
3. See *The New Cambridge Modern History* 1 (Cambridge: University of Cambridge Press 1957), pp. xxiv–xxv.

4. It is as well to remember that the Elizabethans did not know themselves as "Elizabethans." The word "Tudor" was probably never used in that time to refer to Tudor monarchs.
5. Drakakis, "The Critical Process of Terence Hawkes," p. 11 (manuscript). I'm also using terms proposed by a variety of critics.
6. DiPietro, Chapter 6, p. 86.
7. Lupton, quoting the Church of Craft mission statement (online), Chapter 3, p. 60.
8. In my *Shakespeare in the Present* (London: Routledge, 2002), pp. 3–22.
9. John Barton and Peter Hall, *The Wars of the Roses* (London: BBC, 1970), pp. viii–ix.
10. Worthen, Chapter 7, p. 150.
11. See Gwyn A. Williams, *When Was Wales* (London: Black Raven Press, 1985), pp. 121–3.

Acknowledgments

The initial ideas for this anthology were gestated in discussions one or both of us had with Terence Hawkes, Evelyn Gajowski, and Lynne Braddock, particularly in the aftermath of the MLA Special Session: Radical Temporalities in Shakespeare Studies at the Modern Language Association Convention, January 7, 2011 in Los Angeles, CA. with papers by Cary DiPietro, Evelyn Gajowski, and Hugh Grady.

In addition, we thank all our contributors for their positive reactions and individual contributions. We thank also Sharon O'Dair, who was very helpful in the late stages of this work.

The Introduction and Chapter 1 by Cary DiPietro and Hugh Grady both contain material from our earlier joint article, "Presentism, Anachronism and the Case of *Titus Andronicus*," *Shakespeare*, 8.1 (2012): 44–73 (http://www.tandfonline.com/doi/full/10.1080/17450918.2012.660277). Chapter 1 is an abridged, recontextualized, and revised version of that original essay. The Introduction contains passages taken and recontextualized from the earlier essay as well. The material is used with the permission of Routledge, publishers of the journal *Shakespeare* in which the original article appeared.

Notes on Contributors

Lynne Bruckner received her PhD from Rutgers University, and is currently Professor of English at Chatham University. She has published on Sidney, Chaucer, Johnson, and Shakespeare. She is first editor (with Dan Brayton of Middlebury College) of *Ecocritical Shakespeare* (2011) and has a chapter, "Nature and the Difference *She* Makes," in *Ecofeminist Approaches to Early Modernity* (eds. Jennifer Munroe and Rebecca Laroche, 2011). She has also published ecocritical articles on contemporary literature and film.

Cary DiPietro teaches at the University of Toronto Mississauga. He is the author of *Shakespeare and Modernism* (2006; reissued 2009), which explores the interactions between two cultural moments, Shakespeare's and that of the early twentieth century. He is also editor of Volume 9 in the *Great Shakespeareans* series (Gen. Eds. Peter Holland and Adrian Poole), published in May 2011. Recent work includes articles and book reviews in *New Theatre Quarterly*, *Shakespeare Survey*, and the journal *Shakespeare*, and a chapter on Shakespeare and George Bernard Shaw in *Shakespeare and the Irish Writer* (ed. Janet Clare and Stephen O'Neill, 2010).

Gabriel Egan is Professor of Shakespeare Studies at De Montfort University. He is the author of *Shakespeare and Marx* (2004) and *Green Shakespeare: From Ecopolitics to Ecocriticism* (2006). His most recent book is *The Struggle for Shakespeare's Text: Twentieth Century Editorial Theory and Practice* (2011). He is working on computer applications for the study of press variants and compositor stints in early Shakespeare editions.

Hugh Grady is Professor of English at Arcadia University. His books include *The Modernist Shakespeare: Critical Texts in a Material World* (1991), *Shakespeare's Universal Wolf: Essays in Early Modern Reification* (1996), *Shakespeare, Machiavelli, and Montaigne: Power and Subjectivity from "Richard II" to "Hamlet"* (2002) and, most recently, *Shakespeare and Impure Aesthetics* (2009). He is the editor of the critical anthology

Shakespeare and Modernity: From Early Modern to Millennium (2000) and co-editor with Terence Hawkes of *Presentist Shakespeares* (2007). He has contributed to the *Cambridge Companion to Shakespeare Studies*, the *Oxford Companion to Shakespeare*, and the *Greenwood Shakespeare Encyclopedia*.

Terence Hawkes is Emeritus Professor at Cardiff University, Wales. He is the author of *Shakespeare and the Reason* (1964, 2005), *Metaphor* (1972), *Structuralism and Semiotics* (1977, 2003), *Shakespeare's Talking Animals* (1973), *That Shakespeherian Rag* (1986, 2005), *Meaning by Shakespeare* (1992), and *Shakespeare in the Present* (2002). He was general editor of the *New Accents* series and *Accents on Shakespeare* and an editor of the journal *Textual Practice*. He was co-editor, with Hugh Grady, of *Presentist Shakespeares* (2007).

Julia Reinhard Lupton is Professor of English and Comparative Literature at the University of California, Irvine, and founder of Humanities Out There. She is the author or co-author of four books on Shakespeare, including *Thinking with Shakespeare: Essays on Politics and Life* (2011). She has also written two trade books with her sister Ellen Lupton on DIY design, including *Design Your Life: The Pleasures and Perils of Everyday Things* (2009). She is currently writing a book on Shakespeare and hospitality.

Mark Robson is Professor of English and Theatre Studies at the University of Dundee. He is the author of *Stephen Greenblatt* (2008) and *The Sense of Early Modern Writing* (2006), co-author of *Language in Theory* (2005), editor of *Jacques Rancière: Aesthetics, Politics, Philosophy* (2005), and has written many essays on Shakespeare and early modern culture. He is co-author of *Shakespeare, Jonson and the Claims of the Performative* (with James Loxley, 2013) and editor of *What Is Literature?* (2013). He is currently working on a book on the poetics and politics of suicide. In 2011–12, Robson was Visiting Fellow at the Institute of Advanced Study in the Humanities at the University of Edinburgh.

Charles Whitney is Professor of English at the University of Nevada, Las Vegas. His "Dekker's and Middleton's Plague Pamphlets as Environmental Literature" appeared in *Representing the Plague in*

Early Modern England (2010). He is the author of *Francis Bacon and Modernity* (1986) and *Early Responses to Renaissance Drama* (2006), which won the 2008 Elizabeth Dietz Memorial Award from *SEL* and Rice University for the Best Book in Early Modern Studies. He has published in *English Literary Renaissance, Journal of the History of Ideas, Borrowers and Lenders, Clio, Shakespeare Quarterly*, and elsewhere. He edited the collection *Thomas Lodge* (2011) and his essay "Shakespeare's Early Reception and Reputation" is forthcoming in the *Cambridge World Shakespeare Encyclopedia*.

W. B. Worthen is Alice Brady Pels Professor in the Arts, and Chair of the Department of Theatre at Barnard College, Columbia University, where he is also Co-Chair of the Ph.D. program in Theatre, Professor in the Division of Theatre, School of the Arts, and in the Department of English and Comparative Literature. His publications include *Drama: Between Poetry and Performance* (2010), *Print and the Poetics of Modern Drama* (2006, 2009), *Shakespeare and the Force of Modern Performance* (2003), *Shakespeare and the Authority of Performance* (1997), *Modern Drama and the Rhetoric of Theater* (1992), *The Idea of the Actor* (1984), and a wide range of articles in *TDR, PMLA, Shakespeare Quarterly, Modern Drama, Theatre Journal, Shakespeare Survey*, and other journals. He is the editor of *The Wadsworth Anthology of Drama*, and a past editor of *Theatre Journal* and *Modern Drama*.

Introduction

Cary DiPietro and Hugh Grady

Shakespeare has attained his iconic place in global culture today through an extraordinary series of recontextualizations and refashionings of his great oeuvre.[1] He continues to have a presence that can be aesthetically powerful—in private readings, in the theatre, and on film—as well as culturally formative—in school and higher education, and in popular culture. This strong Shakespearean presence in the contemporary world may evoke for some the idea of universal genius, as the "timelessness" implicit in the characterization of his friend by the contemporary playwright and poet Ben Jonson, who famously wrote that Shakespeare was "not of an age, but for all time." However, it is the contention of this volume that, far from creating a sense of timelessness, the omnipresence of Shakespeare in our multicultural present bespeaks instead something more remarkable: our ability to reshape and rethink Shakespeare across time and space, to turn the reading and watching of the plays into a creative encounter between 400-year-old texts and active, creative readers and audiences in the present, passionately involved in appropriating and reunderstanding these "timeless" works.

Of course, set against Shakespeare in the present is a Shakespeare whose temporal and cultural alterity foregrounds the distance between present and past, as well as the myriad cultural differences of our post-colonial, post-national global society. Even when resisted, though, the presence of Shakespeare now presses upon us with an urgency felt in the immediacy of our engagements. Now is a moment—always fleeting, ever changing—precariously positioned between what has (just) happened and what will be; moreover, the necessary urgency of now implies some necessity of agency, that we can somehow and perhaps should intervene to determine how the consequences of things that have happened will unfold in the future—that we have to act now! Where, then, does Shakespeare figure in the much more urgently felt immediacies of our changing world, in light of the markedly precarious state of the world's politics, ecology, and economy? By the same token, how do economic, environmental, and institutional pressures interpenetrate Shakespeare as a cultural enterprise—in performance, film, popular culture, global appropriation—and no less in academic criticism? What is gained or lost by bridging the 400 years of chronological distance that separate us from Shakespeare as a historical object and addressing Shakespeare in the urgency of now?

Ever since Martin Luther King, Jr. first evoked the "fierce urgency of now" in the American civil rights movement in the early 1960s, his trope has become ubiquitous.[2] It continues to be a powerful slogan for civil rights and political protest. It is frequently intoned by global anti-poverty and social equality activists. Barack Obama repeatedly evoked it during his 2008 presidential campaign of hope and change. With good reason, the urgency of King's phrase resounds strongly when employed in the global environmental movement, for example in Al Gore's *An Inconvenient Truth*.[3] Far from becoming a cliché, however, the repeated appropriation of King's coinage exemplifies how the recontextualization of words spoken in different places and times can retain the force of their original utterance—in this case, the persuasive power and beauty of King's speeches, the legacy of his advocacy, and the magnitude of the sense of loss produced by his assassination—even while they are translated into new and ever-shifting contexts. As such, the legacy of King's words demonstrates through analogy a fundamental principle exemplified in the approach to Shakespeare's plays by the essays collected in this volume: that the significance of texts is never static or "timeless," but rather involves a negotiation and constant renegotiation between horizons of interpretation and an ever-shifting present, from which we view the past with new understandings, with different interpretive lenses, with different senses of what is important and relevant, and what is not.

The essays in this volume address in a variety of ways the intersections between Shakespeare, history, and the present, a variety that includes a range of methodological approaches, some well established and others providing decidedly new interventions. In doing so, we hope that the essays recapture the lost urgency that theory and cultural studies inspired when they first had a full-force impact on literary criticism. The multiplicity and variety of dialogue that literary theory produced were marked in Shakespeare studies by collections of essays such as *Political Shakespeare, Alternative Shakespeares, Shakespeare and the Question of Theory, The Matter of Difference,* and *Shakespeare, Theory, and Performance*.[4] Starting in the mid to late 1990s, the New Historicism and cultural theory began to evolve from their earlier emphasis on literary theory into what was called post-theoretical criticism—a turn to the new, but also a return to the literary and historical interests of a prior generation of criticism. Instead of disappearing, however, theory has reemerged in several new guises—in a new theoretical discourse about citizenship and states of emergency drawing on the Italian theorist Giorgio Agamben and the controversial early twentieth-century German political theorist Carl Schmitt; in the applied deconstruction of the late works of Jacques Derrida; in a renewed interest in aesthetic theory drawing on Derrida, Theodor Adorno, and Walter Benjamin; and in reinvigorated, well-established theoretical traditions like feminism, Marxism, and ecocriticism, often in dialogue with some of the newer approaches. All of these theoretical innovations, however, draw from the discourses of our present historical moment, and in that sense represent another counter-discourse that emerged in the wake of the apparent triumph of historicism, the movement known as Presentism.

Not all of the writers in this volume will necessarily identify with this designation, no less because the critical application of the term "Presentism" continues to be confused with its original meaning as a pejorative designating a naïve approach to the past that fails to take historical differences into account. Nevertheless, taken together, the essays collected here continue the project of Presentism reasserted in the relatively recent works of Terence Hawkes, Hugh Grady, Ewan Fernie, and many others.[5] However, Presentism, as Grady and Hawkes wrote in the Introduction to their critical anthology *Presentist Shakespeares*, was not intended as a term designating only one specific critical methodology. It was meant instead to be a "big tent" under which a number of different contemporary critical tendencies could be grouped—tendencies with the shared view that a wholly historicist approach to literary criticism is reductive of the complexities of reading in the present. In many ways, they argued, the New Historicism and the Cultural Materialism of 1985 to the recent past were already Presentist: self-conscious of their situation in our own culture, making use of forms of theory that were developed far after the age of Shakespeare, and very much engaged directly and indirectly with cultural and political issues of our own times. Nevertheless, it was evident already in the mid to late 1990s, and became obvious by 2005, that the trend in the field had developed away from this Presentist dimension of what was beginning to be called simply "materialist" criticism and toward something more and more similar to positivist "old historicism."[6] That was the context in which *Presentist Shakespeares* was conceived and developed, and a number of different kinds of Presentism were offered in that initial anthology and in several subsequent works. And of course there were many like-minded scholar-critics working independently along the same lines. A variety of different approaches to the best way to work with the dialectic of past and present were and are in evidence, as can be seen quite clearly in the present volume.

The essays collected here share an approach to the past based on a self-conscious positioning of the perceiver in the present, aware of historical difference but aware as well of the approachable but real epistemological barrier between ourselves and the past—and deliberately choosing to highlight our presentness, whether as a methodological starting point, the inevitable horizon of interpretation, or its enabling condition. As such, the essays share a set of general principles, but they are also a response to the specific current situation in English studies. We are still oscillating between two poles of English studies that kept reasserting themselves in different forms throughout the twentieth century and continue into the twenty-first, an oscillation that has to do with two competing missions for the field and two different emphases between the original meanings of the texts at their moment of origin and their meaning for us in our present. Without historical consciousness, we are in danger of succumbing to a false universalism. However, without a firm understanding that the meaning of the past is rooted in our reconstruction of it in the present, we are in danger of immersing ourselves in an empty search for facts and differences for their own sake.

It was the eighteenth-century German Romantic theorist Johann Gottfried Herder who in effect invented historicism by emphasizing changing ideologies, assumptions, and mental frameworks as history developed from one era to the next. The term "presentism" developed within German historicism as a pejorative, indicating the fallacy of not taking into account the profound differences in mental outlooks between one era's "worldview" and another's.[7] Ultimately, the new consciousness of the possibility of committing a "presentist" error led to the development of professionalized research agendas for the new academic field of literary studies that developed in the late nineteenth and early twentieth centuries—agendas involving precisely the attempt to reconstitute the vanished mental frameworks that underlay the literary masterpieces studied in the new setting of the modern research university. Shakespeare studies was more than typical of this development; the study of Shakespeare helped lead the way. One of Herder's best-known arguments for the need to critique Enlightenment notions of universal rationality and develop a more historicist understanding of the cultural works of the past was his long essay "Shakespeare," published in 1773, in which he championed Shakespeare against neoclassical critics and their belief that universal reason had established one correct strategy for writing tragedy.[8]

Historical criticism, as is well known, was challenged in the early twentieth century by the Cambridge and American New Critics, only to return, in a radically new form influenced by the rise of critical cultural theory, in the New Historicism and Cultural Materialism that have shaped contemporary Shakespeare studies. More recently, the enthusiasm for theory (as we noted above) has waned considerably, and the 1990s and much of the 2000s have walked a tightrope called "post-theory," which has attempted to retain the pragmatic hermeneutic techniques of theory without concerning itself with theory per se. As a result, it is becoming harder and harder to distinguish much recent historicist criticism from an earlier generation's old historicism. In short, in our own time, as happened earlier in the twentieth century, the force of professional routine and the dynamics of publication and credentialing are at work to domesticate methods that once challenged complacency as the New Historicism and Cultural Materialism of the 1980s have slowly evolved into today's deradicalized historicisms. Behind the calls in recent years for a renewed scholarship of facts can easily be discerned a professionalist agenda of self-reproduction. Of course, a scholarship of facts can provide matter for dissertations and journal articles necessary in an era of unprecedented expectations for publication by young scholars. We all know the market forces and professionalist processes through which this situation evolved, and certainly it is a reality that must be attended to. However, a scholarship of facts forms an immensely instrumental agenda for Shakespeare studies, one that threatens to forget the socially critical mission of literary education in our society. For the academic study of literature is only an end to a larger means in modern liberal societies. If universities and colleges fail to *apply* the study of literature to issues of value, to political debates, to larger issues of meaning in the present, then they will have failed one of their crucial social functions. We live in a world where the institutions through which political society has conducted its debates and probed larger questions of meaning are in crisis. Newspapers, television, radio, and in general the intermediate citizen-bodies that in the past constituted democratic civil society are weakening and succumbing to practices that marginalize rationality in favor of sensation, deliberate distortions, and continual public hysteria. Colleges and universities cannot solve this problem by themselves, but they can certainly contribute to a solution by maintaining and protecting arenas of rational discourse, debate, and critical reflection on values and politics.

This is what the writers in this volume of essays do. They recognize that the stakes are high. They understand that the work we do is not only at a crisis point, one that is urgently felt in the lived realities of teaching and studying in the university today, but that this work—the questions we ask of literature, the methods we use to interrogate it, and the meanings we derive from it—circulates in and provides arenas of critical discourse and debate, in communities shared with students, colleagues, peers, readers, audiences, and so on. We hope that by forging analogies between the felt immediacies of our world now and the historically situated texts of Shakespeare's plays, the essays presented here will help to forestall a deradicalized historicism by emphasizing, rather than the *facts* of the past, the ever-shifting nature of historical context and, rather than the inevitable inescapability of our presentness, its necessity. The chapters below demonstrate, each in its own way, that those same analogies can lead us through Shakespeare's plays to new understandings of our own world and its urgently felt crises, and that critical reflection and discourse continue, as ever, to be urgently needed *now*.

Notes

1. The present Introduction draws on arguments recontextualized and revised from our joint essay, "Presentism, Anachronism and the Case of *Titus Andronicus*," *Shakespeare*, 8.1 (2012): 44–73. Some verbatim passages from that article, however, are also included here.
2. King coined the expression in his famous "I Have a Dream" speech, delivered on the steps of the Lincoln Memorial in Washington on August 23, 1963. He also invoked it in a later speech, "Beyond Vietnam," delivered at a meeting of Clergy and Laity Concerned at Riverside Church (New York City, April 4, 1967)—not without controversy, to criticize America's military involvement in the Vietnam War. See Martin Luther King, Jr., *A Call to Conscience: The Landmark Speeches of Dr. Martin Luther King, Jr.*, ed. Clayborne Carson and Kris Shephard (Atlanta, GA: IPM, 2001), pp. 82 and 162 respectively.
3. Quoting King's speech in 1967. Al Gore, *An Inconvenient Truth: The Planetary Emergency of Global Warming and What We Can Do about It* (New York: Rodale Press, 2006), p. 10.
4. Jonathan Dollimore and Alan Sinfield, eds., *Political Shakespeare: New Essays in Cultural Materialism* (Ithaca, NY: Cornell University Press, 1985); John Drakakis, ed., *Alternative Shakespeares* (New York: Methuen, 1985); Patricia Parker and Geoffrey Hartman, eds., *Shakespeare and the Question of Theory* (New York: Methuen, 1985); Valerie Wayne, ed., *The Matter of Difference: Materialist Feminist Criticism of Shakespeare* (Ithaca, NY: Cornell University Press, 1991); James C. Bulman, ed., *Shakespeare, Theory, and Performance* (New York: Routledge, 1996).
5. The term "Presentism" used in a positive sense to describe critical methods that acknowledge the productive influence of the present on interpretation first appeared in Hugh Grady, *Shakespeare's Universal Wolf: Studies in Early Modern Reification* (Oxford: Clarendon, 1996), pp. 4–8. The term was taken up and applied to his own related critical methods by Terence Hawkes in *Shakespeare in the Present* (London: Routledge, 2002) and further discussed by Grady in *Shakespeare, Machiavelli, and Montaigne: Power and Subjectivity from "Richard II" to "Hamlet"* (Oxford: Oxford University Press, 2002), pp. 1–25. Presentism was further defined by Ewan Fernie, "Shakespeare and the Prospect of Presentism," *Shakespeare Survey*, 58 (2005): 169–84 and exemplified in two critical anthologies: Hugh Grady and Terence Hawkes, eds., *Presentist Shakespeares* (London: Routledge, 2007) and Evelyn Gajowski, ed., *Presentism, Gender, and Sexuality in Shakespeare* (New York: Palgrave, 2009). There are of course any number of critics and critical methods employing Presentist principles without

using that term. If there is a manifesto for contemporary Presentism in Shakespeare studies, it is Terence Hawkes, *Shakespeare in the Present* (2002), particularly the brief Introduction (1–5); although all of Hawkes's works of recent years, including *That Shakespeherian Rag: Essays on a Critical Process* (London: Methuen, 1986) and *Meaning by Shakespeare* (London: Routledge, 1992), are examples of his particular version of Presentism.
6. For an extended argument along these lines, see Hugh Grady, "Shakespeare Studies, 2005: A Situated Overview," *Shakespeare: A Journal*, 1.1 (2005): 102–20.
7. In contrast, theoretical presentism in the positive sense—ironically for us, using the term "historicism" as its self-designation—goes back at least to the early twentieth-century Italian philosopher of history Benedetto Croce, who wrote, for example, "The practical requirements which underlie every historical judgment give to all history the character of 'contemporary history' because, however remote in time events there recounted may seem to be, the history in reality refers to present needs and present situations wherein those events vibrate" (*History as the Story of Liberty*, 1938; trans. Sylvia Sprigge (New York: Norton, 1941), p. 19; see also his *History: Its Theory and Practice* (1916), trans. Douglas Ainslie (New York: Russell and Russell, 1960). And of course, a milestone work of a previous generation with specific Presentist principles is Jan Kott's *Shakespeare Our Contemporary*, trans. Boleslaw Taborski (Garden City, NY: Doubleday, 1964). Many of the criticisms of historicism and New Historicism now deployed by a variety of Presentists were first elaborated by Howard Felperin, *The Uses of the Canon: Elizabethan Literature and Contemporary Theory* (Oxford: Clarendon, 1990).
8. Johann Gottfried Herder, *Shakespeare*, trans., ed. Gregory Moore (Princeton: Princeton University Press, 2006).

1
Presentism, Anachronism, and *Titus Andronicus*

Cary DiPietro and Hugh Grady

I

Shakespeare's plays and poems in their own time reflect a fractious, often violent, and uncertain moment in the shift from feudalism to modernity, a moment that continues to resonate in our own, often violent and precarious moment in late modernity.[1] In the early, extremely violent play *Titus Andronicus*, this convergence is particularly apparent, and it has become even more so in the wake of the attack on the World Trade Center in New York on September 11, 2001. We want to make use of this convergence to exemplify one version of the Presentist criticism discussed in the Foreword by Terence Hawkes and in our Introduction. As we noted, there is no one single kind of Presentism, but rather a multiplicity of possible approaches. In this essay, we offer one example of a specific kind of Presentism, one that acknowledges the importance of scholarly attempts to understand the contexts of the texts that come down to us—while also acknowledging that such historicist efforts nevertheless are always already implicated in the assumptions and values of the "now" within which they are created. The "timelessness" of literature, we have learned, is a façade for our reconstructions of the past at our specific historical moment—and all too often a façade concealing unspoken assumptions from our own time. Thus, it is important instead to see, as the previous generation of critical practice has demonstrated in detail, that all literature arises from specific historical moments and is imprinted with the "timeliness" of its originating era. What Presentism would add to that insight, however, is the equally crucial truth that we encounter these historical works outside of their moment of origin, and they have meaning for us because their very otherness is a challenge to our own thinking, feeling, and values—which, however, constitute the only ground from which we can contemplate them. Any reading of works of the past has to work within this dialectic. There is never a moment of "timelessness"; there is instead a complex negotiation between then and now, and one that has to be continually renegotiated as our "now" changes in the wake of developing history. Thus, contrary to what some of its critics claim, Presentist criticism is deeply implicated in defining a constantly changing interaction between past and present, not seeing them as static and unchanging.

What we are advocating here is a kind of "allegorical" approach, inspired by Walter Benjamin's theory of allegory and the application of it to literary analysis of Richard Halpern.[2] Two aspects of the allegory as defined by Benjamin are relevant here. The first is its informing quality, productive of an open, unfinished text. As Benjamin puts it, "Allegory has to do, precisely in its destructive furor, with dispelling the illusion that proceeds from all 'given order,' whether of art or of life: the illusion of totality or of organic wholeness which transfigures that order and makes it seem endurable. And this is the progressive tendency of allegory."[3] The second is its quality of layered, multiple meanings, meanings that overlay each other, are not identical with each other nor capable of being organically unified with each other, but do not cancel each other out. In the seventeenth-century baroque *Trauerspiele* from which Benjamin derived much of his theory of allegory, the plays are always set in a specific historical time, different from the historical era in which they were being written. History in these plays, Benjamin wrote, is thus revealed to be in ruins, and the plays are built from these ruins, thus "history has physically merged into the setting" in the form of "ruins."[4] "Allegories are," writes Benjamin, "in the realm of thoughts, what ruins are in the realm of things."[5] They disclose a world in decay, but they show how the elements of decay can be reborn as new art in a new and different era. Our own readings of the texts of the past share in this allegorical quality. They are ruins for us, fragments of history surviving into our own time. And their meaning shifts as we back into history.

We offer a reading of Shakespeare's use of anachronisms in *Titus Andronicus* to explore the relationship between historical difference and critical practice, and also to exemplify one approach among many that might be identified with what has come to be known as the critical movement Presentism. Anachronism presupposes at one level a sameness between past and present, a sameness that is for the historian troubling, a temporal error. What we will argue, by comparison, is that the construction of an analogy between past and present involved in a conscious use of anachronism allows us to reevaluate what we know of the past in present terms. The real error is to assume that through disinterested, empirical analysis of the raw "material" of the past we can come to an ever more objective or true understanding of it. Historicist and materialist scholars no doubt understand this epistemological barrier, yet an assumption about the historical "truth" of the past continues to be a chimera of literary scholarship. The alternative, we will argue, is to acknowledge that we read the past through the lens of our own ideological positions and articulate it from within contemporary discursive paradigms; a conscious, critical anachronism allows us to dialogue pragmatically with a past that we can only reconstruct incompletely and never impartially, but, more importantly, it is through such critical and creative contexts that we can come to understand what is aesthetically powerful about Shakespeare's plays for us now.

Titus Andronicus, a revenge tragedy composed at some point in the early to mid-1590s, is an excellent example of such aesthetically powerful anachronism, no less because of the resonance it has for us post–9/11. The play's extreme aesthetics of shock as well as its linkage of racial stereotyping to acts of violence, primarily through the figure of the stage Moor, give the play new meanings for us today. Moreover, Shakespeare himself employs his own kind of anachronism to much the same effect. Although one of his four Roman plays whose fictionalized setting and characters derive indirectly from a number of Latin textual sources, *Titus* also expresses its moment of historical origin in an early modern Europe in complex interrelations with the Muslim world, thereby expressing as well the ethno-political violence and instability that were part of the early modern European–Islamic interaction. The play thus focuses the Roman characters and Latin textual antecedents through the lens of its many anachronisms, producing often explicit analogies between the classical past the play represents and an Elizabethan present.

Using this notion, then, we offer an alternative reading that, rather than exploring the classical setting through Shakespeare's use of Latin sources in Seneca and Ovid as a locus for the play's meaning, emphasizes instead the play's own historical allegory through its presentation of anachronisms to Elizabethan audiences—and, moreover, anachronisms that correlate that experience of the play with a future present: our own time. In particular, what make this play's use of terror in its aesthetic appeal seem so contemporary are its references to the complex figure of "the Moor" and our own era's associations of terrorism with the complex matrix of economic, political, and social realities of today's Middle East. This association has contributed greatly to the neatly polarized antagonism between Muslim East and Imperialist West, a "clash of civilizations." This positioning would seem to exemplify a "violent hierarchy" in which one extreme binary difference effectively suppresses our awareness of an inextricable web of differences, an exemplary demonstration of Jacques Derrida's *différance* in the construction of the Other.[6] Terror, as much as it depends on violence or the threat of violence, also depends on a static binary that serves rhetorically to amplify difference, heightening the *fear* of the Other to *terror*.

A critical and productive use of anachronism, a deliberate "Presentism," offers one way of disrupting that "violent hierarchy" between present and past, collapsing the distance between them in a double gesture that both inverts and defamiliarizes. When we think of contemporary acts of terrorism, we feel the unnatural tension and violent emotion that are amplified by our sense of the presence of terror in the present. If *Titus Andronicus* resonates in our own time, to what degree, then, did Elizabethans share in a similar presence of terror, generated by experiencing not a radical fundamentalist or a political terrorist, but an Orientalized, theatrical Moor staging violence?

II

Shakespeare's *Titus Andronicus* constitutes a promising text for discussing these issues because its many anachronisms produce often explicit analogies between the classical past the play represents and an Elizabethan present. These analogies exemplify Benjamin's theory of allegory, in which multiple meanings overlay each other and, though not identical with each other, are nevertheless woven into a "timely" history. The many fragments of classical texts—a quotation of Horace's *Odes* in a letter, the use of Ovid's *Metamorphoses* as a stage prop, an allusion to Livy at the moment of Titus's murder of Saturninus—are the ruins from which the play is built, "physically merged into the setting" of the play and with meanings that shift with their iteration on the Elizabethan stage. What Benjamin describes as the destructive furor of allegory, its open-endedness resistant to a unified organic order, is realized not only through the play's pervasive use of anachronism, but by the anarchic violence of its action and its disruption of the Roman mythos. Any desire to recognize in the play a unified idea of "Rome"—as some critics have done, to read the play in the more traditional sense of allegory as an allegorical distillation of the whole Roman Empire[7]—is made impossible by the fragmentary use of multiple classical sources, by the very hybridity of what Titus, when alluding to Livy before his murder of Lavinia, calls a "pattern, precedent and lively warrant" (5.3.43) for his own actions.[8] The disruption of the Roman mythos is further mirrored by the events of the play, which sees Rome invaded by Goths and re-formed into an uneasy political union with them at the end of Act 5. The disruptive politics of the play's conflict do for Rome what anachronism does for the play's presentation of Roman history, taking the fragments and re-forming them into a new work.

The play's representation of a classical past thus showcases the irreducibility of the present; and so it constitutes an instance, albeit in a creative aesthetic context, of Shakespeare's own Presentism. Indeed, it is Shakespeare's creative amalgamation of neoclassical humanism and Latin sources that brings the past into view through a historical context particular to the play's Renaissance audience. So too are our own contemporary encounters with the play, as well as the past it represents, subject to shifting historical contexts. Once again, *Titus Andronicus* is also an exemplary case study of such shifting contextual paradigms inasmuch as its place in the Shakespeare canon has shifted dramatically in recent years. Where once it was considered an embarrassment, an instance in which the neoclassical evaluation of Shakespeare as a barbarian victim of a barbarous age still applied, today the play has emerged as a much-discussed text with surprisingly deep cultural resonances and aesthetic integrity. Because the play's once-scandalous extreme violence is suddenly both politically relevant and aesthetically powerful—in performance, on film,[9] and in the study—it is a prime example of one of the fundamental principles on which Presentist critical theory is based: that the meaning and significance of texts is never static or "timeless," that both shift as the play is inscribed and reinscribed in the series of historical and cultural contexts provided by the aging of the work and its relocation in different cultural contexts. It also provides an important example of how "historical context" itself—the supposed binary opposite of "Presentist criticism"—is something that shifts radically as our present history leads us to view the past with new understandings, with different interpretive lenses, with different senses of what is important and relevant, and what is not.

To read the play in terms of the disruptive politics of its conflict is necessarily to read it through a Presentist lens and, more specifically, through the violence and turbulence of global politics post–9/11. As an instance of a Benjaminian allegory that violently disrupts the illusion and organic wholeness of history, the play offers a timely critique of the destructive binary between civilized Occident and barbaric Orient on which its plot and characters are built. The play's horrifying representations of violence on stage combined with its rhetorically ornamented descriptions of off-stage violence—from ritual human sacrifice and filicide, to rape, dismemberment, decapitation, and cannibalism—are thus, in a Presentist sense, contiguous with the many representations of violence that circulate in contemporary mass media[10]: one thinks of the well-known, grainy digital images of Abu Ghraib detainees, for example; or the staged video murders of kidnapped foreign nationals in Saudi Arabia and Iraq, committed in response to the intervention of the American military complex post–9/11 in Islamic states. Indeed, the similarities between the play's and more contemporary representations of violence are striking: theatrical uses of costume and disguise, scripted declarations of revenge, and the performance of otherwise unimaginable acts of violence, horrifying tableaux of torture, murder, and dismemberment. The play more or less begins with its own ritualized revenge killing: the slaying of Alarbus, eldest son of the captured Goth Queen, Tamora. After Alarbus is led off stage by Titus's sons to be executed, Tamora, having pleaded with Titus to spare her son, exclaims "O cruel, irreligious piety" (1.1.133), an oxymoron that we might readily use to describe contemporary, religiously motivated violence.[11]

The idea of nonidentical but contiguous histories overlaying one another in our reading of historically situated texts requires a kind of temporal double-consciousness, a concurrency between present and past that is, by another name, anachronism. Nicholas Moschovakis has argued that anachronism provokes a "reevaluation in present terms of subjects otherwise regarded as past." He quotes Clifford Ronan to argue that anachronism transforms "the Then" into "a Now that urgently must be dealt with."[12] To be sure, presence has become highly suspect in the wake of Derrida, who of course critiques the idea of metaphysical presence in part by showing how any use of a sign at a single moment of time implicates it simultaneously in both the past and the future. When Derrida quotes Hamlet's "The time is out of joint," he also describes the sense of lateness that inheres in present experience, the sense that the present always comes after something before it, just as our experience of Shakespeare is always already shaped by a moment of intention or origination that has passed.[13] Derrida later uses the term "anachronism" to describe this "out of joint" quality, a term he also employs to explain how historical texts continue to have meaning in later historical contexts.

In an oft-quoted moment in a late interview, Derrida uses the example of Shakespeare to speak about the text's relationship to history, a passage worth quoting in full:

> Here the example of Shakespeare is magnificent. Who demonstrates better that texts fully conditioned by their history, loaded with history, and on historical themes, offer themselves so well for reading in historical contexts very distant from their time and place of origin, not only in the European twentieth century, but also in lending themselves to Japanese or Chinese transpositions?
>
> This has to do with the structure of a text, with what I will call, to cut corners, its iterability, which both puts down roots in the unity of a context and immediately opens this non-saturable context onto a recontextualization. All this is historical through and through.[14]

Using the example of Shakespeare, Derrida emphasizes the historicity of history itself, and, in the process, he opens up the literary text by way of what he calls its iterability, a term he had defined in a relatively early work in this way:

> Every sign, linguistic or nonlinguistic, spoken or written (in the usual sense of the opposition), as a small or large unity, can be cited, put between quotation marks; thereby it can break with every given context, and engender infinitely new contexts in an absolutely nonsaturable fashion. This does not suppose that the mark is valid outside its context, but on the contrary that there are only contexts without any center of absolute anchoring.[15]

That is to say, no text exists outside of a context, but every text possesses the potential for location in a different context from that from which it originates. In addition, the concept of iterability underlines the inevitable distance between its original contexts and subsequent recontextualizations—and the impossibility of overcoming this distance. To take the example most relevant here, every reading of Shakespeare in our own time is a citation, a relocation of a text from its original to an entirely new context—including all "historicist" readings, which necessarily construct new contexts in our present. Thus, as Derrida suggests, all reading is historical through and through, but there is no direct access to any past context. Derrida, then, in effect defines a kind of Presentism, and indeed, even a kind of textual "presence" constituted by different iterations of the same text at multiple historical moments.

This is not the metaphysical presence of his essay "Différance." There, he saw presence as a kind of false guarantor of an (illusory) direct access to the real, arguing that such presence must be rethought as an effect produced by différance:

> Différance is what makes the movement of signification possible only if each element that is said to be "present," appearing on the stage of presence, is related to something other than itself but retains the mark of a past element and already lets itself be hollowed out by the mark of its relation to a future element. This trace relates no less to what is called the future than to what is called the past, and it constitutes what is called the present by this very relation to what it is not, to what it absolutely is not; that is, not even to a past or future considered as a modified present. In

order for it to be, an interval must separate it from what it is not; but the interval that constitutes it in the present must also, and by the same token, divide the present in itself, thus dividing, along with the present everything that can be conceived on its basis, that is, every being.[16]

Our idea of the "present," then, must take account of these paradoxes and refuse to be conceived as radically separate from the past and future of which it bears traces. "Presentism" must embrace these dynamics, seeing every iteration as carrying traces of the past and of a yet-to-be future. Thus Derrida, in theorizing Shakespeare's "iterability," embraces the moving "now" of a text in changing historical circumstances.[17]

The clearest instance of the anachronism of the play for Elizabethan audiences—and, as it happens, persuasive evidence of the aesthetic experience of the play in the now of performance—is provided not by the text, but by what is arguably the only known visual evidence of a Shakespeare play in original performance, the well-known sketch by Henry Peacham. As a record of performance, the sketch is highly unreliable; the date (1595), the attribution to "Henricus Peacham," and the annotation that accompanies the illustration in the Longleat manuscript are all spurious. Moreover, the tableau that the sketch presents does not correspond to the episode in Act 1 from which it is purportedly drawn: Aaron should be bound and kneeling, if present at all; the Goth Queen Tamora should have three rather than two sons kneeling behind her; and Titus should be accompanied by his own sons, not to mention numerous other characters present in the scene.[18] Nevertheless, what the sketch does show us, even as an unreliable record of original performance, is that anachronism was a readily recognizable feature in the presentation of Rome to Elizabethan audiences. Though Titus is dressed in something resembling a Roman tunic and sash, the Roman soldiers behind him appear in the attire of Elizabethan infantry and Tamora is dressed in costume more appropriate to the medieval settings of Shakespeare's English histories. Aaron is also portrayed, starkly black, dressed in a loose-fitting tunic and threatening Titus and the Romans with his sword. The visual presentation of Aaron as a threatening and dangerous, sword-wielding antihero, in combination with his blackness, recalls the equation between villainy and skin color that Aaron makes in an aside in Act 3. Just before he exits with Titus's recently chopped-off hand, he states, "Oh how this villainy / Doth fat me with the very thoughts of it. / Let fools do good and fair men call for grace. / Aaron will have his soul black like his face" (3.1.203–6). In a complex interplay between past and future, the sketch thus looks forward through the threatening figure of the stage Moor, sword at the ready, to the murders and violence that Aaron will commit later in the play, even as it looks back through the reconstitution of Peacham's memories to an original performance that it only approximates, and arguably not very well—an exemplary instance of the moving now of the text.

Such visual anachronisms in performance as the Elizabethan military costumes disrupt in a not dissimilar way the temporal consistency of the play's narrative, its representation of a past through narrative setting. Similar anachronisms in the play, such as the many Christian oaths or allusions to Christian rites such as christening (4.2.73), function in performance to collapse or disrupt the narrative by drawing attention to the now of Elizabethan London. When in Act 4 the clown swears the oath "God forbid" (3.90), for example, he becomes a curiously English interruption of the Roman setting by recalling the stock character and comic conventions associated with courtly clowning in the late medieval English court, as appropriated into the early modern theatre. The clown in particular stands out from the rest of the characters in the play partly as a result of his proverbial, comical prose, the fluidity of which contrasts starkly with the highly stylized rhetoric employed by the other characters. As another example, when Demetrius receives a scroll with a Latin inscription delivered to him from Titus, he states: "O, 'tis a verse in Horace, I know it well: / I read it in the grammar long ago" (4.2.22–3). Not only does he recall anachronistically *Lily's Grammar* of 1540 in which the quotation appears twice, he reminds his Elizabethan audience of the humanist curriculum initiated in the early Tudor period, which provides the lens through which the play's Roman setting comes into view. The observation of these anachronisms is, of course, nothing new; for nineteenth-century detractors, such anachronisms, "ludicrous" historical inaccuracies, were among the barbarisms for which Shakespeare needed to be excused, or on the basis of which Shakespeare's authorship could be questioned.[19] We would argue, by comparison, that Shakespeare's anachronisms are not only deliberate, but aesthetically powerful, precisely because they collapse orders of time by drawing connections or analogies between Roman past and English present. The evidence offered by the Peacham sketch confirms the sense of "double time" that such anachronisms as the clown produce, and they are deliberate to the extent that the play is not motivated by the kind of antiquarianism found in contemporary post-historicist evaluations of Shakespeare. The assumption for Shakespeare is not that the Roman past can or ought to be recreated and represented on the stage with a view to historical authenticity, or that the imposition of the present through anachronism is an "error" of such authenticity; rather, the readily apparent inclusion of anachronism argues that the staging of history is a conscious reforming and transvaluing of the past—*neo*classicism as opposed to antiquarianism. Shakespeare's creative Presentism is the vehicle by which the past becomes meaningful for Elizabethan audiences.

Shakespeare's neoclassicism is anachronistic because it articulates the past through the present, drawing attention to the way in which classical *topoi* and rhetorical forms are expressed in and through a modern English idiom. As much as the stylized verse and Latin tags lend the play historical character, the language is simultaneously an expression of the fashionable neoclassical style of "English poesy" championed by George Puttenham and other English stylists such as George Gascoigne and Philip Sidney. Puttenham's argument in 1589 in *The Arte of English Poesie* in particular is predicated on the similarity of English to Greek and Latin: "our language being no lesse copious pithie and significative then theirs, our conceipts the same, and our wits no lesse apt to devise and imitate then theirs were."[20] In fact, English has more "diversities" such as rhyme, he argues, and "Poesie therefore may be an Art in our vulgar, and that verie methodicall and commendable." Both Sidney's unfinished prose romance *Arcadia* and the first book of Edmund Spenser's *The Faerie Queene* were printed in 1590, within two or three years of the composition of *Titus*, and both craft Tudor allegories by translating the Virgilian and later Italian pastoral into distinctly "Englished" settings and language, much in the same way that Protestant exegetical writings diversely appropriate the Roman pastoral into a post-Reformation Christian allegory. In a similar fashion, *Titus* contemporizes its Latin antecedents, no less by appropriating pastoral *topoi* into a tragic form. The precedent is provided by Shakespeare's source in Ovid's *Metamorphoses*, whose violent conflicts are set in the idealized landscapes of the Roman pastoral genre typified by Virgil's *Eclogues* and Longus's *Daphnis and Chloe*; in the spirit of Roman pastoralism, Ovid amplifies the danger of the libidinal pleasures his characters pursue, with often tragic results. While Shakespeare's contemporaries convert the Roman pastoral to a mythology arguably more consistent with post-Reformation Protestantism and Tudor ideology, Shakespeare overlays his own use of the Ovidian disruption of the pre-Christian Roman pastoral with Christian religious anachronisms. The result is an effect of juxtaposition where both the subversion of pastoral idealism and Christian anachronism heighten the irony of the "irreligious piety" observed by Tamora in Act 1.

Shakespeare employs language in the same way as he employs his historical sources, taking fragments and ideas and combining them into a new form with little concern for their integrity. Again, there is no antiquarian imperative in Shakespeare's use of Latin antecedents; instead, he employs them in a way that draws attention to and makes creative use of the interpretive traditions that are embedded in them. In this manner, the highly patterned rhetoric emulates the style of Seneca, recalling both the Latin curriculum of the English grammar and the neoclassical style pioneered by Thomas Kyd in the popular precursor to this revenge tragedy, *The Spanish Tragedy* (c. 1587). Moments of complexly patterned metaphoric language in Titus's speeches, for example, are an undeniable pastiche of the "woes" expressed by Kyd's Hieronimo. Another of the play's more remarkable anachronisms occurs in Act 4, when a codex-format book of Ovid's *Metamorphoses* is brought on stage, a moment that recalls a similar episode in *The Spanish Tragedy* when Hieromino enters reading a volume of Seneca's plays, which he proceeds to quote as he contemplates his own revenge in soliloquy (3.13.1–44). In *Titus*, however, the book is out of place in the Roman setting of the play. Not only is it not a Latin scroll as it ought to be if the play were accurately "historical," but as a stage prop that is recognizably contemporary for Elizabethan audiences—composed of paper, bound with a contemporary binding, and possibly even printed—it offers a visual anachronism in performance not unlike the Elizabethan dress of the Peacham sketch. The episode in Book Six of Ovid's *Metamorphoses* involving Philomela is alluded to at several earlier points in the play, most memorably in Marcus's ekphrastic speech in Act 2 when Lavinia first appears after her rape and mutilation by Chiron and Demetrius. Ovid's Philomela becomes the literary counterpoint against which Marcus measures the visual evidence of the crimes done on Lavinia's body, as he observes that

> Fair Philomela, why she but lost her tongue…
> A craftier Tereus, cousin, hast thou met,
> And he hath cut those pretty fingers off,
> That could have better sewed than Philomel. (2.3.38, 41–3)

Marcus's description of Lavinia provides a measure against which Shakespeare amplifies the Ovidian horrors for an English audience, in essence outperforming Ovid by doubling the number of her rapists and the amputations they perform on her. While the Latin source is interwoven into the narrative fabric of the play, the anachronism of the early printed book on stage calls attention to the presence of Ovid in the literary culture of early modern England. Lavinia turns the pages with her stumps in Act 3, reminding audiences of their own experience of reading Ovid's books. Bearing in mind that printed bound books had, in little more than a hundred years, almost entirely replaced the practice of the scribal copying and binding of large manuscripts, we might even speculate that the book on stage is Arthur Golding's "Englished" version of the 1560s, reprinted in a new volume as late as 1587.[21] The question of whether the audience could distinguish from the auditorium of The Rose the difference between a print and a manuscript book is immaterial; the well-established habit of print reading is embedded in the "always already read" of the text.

The anachronism of the book thus instigates a dynamic tension between past and present that mirrors the play's temporal binary of neoclassicism, a tension between, on the one hand, the narrative the play seeks to represent and, in this case, greatly amplify—a narrative that would seem locked in a past that has always already been written and is fixed in print—and, on the other hand, the anachronism of the book whose presence emphasizes the significances that Ovid has for audiences in the now of Elizabethan performance: as a marker of humanist culture, as a commodity for exchange in London's marketplace, and as a source for dramatic writing, among other uses. The numerous allusions to the Philomela narrative, well known to Elizabethan literary readers, also look forward by foreshadowing the final events of the play, its filicide and cannibalism; while Philomena is revenged by her sister Procne, who kills her own son Itys and feeds him to his father Tereus, Titus eventually kills Chiron and Demetrius, draining their blood and crushing their bones to a paste to make pastry, baking them in a "pasty"—a common English meat pie, yet another anachronism—and feeding it to their mother Tamora, all before killing her and his own daughter. The hewing and chopping, the violating of bodies, and their re-presentation and recombination into new forms, whether an ekphrastic oratorio or an unsavory meat pie, completes the Presentist triptych of Shakespeare's neoclassicism, combining allusion, metaphor, and linguistic invention.

Not unlike the later *Trauerspiele*, in which, as Benjamin describes, history is physically merged into the setting of the play in ruins, in *Titus* the many anachronisms are temporally incongruent, but they also work spatially to interpenetrate the setting of the play. The figure of Aaron in the Peacham sketch is aesthetically powerful not because he disrupts the historical narrative of the play—its Roman setting in the past—but because he has presence in the now of performance in early modern London, as well as a spatial relationship to early modern playgoers. This is especially evident in those soliloquies and asides in what seem instances of direct address to the audience, when Aaron steps, as it were, out of the setting to give us the information that is necessary to the play's dramatic irony. Not unlike the clown, he is a figure who instigates a sense of double time or synchronicity, because he stands apart from the Roman setting. Aaron as a Moor is chronologically "out of place" in ancient Rome: the English word "Moor," though it has a Greek cognate and one in early medieval Latin, is in English usage of later medieval and early modern provenance, and Moors were not in Shakespeare's time generally associated with the classical world. As an embodied anachronism, Aaron calls to mind for early English audiences their spatial, geohistorical relationship to an early modern Mediterranean and the potential for an escalation of violence and political disruption that it betokens, just as in our own time, the play's moments of violence call to mind our own experiences of terrorism.

III

Reading the play's anarchic violence through the lens of contemporary politics is a way to make the play our own, to add meaning to a text already saturated through the continuous, 400-year-old history of its reception. However, it also helps to draw attention to how the play itself collapses through anachronism the temporal binary between past and present. An important part of what makes the play particularly relevant post–9/11 is the sense in which it looks forward to problems in our own world. Primarily through the figure of Aaron the Moor—the chief perpetrator of terror—the play continually references for us the Islamic world associated in contemporary culture as the very land and source of terrorism. But the analogy comparing the play's violence with contemporary terrorism is motivated by more than a mere retrospective resonance. The anachronism challenges us to reevaluate the historicity of historically situated texts; in other words, to reiterate an earlier point, it requires a pragmatic negotiation of a dialectic between the text's historical identity in a "then" and its timeliness for us "now" as a work of art, as distinct from what critics of Presentism argue to be the temporal or anachronistic error of presupposing its "timelessness." In the case of *Titus Andronicus*, while a historical recontextualization is motivated by the resonance of the play's violence in our post–9/11 world, that resonance is nevertheless firmly rooted in a historically situated ideological encounter between East and West.

Our reading of *Titus Andronicus* borrows the revisionist impulse of contemporary postcolonial critique—which is yet another exemplary instance of the way in which historical context shifts according to the priorities and values, often urgently political, of the present— specifically in its identification in the play of the ideological binary described by Edward Said in his now classic work *Orientalism*.[22] Although Said is principally concerned in his study with the colonial discourse of the eighteenth and nineteenth centuries as it manifests in and through literary texts, his cultural theory usefully characterizes the play's rhetorical, iconographic, and contemporary-sounding constructions of race and a kind of proto-Orientalism. His term Orientalism refers not to an ontologically stable Orient, nor even to the changing historical and cultural relationship of Europe with Asia and North Africa through the modern period, but, more specifically, to a cultural enterprise, a set of Foucauldian discursive practices, that combines to construct the Orient as what has come to be understood as a version of the Other, inferior and alien, a mirror image of the West. The Orient becomes, rather than a fact of natural geography or history, a fact of human production, what Said calls "geography of the imagination." And as he suggests in the preface to the most recent edition of *Orientalism* (published not long before his death), this imaginary line dividing Orient from Occident continues to manifest in the hyperbolic rhetoric of the "clash of civilizations," though such rhetoric has also become a key discursive strategy in the operation of global terrorism.[23]

Said has often been criticized for offering a totalized account: if a theory of Orientalism concerns the diverse ways by which Western discourses construct an Orient that serves as colonial subject to Western imperialist rule and ambition, then a homogenized "East" is always already subordinate to a European empire that is seen as both dominant and inevitable. Indeed, the objections commonly raised to *Orientalism* might also be readily applied to a reading of *Titus Andronicus* that seeks to establish the play's continuity with the present by reading in it the historical relations between East and West. It might be said that an "early modern Orientalism" homogenizes or flattens out the heterogeneity and diversity of transnational and transcultural encounter in favor of an anachronistic colonial model, and that the theory itself therefore constitutes an act of colonizing historicism; this has been the argument of a number of critics within Shakespeare and early modern studies, including Daniel Vitkus, Emily Bartels, and Jonathan Burton.[24] It has even been argued that Said's critique of Orientalism fails to account for the temporal binary that is often encoded in Orientalist discourse that posits the West as present and the Orient as a pre-modern or pre-Westernized "not yet."[25]

These are unfair criticisms in many ways; Said was interested, after all, precisely in identifying and critiquing this domination as his major contribution to intellectual history. Moreover, Said understood the impossibility of stabilizing or objectifying such constructed entities as "the Orient"—or for that matter, a "Shakespeare" outside of the myriad interpretations of Shakespeare. In fact, there is a wonderful moment in a later article when he compares the epistemological problem of positing an Orient to that of the interpretation of Shakespeare:

> Similar problems are commonplace in the interpretation of literary texts. Each age, for instance, re-interprets Shakespeare, not

because Shakespeare changes, but because despite the existence of numerous and reliable editions of Shakespeare, there is no such fixed and non-trivial object as Shakespeare independent of his editors, the actors who played his roles, the translators who put him in other languages, the hundreds of millions of readers who have read him or watched performances of his plays since the late sixteenth century. On the other hand, it is too much to say that Shakespeare has no independent existence at all, and that he is completely reconstituted every time someone reads, acts, or writes about him.[26]

Said, in other words, is a Presentist when he observes that "even so relatively inert an object as a literary text is commonly supposed to gain some of its identity from its historical moment interacting with the attentions, judgements, scholarship, and performances of its readers."[27] The point he argues is a variation on the argument against "timelessness" above: that no one trying to understand a historically constituted set of objects—a body of plays written at a specific point in history by a man called Shakespeare, the peoples and cultures that constitute what has been called the Orient—can do so by standing at an Archimedean point outside of them. Rather, it is precisely because they defy neutral or disinterested definition that they prevail on us to make the attempt to understand them.

Still, the weight Said gives to the idea of the West's domination over the East is, if problematically homogeneous from his starting point in the eighteenth century, particularly untenable in the early modern period, when the power relations between European countries and their neighbors to the East and South were far from those of simple domination and subjugation; when England, in the shadow of European empires such as those of Spain and Portugal, was yet to establish itself as a powerful empire, especially in the Near East. Early modern English colonialist discourse therefore more often betrays the anxiety, inferiority, and ambition that the English felt in relation to their immediate neighbors in Europe, and political tensions that were amplified not by the anti-Islamic dogmatism of contemporary religious tracts, but by more pressing rivalries between Catholics and Protestants.[28] Of course, these European rivalries would be battled out in the new world through the seventeenth century, but they also inflect English encounters with an early modern Orient.

Importantly, that Orient is constructed in the early modern period not in terms of England's relation to the East—starting on an axis point in the Middle East and moving eastward, as in eighteenth-century Orientalist writing—but in relation to an Orient constructed in the period through England's complex relation to a fluid and diverse Mediterranean.[29] The name Mediterranean, taken from late Latin, suggests the literal translation "middle earth" as well as the more prosaic "between the lands," and thus signifies the geographical regions surrounding the Mediterranean Sea as much as the sea itself. Such a meaning situates Europe lexically at the centre of an imaginative geography, one not divided along an East–West axis, but one that is rather a fossil of an older cultural memory with important ideological, legitimizing functions for the English state. In the Renaissance, England was situated both within and against this Mediterranean. England shares with the early modern Mediterranean a cultural and political memory that is, in England's own myths of origin, traced from the classical to Renaissance periods in a westward-moving relocation of empire from Troy to Rome to London.[30] At the same time, Rome and its Catholic allies in Southern Europe are separated from England by religious schism and imperialist aspiration and rivalry. The same dichotomy characterizes England's relationship to the Levant, the broad geographical area along the Eastern side of the Mediterranean encompassing modern Palestine and Israel. The Levant, and especially Jerusalem, is the religious center of Christianity, but at the same time its geography is historically composed of multiple ethnicities and religious traditions. Such fluidity runs counter to England's own aspirations under Elizabeth in the post-Reformation period to homogenize and extend its religious and cultural identity, precisely what the powerful Islamic Ottoman Empire was now doing in the Levant, extending its power from Turkey all along the eastern side of the Mediterranean.

Indeed, far from being a colonizing oppressor, England under Elizabeth, despite many cultural anxieties and strong religious prejudice, was increasingly developing profitable trade routes through the Mediterranean in a period when commercial relations with North Africa, and especially Morocco, were thriving. England was also finding itself increasingly allied with the Barbary states against the Catholic European powers. Long before England had established itself as a global empire, the busy trade routes on the Mediterranean offered the greatest transcultural traffic between England and non-European peoples.[31] Such trade routes, however, were extremely hazardous given the simultaneous increase in piracy by Barbary corsairs (backed by the Turkish) and renegadoes (Christian converts to Islam, many of them English, operating out of North Africa).[32] By the late sixteenth century, several hundred English had already been captured and either converted or sold into slavery or both, and in the very same North African states with which England was trading commercially, far more in number than any non-European peoples who had been captured or enslaved by the English at this point in time. Such were the perils for ambitious English entrepreneurs, navigating their commodities in a turbulent sea of religious antipathies, cultural stereotypes, and tangible threats to their security.

A play contemporary with *Titus Andronicus*, George Peele's *The Battle of Alcazar*, demonstrates England's over-determined relationship to the regions surrounding and beyond the Mediterranean. The play dramatizes the 1578 battle, near the modern city of El-ksar-el-Kebir outside of Morocco, between the armies of King Sebastian of Portugal and Abd Al-Malik, the sultan of Morocco. Having assumed the title "Most Obedient King," demonstrating his zealous obedience to the Catholic Church, King Sebastian sought to wage a series of religious crusades against the Islamic North African principalities. England's presence in the battle was provided by the recusant Catholic Thomas Stukeley, a notorious English soldier who had turned to open mutiny against Queen Elizabeth in 1570; Stukeley was, it was rumored, a bastard son of Henry VIII. While traveling from Rome to Spain and on toward Ireland to stake his claim there against the English, Stukeley stopped in Lisbon and was persuaded by King Sebastian to join his mercenary army with the Portuguese to fight alongside the Moors against Morocco. Peele's play, set mostly in and around Morocco, draws on the notoriety of Stukeley in England as a recusant and seditious Catholic, as well as on England's anxieties about Catholic empires such as Spain. Not only does the play stage the defeat of Stukeley and celebrate the near obliteration of the Portuguese army in their Catholic crusade, it also prepares the audience for the rise to power of the subsequent sultan, Ahmad al-Mansur, who was by this point in the reign of Elizabeth a political ally against the Spanish and an important commercial trading partner. *The Battle of Alcazar* thus reflects the complex intersection of cultural and religious bias with the material realities of trade and political alliance between England, Catholic Europe, and North Africa.

Given Stukeley's involvement, the battle of El-ksar-el-Kebir became a popular subject in English pamphlets and ballads through the late 1570s and 1580s, and, combined with Peele's dramatic account of it in *The Battle of Alcazar*, began a trend for representing Moors on the stage in England.[33] Much recent scholarship has sought to establish the cultural and ideological location of such theatrical Moors, to reveal how differing instances of the use of the terms "Moor" and "Blackamoor" signal English misperceptions and misunderstandings that see Moors associated variously with geographically specific ethnicities, from the Berbers of North Africa to sub-Saharan Africans, as well as with geographically and ethnically indeterminate stereotypes about appearance, behavior, and religion.[34] Far from being determined by fixed notions of race, representations of the Moor on the English stage reflected the transcultural heterogeneity, the mixing of race in the traffic across and around the early modern Mediterranean; even while, on the other hand, representations of the Moor served to construct race—and racism—in terms of an equivalency between blackness and barbarism.[35] We see this process at work in the *Battle of Alcazar*, which stages competing constructions: Abdelmelec is the "brave barbarian," unlike his nephew, "the barbarous Moor, / The negro Muly Hamet."[36] Commonly, theatrical constructions of the Moor are contextualized in relation to contemporary English travel narratives, such as the second volume of Richard Hakluyt's 1599 *Principal Navigations*, revised from early editions to include expanded sections on Africa, and the 1600 English translation of Leo Africanus's *Geographical History of Africa*.[37] The dates of these particular travel narratives are often invoked to account for the remarkable differences between Shakespeare's Aaron and the later Othello: while Othello is associated explicitly with the Barbary coast and suggests Shakespeare's familiarity with such travel narratives at the turn of the seventeenth century, *Titus Andronicus* was written between about 1590 and 1594, just prior to the most popular travel narratives of the period and, importantly, before such well-known political events as the first Moroccan embassy to London in 1600. The difference is encapsulated well by Ania Loomba: "Aaron leads us to literary, religious, and theatrical traditions that had equated black skin with godlessness and sin... *Othello* invites us to consider how that lineage is also intertwined with the long history of Christian interactions with various kinds of Moors."[38] What leads to this conclusion is her observation that "religion and skin colour intersect in the development of race as a concept": while Aaron's depravity is associated with his skin color and, therefore, with uses of the term Moor that signify his African blackness, Othello, although the play never comments directly on his religion, "cannot be understood without understanding attitudes to Turks and Muslims."[39] To be sure, Othello is a considerably more complex character than Aaron, heroic and idealized, but at the same time susceptible to being interpreted in racist terms as well—as the history of *Othello* criticism plainly establishes.[40] However, there is a curious geographical displacement in Loomba's argument that reads Aaron exclusively in terms of racial constructions of sub-Saharan African blackness and situates Othello in early modern encounters with Islamic Europe, Arabia, and North Africa. If we allow instead that Aaron, like Othello, must also be understood in terms of contemporary constructions of Turks and Muslims, then his otherwise curious presence in the play sheds a very different light on the violence of its "irreligious pieties."

If Aaron is anachronistically out of place in Shakespeare's Rome, his place in the Elizabethan theatre can thus be clarified by the complex geopolitical relationship between England and North Africa dramatized by Peele's *The Battle of Alcazar* and the imaginative geography of the Mediterranean that we find there.[41] There are, indeed, undeniable similarities between Aaron and Peele's Muly Mahomet, a name that resurfaces in *Titus Andronicus*; "Muly," Aaron tells us, is his countryman, and this is the one concrete reference to Aaron's geographical identity.[42] If both Aaron and Muly Mahomet are racially coded in a way that equates blackness with villainy, Muly Mahomet's name further links the Moor to characterizations of Mohammed in anti-Islamic polemical tracts. Both are driven by an insatiable desire for revenge against a principal enemy, but eager to see either of their enemies destroyed: for Muly Mahomet, either Abdelmelec or his Portuguese allies; for Aaron, both Titus and Saturninus. In both plays, revenge is associated with appetite and consumption: to fuel their revenge, Muly Mahomet kills a lioness to feed his wife, Calypoli; revenge in *Titus Andronicus* is linked to sexual desire, violation, and oral consumption in numerous figurative and disturbingly literal ways.[43] Orality is also allied to rhetorical skill: both Muly Mahomet and Aaron speak in strikingly lyrical verse, rich with allusion to classical and mythological figures. They speak our language, with a rhetorical dexterity and in a cultural lexicon that is not incomprehensible and alien, but chillingly familiar. Both characters are dramatic instances of an early modern figuration of the non-European barbarian who is derived from the long tradition of anti-Islamic rhetoric and characterizations of Mohammed, in combination with a burgeoning discourse of racial difference: they are exotic and erotic, powerful and soulless, seductive and dangerous.

Insofar as Peele's play participates in the definition of an English sense of self and nationhood in its staging of a Moorish battle, the play also reflects England's complicated relationship to the early modern Mediterranean. Peele's play, in particular, is marked by different modes of transnational exchange with both Europeans and non-Europeans. As many have noted about other examples of early Elizabethan drama, especially such plays as Marlowe's two-part *Tamburlaine*, *The Battle of Alcazar* is evidence of an increasingly cartographic understanding of the world. The map becomes a projection onto a spatial field of early modern transnationalism, reflecting both actual and imagined economic and cultural exchange, as well as colonial desire and anxiety; similarly, through its drama, the theatre participates in the construction and articulation of geographical and ethnographic discourses of similarity and difference. There is no reason to exclude *Titus Andronicus*, despite its classical matter, from this paradigm, especially when we position it spatially in the intersection of discursive and cartographic imaginings in early modern England. Such transnational encounter and exchange are staged in *Titus Andronicus*, but they are also the impetus to further conflict, violation, and miscegenation in Shakespeare's Rome. Act 1 concludes with Tamora wedded to Saturninus, "incorporate in Rome, / A Roman now adopted happily" (1.1.467–8), even while she plots with Saturninus to "find a day to massacre them all" (1.1.455). When all have exited but Aaron, he then steps forward to speak for the first time, to reveal in soliloquy how he will "wanton with this queen, / This goddess, this Semiramis, this nymph, / This siren that will charm Rome's Saturnine / And see his shipwreck and his commonweal's" (1.1.520–24). Taking the window opened by Titus, Aaron imagines his own version of social-psychological warfare, plotting and waiting to instigate the kind of counter-hegemonic violence disruptive of the political status quo that we now call, some 200 years after the word's coinage during the French Revolution, "terrorism."[44]

If *Titus Andronicus* resonates more powerfully than Peele's play in our own cultural paradigm, the reason is that we can map its violent hierarchies—the extreme binary differences that efface or erase the myriad differences between people—more readily onto our own. The play's destructive reciprocity of retaliation and revenge, its ambivalence toward national and political formations, its anxieties about cultural and racial hybridity, its self-negation of values and moral precepts in the encounter with an Other in mirror image: all of these themes challenge and complicate the project of nation-building and Empire in England before they had barely begun, and these themes continue to resonate for us in the wake of Europe's post-colonial legacy. If England lacks a presence in Shakespeare's Rome, England is present in the experience of the play in the now of the Elizabethan theatre: when Aaron steps forward to direct his speech toward the audience, he crosses a temporal boundary between the play's Roman past and England's present, as he anticipates a future of violence and destruction.

Notes

1. This chapter has been revised and recontextualized from an earlier essay, "Presentism, Anachronism and the Case of *Titus Andronicus*," *Shakespeare*, 8.1 (2012): 44–73 (http://www.tandfonline.com/doi/full/10.1080/17450918.2012.660277). We thank Routledge, the publishers of the journal, for permission to reproduce the material here.
2. Richard Halpern, *Shakespeare Among the Moderns* (Ithaca, NY: Cornell University Press, 1997), pp. 1–14.
3. Walter Benjamin, *The Arcades Project*, ed. Rolf Tiedemann, trans. Howard Eiland and Kevin McLaughlin (Cambridge, MA: Belknap, 1999), p. 331.
4. Walter Benjamin, *The Origin of German Tragic Drama*, trans. John Osborne (London: New Left Books, 1977), pp. 177–8.
5. Ibid., p. 178.
6. See Jacques Derrida, *Writing and Difference*, trans. Alan Bass (London: Routledge, 1981); and *Of Grammatology*, trans. Gayatri Chakravorty Spivak (Baltimore, MD: Johns Hopkins University Press, 1998, corr. ed.).
7. Jonathan Bate addresses the tradition of allegorical reading in his Arden Introduction by quoting T. J. B. Spencer in "Shakespeare and the Elizabethan Romans": "The play does not assume a political situation known to Roman history; it is, rather, a summary of Roman politics. It is not so much that any particular set of political institutions is assumed in *Titus*, but rather

that it includes *all* the political institutions that Rome ever had," in William Shakespeare, *Titus Andronicus*, ed. Jonathan Bate (London: Cengage Learning, 1995), pp. 16–17. See also Naomi Conn Liebler, "Getting It All Right: *Titus Andronicus* and Roman History," *Shakespeare Quarterly*, 45/3 (1994): 263–78. For a fully developed allegorical reading of the play's use of Rome, see Heather James, *Shakespeare's Troy: Drama, Politics and the Translation of Empire* (Cambridge University Press, 1997).
8. All textual references are to Bate's Arden edition, cited above.
9. Julie Taymor's 1999 film *Titus* has been the stimulus for several reconsiderations of the play; for an overview of the critical fortunes of the play before and since Taymor's film, see Jane Kingsley-Smith, "*Titus Andronicus*: A Violent Change of Fortunes," *Literature Compass*, 5.1 (2008): 106–21. Among the many notable critical discussions of the film are Thomas Cartelli, "Taymor's *Titus* in Time and Space: Surrogation and Interpolation," *Renaissance Drama*, 34 (2005): 163–84; Courtney Lehmann, "Crouching Tiger, Hidden Agenda: How Shakespeare and the Renaissance Are Taking the Rage Out of Feminism," *Shakespeare Quarterly*, 53.2 (2002): 260–80; Courtney Lehmann, Bryan Reynolds, and Lisa Starks, "'For Such a Sight Will Blind a Father's Eye': The Spectacle of Suffering in Taymor's *Titus*," in *Performing Transversally: Reimagining Shakespeare and the Critical Future*, ed. Bryan Reynolds, Janelle Reinelt, and Jonathan Gil Harris (New York: Palgrave Macmillan, 2003), pp. 215–243; and Carol Chillington Rutter, "Looking Like a Child – Or – '*Titus*': The Comedy," *Shakespeare Survey* 56 (2003): 1–26.
10. There is of course another range of contemporary contexts highly relevant to our understanding of this play, those involving the important issue of violence against women. For reasons of focus we limit ourselves to a different constellation of issues here. For an informative summation and discussion of the relevance of feminist connections of the play to Presentism, see Evelyn Gajowski, "Lavinia as 'Blank Page' and the Presence of Feminist Critical Perspectives," in Hugh Grady and Terence Hawkes, *Presentist Shakespeares* (London: Routledge, 2007), pp. 121–40. There are too many feminist assessments of the play to cite them comprehensively here. Of particular note, however, are Sara Eaton, "A Woman of Letters: Lavinia in *Titus Andronicus*," in *Shakespearean Tragedy and Gender*, ed. Shirley Nelson Garner and Madelon Sprengnether (Bloomington: Indiana University Press, 1996), 54–74; Douglas E. Green, "Interpreting 'her martyr'd signs': Gender and Tragedy in *Titus Andronicus*," *Shakespeare Quarterly*, 40 (1989): 317–26; Bernice Harris, "Sexuality as a Signifier for Power Relations: Using Lavinia, of Shakespeare's *Titus Andronicus*," *Criticism*, 38 (1996): 383–406; and Cynthia Marshall, "'I can interpret all her martyr'd signs': *Titus Andronicus*, Feminism, and the Limits of Interpretation," in *Sexuality and Politics in Renaissance Drama*, ed. Carole Levin and Karen Robertson (Lewiston: Edwin Mellen Press, 1991), pp. 193–213. These sources are noted, among others, by Deborah Willis in "'The Gnawing Vulture: Revenge, Trauma Theory, and *Titus Andronicus*," *Shakespeare Quarterly*, 53 (Spring 2002): 21–51 (n. 2).

11. Nicholas Moschovakis reads the opening sacrifice using the trope of anachronism to argue that the ironic "piety" that Titus and the Andronici exercise forces the Elizabethan audience to ask whether persecution and murder done in the name of post-Reformation Christianity are any more defensible than the play's ritualistic violence, which they "must reject as anachronistically pre-Christian or idolatrously un-Christian"; see his "'Irreligious Piety' and Christian History: Persecution as Pagan Anachronism in *Titus Andronicus,*" *Shakespeare Quarterly*, 53.4 (Winter 2002): 460–86; 461.
12. Qtd. in Moschovakis, "'Irreligious Piety,'" 461.
13. Derrida opens *Spectres of Marx: The State of the Debt, the Work of Mourning, and the New International* (London: Routledge, 1994) with a quotation from Act 1 of *Hamlet*, and the "time is out of joint" trope is developed throughout.
14. Jacques Derrida, "This Strange Institution Called Literature, An Interview with Jacques Derrida," in *Acts of Literature*, ed. Derek Attridge and Jacques Derrida (London: Routledge, 1992), pp. 33–75; pp. 63–4.
15. Jacques Derrida, "Signature Event Context," in *Margins of Philosophy* (Chicago: University of Chicago Press, 1982), p. 320. Mark Robson uses this example in his critique of Presentism in "Shakespeare's Words of the Future: Promising *Richard III*," *Textual Practice*, 19.1 (2005): 13–30. We agree with Robson's use of Derrida to help conceptualize the radical temporality of readers negotiating centuries-old texts. However, Robson does not develop the possible connection to the case of Presentism, a term that he understands to mean a kind of "pure" anachronism—not only an admission "of the ineradicability of reading one's own contextual determination," but a thoroughgoing disavowal of the text's historical determination (13). But this critique, we believe, is based on a one-sided understanding of Presentism that ignores its "moment" of negotiating with a text's past; and in its encounter with the text, defining not only the text's congruence with our present ideologies, but also its resistances to them, its status as art in relation to an ideology that cannot capture it.
16. Jacques Derrida, "Différance," in *Literary Theory: An Anthology*, ed. Julie Rivkin and Michael Ryan, 2nd edn. (Malden, MA: Blackwell, 2004), pp. 278–99; p. 287.
17. Ewan Fernie has defined this aspect of Presentism succinctly. Presentists, he writes, "mustn't merely cater to and confirm present values. But any really responsive engagement with Shakespeare's inimitable and even alien presence in the present will in fact creatively confront, unsettle and transcend routine modes of thinking." Ewan Fernie, "Action! *Henry V*," in Grady and Hawkes, *Presentist Shakespeares*, pp. 96–120; p. 97. For Fernie, the irreducibility of the literary work's presence to antiquarian interests is the condition that ultimately distinguishes us as literary critics from mere historians, and so the need to revalue the presence of the text in the present is, as we have been arguing, a matter of disciplinary urgency.

18. Some historians have suggested that Peacham recalled the episode from memory many years after performance, that he confused his memory of performance with a reading of the subsequent first Quarto edition (1594) or a ballad version of the story, or even that Peacham had another dramatic version of the play in mind. For the latter argument, see June Schlueter, "Rereading the Peacham Drawing," *Shakespeare Quarterly*, 50.2 (Summer, 1999): 171–84.
19. See, for example, J. M. Robertson, who answers earlier nineteenth-century detractors of anachronism, in *Did Shakespeare Write Titus Andronicus* (London: Watts & Co., 1905), especially pp. 211–12.
20. George Puttenham, *The arte of English poesie Contriued into three bookes: The first of poets and poesie, the second of proportion, the third of ornament* (London: Printed by Richard Field, dwelling in the black-Friers, neere Ludgate, 1589), p. 3; from the Huntington Library Copy, *Early English Books Online*. Online.
21. The first four books were printed in 1565, and reprinted with the remainder in 1567. They were printed by Robert Waldgrave in 1587 under the title "The xv. Bookes of P. Ovidius Naso, entitled, *Metamorphosis*, a worke very pleasant and delectable, Translated out of Latin into English meeter by Arthur Golding gentleman." They were reprinted again in 1593, possibly after the composition of *Titus Andronicus*.
22. Edward W. Said, *Orientalism* (New York: Vintage Books, 2003).
23. Said, in "Preface (2003)," *Orientalism*, p. xiii.
24. Daniel Vitkus explores the viability of reading Orientalism back to early modern Europe in "Early Modern Orientalism: Representations of Islam in Sixteenth- and Seventeenth-Century Europe," in *Western Views of Islam in Medieval and Early Modern Europe*, ed. David R. Blanks and Michael Frasetto (New York: St. Martin's Press, 1999), esp. p. 209. Jonathan Burton has offered a more pluralistic model of transcultural encounter between Europe and North Africa under the rubric of "trafficking," in *Traffic and Turning: Islam and English Drama, 1579–1624* (Newark, DE: University of Delaware Press, 2005). More recently, Burton has suggested that "it is an old saw to argue against Edward Said's contention that Orientalism can be traced back as far as the European Renaissance. A virtual army of critics indicates instead that not only were relations between 'the East' and 'the West' often characterized by European compromise, deference, and a desire for exchange, nothing resembling discursive coherence in regard to 'the Orient' was even possible before the eighteenth century," "Emplotting the Early Modern Mediterranean," in Goran Stanivukovic, ed., *Remapping the Mediterranean World in Early Modern English Writings* (London: Palgrave Macmillan, 2007), pp. 21–40; pp. 22–3. In his discussion of this point, Burton cites a number of the sources we cite here below. Several of the essays in the earlier *Post-Colonial Shakespeares*, ed. Ania Loomba and Martin Orkin (London: Routledge, 1998), also anticipate more recent objections in the vein of Burton's.

25. In *Provincializing Europe: Postcolonial Thought and Historical Difference* (Princeton University Press, 2000), Dipesh Chakrabarty argues that the very act of historicizing masks European assumptions—originating in the German philosophical tradition and culminating in the post-modernist critique of capitalism—about historical development and the colonial encounter: "Historicism is what made modernity or capitalism look not simply global but rather as something that became global *over time*, by originating in one place (Europe) and then spreading outside it. This 'first in Europe, then elsewhere' structure of global historical time was historicist... Historicism thus posited historical time as a measure of cultural distance (at least in institutional development) that was assumed to exist between West and the non-West" (7).

26. Edward W. Said, "Orientalism Reconsidered," *Cultural Critique*, 1 (Autumn 1985), 89–107; 92.

27. Ibid., 92.

28. Vitkus, in particular, has made the very important point that the postcolonial reading of Shakespeare often fails to account for the difference between the material realities of failed colonial enterprises (as, for example, England's foundering claims in Ireland under Elizabeth, or England's disastrous first attempts to establish colonies in America under James) and discursive fantasies of empire. See his *Turning Turk*, esp. Chapter 1, pp. 1–24. See also Matar, *Turks, Moors, and Englishmen*, esp. Chapter 10.

29. Much recent scholarship has turned to the question of England's place within and against the Mediterranean, particularly as represented in early modern drama; see, in particular, Jerry Brotton, "'This Tunis, sir, was Carthage': Contesting colonialism in *The Tempest*," in Loomba and Orkins, *Post-Colonial Shakespeares*, pp. 23–42; Richard Wilson, "Voyage to Tunis: New History and the Old World of *The Tempest*," *ELH*, 64: 2 (1997): 333–57; and, most recently, Stanivukovic, *Remapping the Mediterranean World in Early Modern English Writings*.

30. This argument has been made persuasively by James, *Shakespeare's Troy*. While the treatment of *Titus Andronicus* is impressive here, the argument proposes an intentional wholeness that depends not only on the assumption of single authorship, but on a consistency and integrity of intention that rarely apply to the changing and often collaborative form of drama in the period.

31. Richmond Barbour, *Before Orientalism: London's Theatre of "the East", 1576–1626* (Cambridge: Cambridge University Press, 2003), considers England's encounters with the East Indies, the establishment of the Charter for the East India Company in 1600, and representations of the East on the English stage.

32. For a full and fascinating account, see Matar, *Turks, Moors, and Englishmen*.

33. See Bartels, "*The Battle of Alcazar*, the Mediterranean, and the Moor," in Stanivukovic, *Remapping the Mediterranean World in Early Modern English Writings*, pp. 97–116, esp. p. 98. See also her more recent book,

Speaking of the Moor: From "Alcazar" to Othello (Philadelphia: University of Pennsylvania Press, 2008).
34. A small but significant sampling of those who address *Titus Andronicus* specifically includes Jack D'Amico, *The Moor in English Renaissance Drama* (Tampa: University of South Florida Press, 1991), pp. 135–47; and, earlier, Anthony Gerard Barthelemy, *Black Face, Maligned Race: The Representation of Blacks in English Drama from Shakespeare to Southerne* (Baton Rouge: Louisiana State University Press, 1987); Emily C. Bartels, "Making More of the Moor: Aaron, Othello and Renaissance Refashionings of Race," *Shakespeare Quarterly*, 41:4 (Winter 1990): 433–54; and Ian Smith, "Those 'Slippery Customers': Rethinking Race in *Titus Andronicus*," *JTD*, 3 (November 1997): 45–58. Other significant discussions of race in early modern England include Mary Floyd-Wilson, *English Ethnicity and Race in Early Modern Drama* (Cambridge: Cambridge University Press, 2003); Kim F. Hall, *Things of Darkness: Economies of Race and Gender in Early Modern England* (Ithaca, NY: Cornell University Press, 1995); Arthur L. Little, *Shakespeare Jungle Fever: National-Imperial Re-visions of Race, Rape, and Sacrifice* (Stanford, CA: Stanford University Press, 2000); and Ania Loomba, *Shakespeare, Race, and Colonialism* (Oxford: Oxford University Press, 2002). Francesca T. Royster emphasizes the complexity of racial constructions in *Titus Andronicus* by focusing on its characterizations of the Goths and Tamora in particular in terms of "hyper-whiteness"; in "White-Limed Walls: Whiteness and Gothic Extremism in Shakespeare's *Titus Andronicus*," *Shakespeare Quarterly*, 51. 4 (Winter 2000): 432–55.
35. Ian Smith, "Barbarian Errors: Performing Race in Early Modern England," *Shakespeare Quarterly*, 49.2 (Summer 1998): 168–86, argues that "speech acts" in early modern plays such as *Othello* are performative markers of racial identity, and, more specifically, that rhetorical "barbarisms" are the linguistic markers of outsiders whose presence represents a transgression of the normal social order. He also provides a critical etymology of the terms "barbarian" and "barbarism."
36. George Peele, *The Battle of Alcazar*, ed. Khalid Bekkaoui (Casablanca: Moroccan Cultural Studies Centre, 2001), p. 43. For discussion of these competing characterizations of the Moor in this play, see Bartels, "*The Battle of Alcazar*, the Mediterranean, and the Moor," esp. p. 107. See also her more recent book, *Speaking of the Moor*.
37. There are also a number of captivity narratives from the period, the majority occurring from the turn of the seventeenth century. These are chronicled by Matar in "English Accounts of Captivity in North Africa and the Middle East, 1577–1625," *Renaissance Quarterly*, 54:2 (Summer 2001): 553–72.
38. Ania Loomba, *Shakespeare, Race, and Colonialism*, p. 45.
39. Ibid., p. 46. This position is given greater scope by Burton in *Traffic and Turning*, esp. Chapter 6.
40. See Grady, *Shakespeare's Universal Wolf: Studies in Early Modern Reification* (Oxford: Clarendon, 1996), pp. 109–30; and more recently Christopher

Pye, "'To throw out our eyes for brave Othello': Shakespeare and Aesthetic Ideology," *Shakespeare Quarterly*, 60: 4 (Winter 2009), 425–47.
41. In his 1984 Oxford edition of the play, Eugene Waith suggests that the character Aaron probably derives from a sixteenth-century European folktale about a wicked Moorish servant who seeks revenge on his master by killing the nobleman's wife and two children, before killing himself. An English version of c. 1569 likely pre-dated the play, but the earliest surviving English text is dated 1693.
42. This reference to Muly may come, in fact, directly from Peele himself, whom Brian Vickers recently claimed to be Shakespeare's co-author in *Titus*; though this has not been accepted in all quarters. See Brian Vickers, *Shakespeare, Co-Author: A Historical Study of Five Collaborative Plays* (Oxford: Oxford University Press, 2002), pp. 449–73. In his Introduction to the Arden edition, however, Bate explores the possibility of collaborative authorship, though he finally dismisses it (82).
43. Among the many notable discussions of violence and orality in the play, the best remains Marion Wynne-Davies's "'The Swallowing Womb': Consumed and Consuming Women in *Titus Andronicus*" in *The Matter of Difference: Materialist Feminist Criticism of Shakespeare*, ed. Valerie Wayne (Ithaca, NY: Cornell University Press, 1991), pp. 129–51. See also the many exemplary essays in Philip C. Kolin, ed., *Titus Andronicus: Critical Essays* (New York: Garland, 1995), especially David Wilburn's "Rape and Revenge in *Titus Andronicus*," pp. 171–94; and Dorothea Kehler, "'That Ravenous Tiger Tamora': *Titus Andronicus*'s Lusty Widow, Wife, and M/other," pp. 317–32.
44. *OED* dates the first English usage of "terrorism" to 1795, following the Jacobin Reign of Terror, to mean "government by intimidation as directed and carried out by the party in power in France during the Revolution of 1789–94; the system of the 'Terror' (1793–4)" ("Terrorism," *OED*, 1).

2
The Presentist Threat to Editions of Shakespeare

Gabriel Egan

I

There are good and bad ways to be Presentist. In the sense used in some of the essays in this collection, the term reappropriates a pejorative word. Historians decry as Presentist any writing that anachronistically imports to the study of the past the concerns of the present. Since the nineteenth century—and under the influence of the empiricist historian Leopold von Ranke (1795–1886), who insisted on the centrality of primary sources—historians have striven for an ideal of scholarship that seeks to understand the past in its own terms rather than applying to it the standards, concepts, and norms of the present. Holding this as an ideal has not blinded historians to the impossibility of achieving it: they were and are quite aware that one cannot entirely leave behind one's present-day assumptions and prejudices in order imaginatively to enter the past without intellectual baggage. The very necessity of attending to one body of evidence rather than another—because rarely can one attend to all the available evidence at once—shapes the narratives that historians write, as Ranke's followers knew.

The key to historical discipline is keeping one's methodological selectivity in view. While not necessarily agreeing that the primary sources could support conclusions entirely opposite to the ones being drawn in a given study, those who followed Ranke would freely admit that alternative narratives might emerge from consideration of other primary sources of comparable value that had not been considered. In evaluating the sources, Rankean historians attempt to imagine what it was like to live at that point in the past and in ignorance of future events known to the historian. One way of failing to do this is teleology, in which events of the past are read as though they inevitably led to the present that embodies their completion, and/or in which historical perspectives available only with hindsight are imputed to agents within those events. Herbert Butterfield found an example of this in what he called *The Whig Interpretation of History* (1931), a nineteenth-century view of British constitutional and social development that celebrated its culmination in the Glorious Revolution of 1688.[1] This was Presentism in the bad sense. Presentism as discussed in several essays in this volume, however, redefines the term on the principle that the historians' ideal of objectivity is at best a self-delusion. According to this new definition, we bring to the past so much baggage from the present that objectivity is impossible, and the most honest approach is to be entirely explicit about this and declare that our interpretations are always utterly shaped by present concerns. The unspoken injunction here is to follow the example of politicized gay criticism that in the 1980s and 1990s reappropriated the term "'queer'": we should declare our Presentism rather than pretending that it does not exist.

In the past ten years, Presentism has become a way of doing literary criticism by explicitly evoking the present concerns that motivate a desire to reread old literature (especially Shakespeare) to discover resonances that it could not have had for its first audiences or readers, because these only became possible as a consequence of what happened between then and now. As such, it is a reaction against the dominant mode of historicist analysis that rose to prominence after the publication in 1980 of Stephen Greenblatt's *Renaissance Self-Fashioning* and the New Historicism that it inaugurated.[2] In 1996, Hugh Grady complained that this historicizing movement had become so dominant that "more 'presentist' approaches—that is, those oriented towards the text's meaning in the present, as opposed to 'historicist' approaches oriented to meanings in the past—are in danger of eclipse."[3] Grady was distinguishing just what a moment in Shakespeare might have meant to early modern readers and playgoers from what that moment might mean to readers and playgoers today. The New Historicism was indebted to Clifford Geertz's literary approach to anthropology, which asked of each activity being studied "What does it mean to these people?"—a question that

Greenblatt projected from the geographical to the temporal domain in order to understand the early moderns.[4]

Done properly, historicism bridges the gap between past meanings and present ones. To treat past meanings as utterly isolated in their own time mistakes the nature of human communication, since if the chasm were unbridgeable then we could make no sense at all of Shakespeare's works. To give a concrete example, Margreta de Grazia and Peter Stallybrass have pointed out that modernizing Shakespeare's spelling tends to flatten into monovocality words that were equivocal in the original. Fluidity of spelling allowed the word we modernize as *hair* in *Macbeth* to attract the forms and senses of "'hair,' 'heir,' 'heire,' 'heere,' and 'here'" and the modern *heir* to trigger "'heir,' 'aire,' 'are,' 'haire,' and 'here.'" Early modern English permitted such multiple associations, while "Modernization requires that this slippage be contained."[5] However, were modern readers truly unable to hear *hair* as *heir* as well as *air*, then the problem would be insuperable: even an editorial footnote could not clarify the point, which would be unintelligible. De Grazia and Stallybrass were right that readers can no longer easily enjoy this equivocality on the page, but it is still recoverable with effort. Most importantly, of course, such multiplicities remain readily active in performance, since the homophones *heir* and *air* are aurally identical.

One kind of literary theory still posits such unbridgeable gulfs between interpretive communities. As Terry Eagleton wittily put it, "Nobody can seriously disagree with Stanley Fish," not because Fish is right, but because according to his model of communication you either share his discursive world and are able to understand and accept what he is saying, or you do not and your objections "present no more challenge to his case than the cawing of a rook."[6] Happily, communication is more interestingly engaged than that. We neither speak past one another as though using different languages nor adopt one another's ideas as self-evident; rather, in conversation we reflect on those differences of opinion that we can grasp, howsoever imperfectly and precariously, and frequently enough we transform ourselves by imaginatively making sense of them. So it is with our attempts to understand the past, and editors of Shakespeare are at the sharp end of the problem of imperfect communication, because their prime objective is to help readers better understand what they are reading.

Presentism shares with Marxist historicist criticism a rejection of the idea that meaning is something transhistorical and transcultural embedded in writing from the past; and both insist on its being generated at the point of consumption by modern readers. Making an edition of Shakespeare gives a practical illustration of the problems that follow from this rejection. Editors want to make works from 400 years ago accessible to modern readers, so they modernize the spelling, which seems like a Presentist activity: privileging of the needs of today over the conservation of the past's alterity. Yet, they usually also want to render the past accurately in all its puzzling alterity—Why were they so cruel to animals? Did they really think the monarch had two bodies?—and that seems like a historicist activity. Like other historians, editors build a bridge to cross the chasm between the past and the present, having first constructed that very chasm in their narratives. It is hard not to suspect that the chasm is constructed to fit the bridge rather than vice versa. That is, as professionals working on the problem, we specify the extent of the past's difference from the present as precisely the amount of difference that we feel able to overcome in our explications. This regrettable tendency may flourish unchecked in purely critical work, but in editing plays it is countered by the need to produce a legible text. Although the editor has at her disposal the tools of an introduction, explanatory notes, and glossaries to assist in the process, the script itself must be clear enough for the ordinary reader to follow the action and understand the characters' actions and motivations. This requirement of clarity generates special problems for textual criticism's engagement with history, as we shall see.

II

The editing of Shakespeare did not became a fully developed scholarly activity until the early twentieth century. The Cambridge–Macmillan complete works of 1863–6 was the first produced by university-employed scholars using an openly expressed bibliographical methodology, arrived at after examining afresh the entire textual situation of Shakespeare.[7] Rather than putting the subject to rest, the entrance of professionals into what had previously been the gentleman-scholar's private domain brought an explosion of new theory and practice in editing early modern drama that soon became known as the New Bibliography, a term coined by the movement's early leader W. W. Greg.[8] In editing Shakespeare, the principles of the New Bibliography reigned virtual unchallenged until the 1980s, when a number of its premises were undermined by the rival New Textualism. The full story of this challenge need not detain us and is told elsewhere.[9] For our purposes there are two key points to be borne in mind.

The first is that the New Bibliography presented itself as disinterested historical investigation into the early editions, unencumbered by twentieth-century preconceptions, while most New Textualists were somewhat Presentist (*avant la lettre*) in their explicit invocation of post-modern concerns with incredulity, incoherence, and instability. The second point is that although disquiet about the approach was voiced in various quarters, the New Bibliographers tended to assume that each play came to fruition in one complete version that remained essentially unchanged during its early life on the stage. This meant that where there exist differing early editions of a play, it was assumed that all were derived from a single original and differ only because varying kinds of corruption entered the text during its aural, scribal, and print transmission. The task then was to recover that original—or get as close as possible to it—by combining evidence from the various debased "witnesses." The New Textualists, by contrast, saw no reason to assume the existence of a singular original, thinking instead that the various early editions might represent distinct versions of the play, separated by authorial and nonauthorial revision that suited the script to the needs of particular times and places. If so, the early editions ought not to be ranked and combined to make a singular modern text, but rather respected for their diversity and given "equal but different" status.

To see the consequences of these divergent approaches, we may take as a test case a multi-text play that has recently been edited twice, once according to essentially New Bibliographic principles and once by the lights of New Textualism. After that, we will consider what these methodologies mean for the editor faced with precisely the opposite problem, because the play survives not in two relatively good early editions but in just one that is highly corrupt. A comparison of the practical effects of these divergent approaches to editing casts new light on the problems to which Presentism addresses itself and throws into relief a peculiar paradox. As literary critics,

Presentists occupy the left of the political spectrum from liberalism to full-blown revolutionary Marxism, and favor interpretations that are politically progressive or radical. However, it is not exactly clear whether these politics are best served by asserting that the past was essentially like the present, in which case its concerns are our concerns and we may draw lessons from the situations described by writers such as Shakespeare, or was essentially unlike the present, in which case we may draw from it the optimistic conclusion that the future may be equally different from the present, too. In editing, the link between theory and practice is even more tenuous. From the test cases examined here, it appears that radical textual intervention may produce a text that is amenable to conservative critical interpretation and that textual conservativism may produce radical readings. The law of unanticipated consequences seems to apply strongly to editing, and the conclusion to this essay will offer some suggestions for how editors might work under these conditions.

In 1595, Thomas Millington published Shakespeare's *Richard Duke of York* in octavo format (O); he used an exemplar of this octavo to republish the play as a quarto in 1600 (Q2). Two years later, Millington transferred his rights in the play to Thomas Pavier, who published a quarto in 1619 (Q3), again set from an exemplar of O. In Pavier's edition the play was paired with *The Contention of York and Lancaster*, which told the preceding story, under the combined title of *The Whole Contention*. When *Richard Duke of York* appeared in the 1623 Folio, it had around 1,000 lines not previously printed and was given the new title *The Third Part of Henry the Sixth*, by which it is now more familiarly known. For editors of the play, the first problem is to establish the relationships between the early editions, and it was from errors in common that they discovered that Q2 and Q3 were merely unauthoritative reprints of O. Only O and F were printed directly from manuscripts, but determining what these were and how they were related to one another is fundamental for using the evidence in O and F to make a modern edition.

In 2001 two modern editions of the play appeared taking different approaches to this problem, one in the Oxford Shakespeare series, edited by Randall Martin, and the other in the Arden Shakespeare Third Series, edited by John D. Cox and Eric Rasmussen.[10] Surveying the differences between the two nonderivative early editions, Martin came to the conclusion that F was printed from the author's own papers (which would reflect the play's form prior to rehearsal and reshaping in performance), while O was printed from a script put together by the actors remembering what they had said and done in performance.[11] Evidence for F's origin in authorial papers are the incompleteness, indefiniteness, and vagueness in its stage directions—although Martin acknowledged recent scholarship that questioned the assumption that only authorial papers would have such unsatisfactory directions—and the presence of actors' names where we should expect characters' names. An instance of the latter is F's direction *"Enter Sinklo and Humfrey, with Crosse-bowes in their hands,"*[12] apparently referring to the Chamberlain's Men's actor John Sincklo, known from other plays. The traditional New Bibliographical explanation is that an actor's name would take the place of his character's name only in the dramatist's papers and that this showed the dramatist making or reflecting a casting decision of some importance. In papers used to run performances of the play, on the other hand, someone in the theatre might gloss the name of a minor character with the name of the actor playing it (just to remind himself), but then both names would appear.

The whole problem of how editors should designate character names for the modern readership engages wider questions about the meaning of variations within the early editions. Under the influence of literary theory, New Textualists are apt to find significance in all kinds of textual variation and to label them as instances of instability and self-contradiction. Leah Marcus thought that when comparing the 1622 quarto and 1623 Folio editions of *Othello*, the important matter is to reveal "how a given text differs from itself."[13] This claim is unintelligible since *differ* and *self* have opposite meanings, but the idea has become a New Textualist shibboleth. Randall McLeod used "non-identity with itself" to describe textual multiplicity[14]; Margreta de Grazia and Peter Stallybrass echoed him by calling multi-version editions of *King Lear* and *Hamlet* symptoms of "the problem of a work's nonidentity with itself."[15] Meredith Skura deflated this New Textualist assumption that variation reveals the ontological vulnerability of texts with an apt theatre-historical comparison: "there are other valid responses to the two texts of *King Lear* besides assuming that there is no *King Lear* or no Shakespeare—just as there are other responses to the two floor plans for the Rose Theater [the original of 1587 and the refurbishment of the 1592] besides assuming that there was no Rose Theater."[16]

In particular, the variation in the names given to a single character in early editions of Shakespeare is diagnosed by New Textualists as an early modern anticipation of the instability of human personality discovered by modernism and post-modernism. In this view, a modern editor who regularizes character names is imposing super-egotistical orderliness where the early documents display the fluidity and chaos of the id. Or, to switch from the modernist language of Sigmund Freud to that of Louis Althusser who combined these ideas with Marxism, an editor who regularizes character names does the work of ideology in giving a fictional coherence to a mere collection of fragmentary social functions that each person fills in society.

According to John Drakakis, only an editor deluded enough to believe in "some stable conception of dramatic 'character'" would want to overrule the naming "instability" (that is, variation) found in the early editions.[17] This kind of reasoning first emerged in the early 1990s when British Cultural Materialists, the group within which Drakakis came to prominence in the 1980s, became aware of the New Bibliographical editorial tradition and rejected it as an ally of conservative criticism. A typical early example is Graham Holderness and Bryan Loughrey's complaint that in the Folio text of *The Taming of the Shrew*, Christopher Sly's speech prefixes identify him as *Beg[gar]* yet modern editors give him the speech prefix *Sly*. Thus, "The substitution of an original emphasis on public identity and social function for a modern emphasis on personality and the individual subject... is a clear instance of modern editors imposing anachronistic values on an early modern text."[18]

In the Folio text of *Richard Duke of York / 3 Henry 6*, Lady Grey is first designated as *Wid[ow]* in speech prefixes and then becomes *Lady Grey*; according to New Bibliography, such variation could occur because in the act of composition (reflected in the author's own papers) Shakespeare would think in relational terms. Hence, to take the most famous example, in the second quarto of *Romeo and Juliet* (1599), Capulet's wife speaks variously as a wife, a mother, and a lady and has corresponding speech prefixes as *Wif[e]*, *Mo[ther]*, or *La[dy]* in different scenes. According to New Bibliography, in a document used for running performances the theatre personnel would regularize this variation to a single identifier to prevent possible confusion about who is meant. In this view, name variation points to the vicissitudes of authorial composition. For New Bibliographers, the clinching evidence for O deriving not from authorial papers or a transcript of them but rather from the actors' recollection of their lines is its garbling of Richard and Clarence's complaint to their brother Edward about the royal marriage settlements he has approved.[19] Although O's rendering of this complaint makes grammatical sense, it is impossible to understand what Richard and Clarence are upset about. A glance at F's version of the same complaint makes it obvious that O has jumbled the names of the brides and grooms. When unjumbled, the basis of Richard and Clarence's grievance is clear: their brother Edward, the new king, has favored the Woodvilles (the existing family of his new wife, the widow Lady Grey) over them. According to New Bibliography, only actors could make such a jumble.

There are other O/F differences, however, that are hard to explain as F representing the authorial script and O representing what was performed by the actors working on and revising this script. Martin found in F a series of metaphors using the wind, sea, and tide as images to represent Henry's rising and falling fortunes, and these images are absent in O. It seems unlikely that before the play was performed someone went through it to delete just these images, or that the actors selectively forgot them when recalling their lines.[20] Rather, it seems that Shakespeare revised the play to put these images in and these revisions also got marked on the manuscript underlying F. Martin found a series of other O/F differences of staging that are best explained by authorial revision, so that memorial reconstruction and authorial revision separate O and F. Since F represents Shakespeare's more considered expression of his intention, Martin took it as the basis for his modernized edition. Martin's position on the provenance of the early editions was squarely within the tradition of the New Bibliography, using its methods for inferring from particular features of the printed text the nature of the manuscript copy from which it was set.

Cox and Rasmussen's view of the textual genealogy was somewhat different. After airing some doubts, they accepted that O was probably made by memorial reconstruction of the script by its actors.[21] They cast doubt on the interpretation of evidence usually understood as showing that the Folio text was printed from the author's papers.[22] Cox and Rasmussen decided that an actor's name (such as *Sinklo*) might appear in theatrical papers if someone made a single document containing all the lines for the many small parts that one actor played in the story and wanted to record his name. Variation in speech prefixes could be introduced in the print shop, either because of type shortage (certain names being avoided because the printer was short of particular letters) or because a different typesetter, with different preferences, took over at the point where the change occurs. More simply, theatre practitioners might not bother to regularize speech prefixes because they did not find it confusing to have to remember that *Widow* and *Lady Grey* are the same person. What follows from Cox and Rasmussen's demurral from the New Bibliography? Their prime conclusion was that they could not be sure that O was based on a memorial reconstruction and F on authorial papers, hence they did "not want to prejudice interpretation by pronouncing one text more authoritative than the other or even by attaching such labels as *original* and *revision*."[23] Yet, their edition was based principally on F with readings from O imported as needed.[24] Martin, by contrast, was clear that the Folio is an expansion and revision of the play represented by O, and thus for him F's variant passages were to be followed except in a few cases of "error, omission, or indispensable clarification."[25] Let us look at what this difference of approach means in practice.

Because they could not tell which early text is more authoritative, there was nothing to stop Cox and Rasmussen importing from O anything they found preferable to the reading in their copy text, F. Thus, the memorable detail of Clifford dying from an arrow in his neck (as recorded in the historical sources) was included in Cox and Rasmussen's edition (taken from O), while Martin, following F, omitted it. Paradoxically, being skeptical about the relative authority of O and F increased Cox and Rasmussen's freedom to depart from their copy. In Act 5, Scene 1, Clarence's abandonment of Warwick's cause and his return to his brothers' side is staged differently in O and F. In O, Clarence enters apparently to assist Warwick in holding the fortified town of Coventry, but when a parley is sounded, "*Richard* and *Clarence* whispers together" and then Clarence "takes his red Rose out of his hat, and throwes it at *Warwike*."[26] In F, however, there is no parley with Richard and no rose throwing, yet Clarence nonetheless breaks from Warwick, so we have to conclude that he intended to do so before the start of this scene.[27]

Martin followed F's action, but because it offers no stage direction for the moment of Clarence's break from Warwick, he invented "*He shows a red rose"* to accompany Clarence's line "Look here, I throw my infamy at thee."[28] This invented stage direction is prescriptive in asserting that what Clarence shows is a rose—nothing in F requires this—but leaves unstated just what he does with it, and so falls short of the required elucidation. Cox and Rasmussen also followed F's action—no whispering between Richard and Clarence, no on-stage change of heart—but they drew on O's wording for their stage directions *"Takes the red rose out of his hat"* and *"Throws it at Warwick."*[29] Thus, Cox and Rasmussen gave weight to specific details of O's stage directions—allowing them to prescribe the action more strongly that Martin did—even though they rejected O's variant action.

Cox and Rasmussen's prescriptive approach might be thought the symptom of an admirable concern for clarity above all other considerations, were it not for aspects of their text that explicitly sacrifice clarity in order to press home a thoroughly modern critical point. For example, they retained F's variability in Lady Grey's speech prefixes, calling her *Widow* in Act 3, Scene 2 because she is known to the audience only as a widow at this point and her widowhood is what attracts Edward. Giving her yet another name, they commented: "In our view, preserving the potent ideological implications of Lady Elizabeth's functional identity as *Widow* in this scene far outweighs the need to iron out this anomaly in the text for the modern reader."[30] Rather than preserving the implications of name variation, this kind of intervention on ideological grounds imposes variation in a distinctly Presentist matter, in the old-fashioned bad sense of the term.

Many characters in Shakespeare's plays have names of which the audience long remains ignorant, if indeed it ever learns them. Viola's name is first uttered, and thus revealed to the audience, in the last ten minutes of performances of *Twelfth Night*, and the king's name in *Hamlet* and the duke's in *Measure for Measure* (Claudius and Vincentio respectively) are never disclosed to the audience. Name variation is endemic in Shakespeare. For example, Bolingbroke is "Harry of Hereford, Lancaster, and Derby" (*Richard 2* 1.3.35–6) and then the Duke of Lancaster before becoming King Henry 4. Editorial consistency of naming in stage directions and speech prefixes nonetheless reflects early performance practice, since despite name variation just one actor took each role. Editorial consistency of naming also clarifies the play for modern readers without distorting performability, since the affected stage directions and speech prefixes are not spoken. Once admitted as criteria for editorial intervention, the ideological potencies of anonymity and name variation allow the plays to speak to our critical concerns, but at the cost of readers' comprehension and of performability.

III

Judging just how far to intervene to repair apparent textual corruption is among the editor's most difficult tasks, and the state of the 1609 quarto of *Pericles*,[31] the only authoritative witness, presents a particularly testing case. The previous year there appeared an anonymous prose novella called *The Painful Adventures of Pericles Prince of Tyre*, which is traditionally attributed to the dramatist George Wilkins and seems to draw on the play as performed.[32] The novella's title page calls it "The true History of the play of *Pericles*, as it was lately presented by the worthy ancient Poet *John Gower*," and a common assumption is that Wilkins collaborated on the play with Shakespeare and then published this prose version of it (drawing also on another source of the story) without the King's Men's permission. Other pieces of evidence can be used to bolster this assumption, such as the fairly clear signs that the play *Pericles* was collaboratively written by Shakespeare and someone else, since stylistically the first two acts of *Pericles* are unlike, and the last three are like, his work elsewhere.

MacDonald P. Jackson showed that Wilkins's style elsewhere matches the first two acts of the play,[33] but as John Klause pointed out, there may be other writers ignored by Jackson whose style would also match the first two acts of *Pericles*.[34] Wilkins's is the presumptive candidate for collaboration if we accept that he wrote the prose novella, but that attribution is not entirely secure. There survive only two copies of *The Painful Adventures of Pericles Prince of Tyre*, neither of which identifies Wilkins as the author, and the only link is that one of them has a dedication signed by him, apparently created as an afterthought during the print run and inserted before binding.[35] Depending on her view of Wilkins's possible involvement in the writing of the play with Shakespeare, an editor might decide that *The Painful Adventures* provides an independent source from which to correct errors in the 1609 quarto of the play, since, if written by one of the two dramatists and reporting what got performed, it might well preserve readings lost in the play quarto.

As Gary Taylor pointed out, the degree to which editors emend a text ought to vary from work to work according to the diagnosed degree and type of corruption in the textual witnesses, but in practice editors tend to be temperamentally inclined to heavy or light intervention that they apply indiscriminately to all the works they handle. As Taylor put it, often the amount of emendation will have "more to do with the emendation-threshold of the individual editor than with the corruption-quotient of the individual texts."[36] In 2004, the Arden Shakespeare Third Series and Oxford Shakespeare published competing editions of *Pericles* that illustrate Taylor's point, the play being emended lightly by Suzanne Gossett and heavily by Roger Warren respectively. In its own way, each edition showed the impressure of modern concerns: Gossett's in respect of modern theory, especially feminism, and Warren's in respect of modern performance. The latter was manifested as an interest in what modern performers do to a script, expressed not merely as a desire to serve their needs but, more radically, as a editorial guide for how far to take emendation in places where the quarto is likely to be corrupt.

Gossett's Preface announced that she wanted to maintain a "typically postmodern diffidence towards proposed solutions to the problems of the play's text,"[37] which in practice meant being reluctant to depart from the 1609 quarto's readings where they are possibly correct and giving little credence at such moments to the prose novella's alternative readings. Warren, on the other hand, entirely accepted the principles first put forward in the "Reconstructed Text" of the play for the 1986 Oxford *Complete Works*,[38] and extensively patched the bad play quarto from the novella. Indeed, Warren went further than the *Complete Works* in the process he described thus: "where the 'verse-fossils' in Wilkins's narrative offer more plausible readings [than the play quarto], the text is reconstructed by re-casting those verse-fossils back into blank verse."[39] Highlighting his involvement in professional productions of the play, Warren claimed that "textual and theatrical issues are interdependent"[40] and reported that "directors have regularly drawn on passages from Wilkins to provide themselves with a more performable script."[41]

A useful illustration of the effects of Gossett and Warren's different philosophies of editing occurs in scene 6 (=2.2), where in preparation for a tournament six knights (including Pericles) present themselves and their ceremonial shields bearing painted devices called *imprese* that are accompanied by foreign-language mottoes. Princess Thaisa describes each *impresa* and reads aloud its motto, and King Simonides interprets their combined meaning. Or rather, that is how the prose novella shows the action: in the play quarto, Simonides unaccountably fails to interpret the second, third, and fifth knights' *imprese* and mottoes. Warren filled the gaps in the play quarto using material from the prose novella, so that all six mottoes are interpreted, while Gossett followed the play quarto and left three of them uninterpreted. Claire Preston showed that the relationship between an *impresa*'s picture and its motto can be likened to the relationship inherent in a simile and to the narration of ostended events,[42] which links this scene to the play's central concerns about aural versus visual meanings. Thus, the incomplete interpretation of *imprese* in the play quarto is of considerable importance to criticism.

Shakespeare himself wrote the text for an *impresa* painted by Richard Burbage for Francis Manners, sixth Earl of Rutland, to use at the tilt on 24 March 1613, the king's accession day.[43] Michael Leslie argued that, unlike the more familiar emblems, *imprese* were intended to be cryptic; where the former speak of universal truths, the latter seek to conceal their meanings, to be paradoxically recondite in a context of public display—a tournament—and so remain mysterious to "all but the most appropriate of readers."[44] An *impresa* was the embodiment of the aristocratic spirit and epitomised its exclusivity, so Simonides's inherent nobility would be demonstrated by his ability to translate the mottoes and make sense of them in relation to the images. There is a contemporary analogue for the play quarto's version of the action: as Inga-Stina Ewbank noted,[45] the fifth act of Thomas Middleton's *Your Five Gallants*—first performed, like *Pericles*, in 1607—dramatizes young men revealing their unworthiness by failing to understand the Latin mottoes of the *imprese* they carry.[46]

Faced with an undeniably corrupt authority for the play, the 1609 quarto, an editor has to decide whether Simonides not interpreting all six *imprese* is one of its many lacunae or to trust its presentation of a Simonides unable to make sense of some *imprese*. Warren's radical intervention of patching the quarto from the prose novella, defended on the grounds that directors do this anyway, made for a psychologically less complex Simonides—he is unproblematically noble—than the flawed one who emerged from Gossett's diffident adherence to the quarto. That is, the cautious editorial approach, Gossett's, made the pyschologically more complex character and Warren's bold approach the simpler.

Such a paradoxical intersection of textual corruption and characterological complexity recurs in scene 19 (=4.5) in which Lysimachus, governor of Mytilene, meets his future wife Marina, Pericles's daughter, when visiting a brothel, and is persuaded by her to repent his lasciviousness. In the play quarto this remarkable conversion seems to happen rather too quickly, in that Marina speaks just 17 lines (comprising 138 words) before Lysimachus says, "I did not thinke thou couldst haue spoke so well… had I brought hither a corrupted minde, thy speeche had altered it."[47] Gossett expressed the editorial tradition in commenting that "her brief lines seem scarcely adequate to bring about his conversion."[48] The prose novella has a longer version of their exchange and Warren drew on it to expand the scene, so that Lysimachus's conversion comes after extensive eloquence from Marina. In Shakespeare, it is possible for a radical change in character to come about suddenly. Romeo speaks just 19 lines to Juliet before she comments, "My ears have yet not drunk a hundred words | Of thy tongue's uttering" and they promptly declare their mutual love (*Romeo and Juliet* 2.1.100–1). Although Juliet underestimates the number of Romeo's words (he has spoken 148 to her), the point is clear: they need few words.

Editorially supplying for Marina more lines by versifying the prose novella (as Warren did on performance grounds) makes for a more eloquent and rhetorically adept young heroine, "more assertive, more 'feminist,'" as Gossett put it.[49] Gossett did not wholeheartedly reject such an approach. Her comment that "editors' commitments, including their sexual politics, have varied radically over the centuries and need not reflect those of the authors" seems like an argument against the approach, but Gossett's main reason for deciding not to draw from the prose novella was that doing so would require confidence about the relationship between the play quarto and the prose novella. In our "postmodern age of fragmentation," she wrote, no one wants to hear an "all-encompassing hegemonic explanation," so Gossett confined herself to "more limited intervention."[50] Yet, as we have seen, the more limited textual intervention can make for psychologically more complex characters, and by contrast Warren's theatrical Presentism smoothes the play's wrinkles and simplifies characters. According to Gossett, because the play quarto shows "indeterminacy, uncertainty, irresolvability," the editor's approach should be "post-modern, post-structuralist,"[51] which puzzlingly can mean just leaving the text alone.

Gossett gave feminism its place in editing, but confined to fairly small changes that she called "inflections," such as respecting the play quarto's lack of a stage direction so that in scene 11 (= 3.1), the midwife who hands Pericles his baby Marina is allowed to stay on stage with him as he bewails the apparent death of his wife, rather than exiting and taking the baby with her. Midwives were well thought of and there is no reason a man should not "emote with a baby in his arms."[52] The lesson here appears to be that whereas a critic may use her Presentist convictions to shape her interpretations in ways that are straightforward and predictable, in editing, the relationship between one's convictions and their effects on the text is indirect and convoluted, leading to unanticipated consequences. Not only are there competing Presentisms—here, theatrical versus theoretical—but their textual outcomes are not predictable from their premises.

IV

At the core of recent debates about editorial intervention is a difference of approach that was fully manifested within the New Bibliography, although critics of this tradition have tended to misrepresent it as a narrow church of inflexible dogma. One of New Bibliography's founders, R. B. McKerrow, advocated "best-text" editing:[53] having chosen the most authoritative early edition, the editor should "reprint this as exactly as possible save for manifest and indubitable errors."[54] New Bibliography's co-founder W. W. Greg disagreed:[55] in "The Rationale of Copy-Text" he argued against "undue deference to the copy-text"[56] and proposed that where authority seems split between two early editions, an editor might get closest to what the author wrote by synthesizing them rather than privileging one over the other. Greg's arguments dominated Shakespeare editing from the 1950s to the 1990s, but since then the New Textualism has deprecated eclecticism in favor of respecting the supposed integrity of the early editions.[57] However, rather than choosing the best early edition, New Textualists have tended to celebrate the differences between early editions, refusing to discriminate. This tendency has spawned modern reprints of unauthoritative early editions—done poorly as "Shakespearean Originals: First Editions" and done well as "The New Cambridge Shakespeare: Early Quartos"—and has encouraged the Arden Shakespeare Third Series to include at the back of each volume, where appropriate, a photofacsimile of an exemplar of the early edition not used as the basis of the modern one.[58]

A logical consequence of refusing to label one early edition as the best is that for a given play, each nonderivative early edition must be presented to the modern reader. This happened with *Romeo and Juliet* in the Oxford Shakespeare edition of 2000, edited by Jill L. Levenson, which provided fully edited versions of the first two quartos, published in 1597 and 1599.[59] For the Arden Shakespeare Third Series *Hamlet*, Ann Thompson and Neil Taylor provided fully edited versions of the bad quarto of 1603, the good quarto of 1604–5, and the Folio text of 1623.[60] Where there is clear evidence of authorial revision, such a policy makes sense. One cannot conflate two editions separated by revision, since it is likely that elements unique to each are alternative ways of handling something—for example, different reasons for Hamlet apologizing to Laertes before the duel in the final scene[61]—and hence combining them produces at best supererogation and at worst contradiction, neither of which the dramatist wanted. But without a hypothesis of revision, there can be no coherent case for respecting the integrity of multiple early editions, since the differences between them can be attributed only to textual corruption.

McKerrow's best-text principle was founded on discrimination: the early edition thought to contain the least corruption (from actors, scribes, and printers) gives us the best chance of recovering what the dramatist wrote. Logically, one cannot combine a respect for the integrity of each edition with a refusal to discriminate between them, since all the plays were at some point reprinted. To reject a reprint in favor of the edition it reprints is an act of discrimination, so an editor's preference for foundational documents over recent ones is itself predicated on the existence of a rank order of editions. An editor who abandons discrimination might as well take the latest Oxford or Arden off the shelf and mark it up with alterations to make a new edition. If one discriminates between editions, as the return to early documents requires, then it makes no sense to cease discriminating as one approaches the earliest editions, just where the task becomes most difficult and most necessary. The discrimination cannot stop when we have worked back to one or more nonderivative editions, since manuscript origins must also be looked into. New Textualists deprecate inquiry into the (now lost) manuscript copy behind each nonderivative early edition on the grounds that such origins are unknowable. This is illogical, since the very act of distinguishing derivative from nonderivative editions is itself an investigation into printer's copy—asking whether it was print or manuscript—and there is nothing special about manuscript copy that puts it off limits to the editor.

The essence of Presentism in its newly minted positive sense is the careful selection of evidence and transparent disclosure of what may be lost or distorted by the selection, which, as Presentists have pointed out, is also historical scholarship executed to the highest standards. Where there exist competing Presentist claims on the editor's attention—as with modern theory and modern performance as we have seen—it is entirely reasonable for an editor to choose between the available imperatives, so long as this is explained and the consequences indicated. The result will be that modern editions of the same play may be markedly different from one another— as the Arden and Oxford *Pericles* editions are—but so long as the premises that gave rise to these differences are clear, the discipline, and indeed the bookselling marketplace, can sustain such variety.

On a very rough average and with notable exceptions, the Arden Shakespeare Third Series has tended to represent the New Textualist trend in editing and the Oxford Shakespeare the New Bibliographical. The exceptions are instructive of the importance of discrimination in the editor's practice. Levenson's refusal to discriminate between Q1 and Q2 *Romeo and Juliet* for Oxford is like Thompson and Taylor's refusal to discriminate between Q1, Q2, and Folio *Hamlet* for Arden, and likewise resulted in an edition in which each early version is represented by a fully edited modernized script. This approach may be criticized for its effect of treating all the differences between the early editions as though they result from revision, when in fact some of them undoubtedly are the effect only of textual corruption. But so long as the editorial premises that give rise to this approach are transparently conveyed to the reader, no harm is done. However, an edition such as Cox and Rasmussen's Arden *3 Henry 6* that eclectically blends two early editions because it refuses to choose between them, and that preserves character name variation on purely ideological grounds, does its readers a disservice.

Except where revision justifies publication of "before" and "after" versions, readers are best served by modern editions that discriminate between early editions and either select for modernization and explication the one likely to contain least corruption, or else draw from two or more early editions the matter for which each is the most authoritative. The recent abandonment of the New Bibliographical principle of discriminating between early editions is Presentist in the worst sense of that term—howsoever it is couched as a celebration of textual plurality and diversity—and it vitiates modern critical editions. Far from suppressing diversity, well-made modern critical editions retain the plays' power to generate new meanings in the present and future.

Notes

1. Herbert Butterfield, *The Whig Interpretation of History* (London: G. Bell, 1931).
2. Stephen Greenblatt, *Renaissance Self-fashioning: From More to Shakespeare* (Chicago: University of Chicago Press, 1980).
3. Hugh Grady, *Shakespeare's Universal Wolf: Studies in Early Modern Reification* (Oxford: Clarendon, 1996), pp. 4–5.
4. Grady later clarified what he meant by Presentism and its good form, which acknowledges and embraces the scholar's historical situatedness and is the same as good historicism (Hugh Grady, "Introduction: Shakespeare and Modernity," in *Shakespeare and Modernity: Early Modern to Millenium*, ed. Hugh Grady, Accents on Shakespeare (London: Routledge, 2000), pp. 1–19). Later still and in collaboration with Terence Hawkes, Grady asserted that historical scholarship in the tradition of Ranke that attempts to reach back to understand the past in its own terms "can't afford to examine the position in the present from which that manoeuvre is undertaken" (Hugh Grady and Terence Hawkes, "Introduction: Presenting Presentism," in *Presentist Shakespeares*, ed. Hugh Grady and Terence Hawkes, Accents on Shakespeare (Abingdon: Routledge, 2007), pp. 1–5; 2). There is some tension between this dismissal of the legacy of Ranke and Grady's earlier assertion that good Presentism and good historicism undertake exactly that examination. Ewan Fernie's intervention in the debate about historicism suggested that rather than going back to the past and detailing its differences from our times, Shakespearians might attend to the opposite movement of his works coming forward in time to meet us now as an outdated yet ever-present alien in our world

(Ewan Fernie, "Shakespeare and the Prospect of Presentism," *Shakespeare Survey*, 58 (2005): 169–84). Evelyn Gajowski too activated both senses of "present" (here and now) when introducing a collection of essays that use Presentism's approach to the otherness of the past—essentially, treating it as a dialogue with the present—to explore new ways of conceiving the othernesses against which normative gender (masculinity) and sexuality (heterosexuality) are defined and challenged in Shakespeare (Evelyn Gajowski, "The Presence of the Past," in *Presentism, Gender, and Sexuality in Shakespeare*, ed. Evelyn Gajowski, (Basingstoke: Palgrave Macmillan, 2009), pp. 1–22).

5. Margreta De Grazia and Peter Stallybrass, "The Materiality of Shakespeare's Text," *Shakespeare Quarterly*, 44 (1993): 255–83; 265–6.
6. Terry Eagleton, "'The Death of Self-criticism': Review of Stanley Fish *Professional Correctness: Literary Studies and Political Change* (Oxford: Clarendon, 1995)," *Times Literary Supplement*, 4834 (24 November, 1995): 6–7; 6.
7. Andrew Murphy, *Shakespeare in Print: A History and Chronology of Shakespeare Publishing* (Cambridge: Cambridge University Press, 2003), pp. 202–6.
8. W. W. Greg, "The *Hamlet* Texts and Recent Work in Shakespearian Bibliography," *Modern Language Review*, 14 (1919): 380–85; 380.
9. Gabriel Egan, *The Struggle for Shakespeare's Text: Twentieth-century Editorial Theory and Practice* (Cambridge: Cambridge University Press, 2010).
10. Randall Martin, ed., *William Shakespeare* Henry VI, Part Three, The Oxford Shakespeare (Oxford: Oxford University Press, 2001); John D. Cox and Eric Rasmussen, eds., *William Shakespeare* King Henry VI Part 3, The Arden Shakespeare (London: Thomson Learning, 2001).
11. Martin, *William Shakespeare* Henry VI, Part Three, pp. 96–113.
12. William Shakespeare, *Comedies, Histories and Tragedies*, STC 22273 (F1) (London: Isaac and William Jaggard for Edward Blount, John Smethwick, Isaac Jaggard, and William Aspley, 1623), p3v.
13. Leah S. Marcus, "The Two Texts of Othello and Early Modern Constructions of Race," in *Textual Performances: The Modern Reproduction of Shakespeare's Drama*, ed. Lukas Erne and Margaret Jane Kidnie (Cambridge: Cambridge University Press, 2004), pp. 21–36; 23.
14. Randall [as Random Clod] McLeod, "Information on Information," *TEXT: Transactions of the Society for Textual Scholarship*, 5 (1991): 241–81; 246.
15. De Grazia and Stallybrass, "The Materiality of Shakespeare's Text," p. 258.
16. Meredith Skura, "Is There a Shakespeare After the *New* New Bibliography," in *Elizabethan Theater: Essays in Honor of S. Schoenbaum*, ed. R. B. Parker and S. P. Zitner (Newark, DE: University of Delaware Press, 1996), pp. 169–83; 171.
17. John Drakakis, "Afterword," in *Shakespeare and the Text*, ed. Andrew Murphy, Concise Companions to Literature and Culture (Oxford: Blackwell, 2007), pp. 221–38; 229–30.

18. Graham Holderness and Bryan Loughrey, "Text and Stage: Shakespeare, Bibliography, and Performance Studies," *New Theatre Quarterly*, 9 (1993): 179–91; 191n18.
19. William Shakespeare, *[Richard Duke of York] The True Tragedie of Richard Duke of Yorke, and the Death of Good King Henrie the Sixt*, STC 21006 BEPD 138a (O) (London: P[eter] S[hort] for Thomas Millington, 1595), D3v–D4r; Shakespeare, *Comedies, Histories and Tragedies*, p6r; Egan, *The Struggle for Shakespeare's Text*, pp. 104–6.
20. Martin, *William Shakespeare* Henry VI, Part Three, pp. 42–3.
21. Cox & Rasmussen, *William Shakespeare* King Henry VI Part 3, pp. 161–6.
22. Ibid., pp. 167–75.
23. Ibid., pp. 175–6.
24. Ibid., p. 146.
25. Martin, *William Shakespeare* Henry VI, Part Three, p. 133.
26. Shakespeare, *[Richard Duke of York] The True Tragedie of Richard Duke of Yorke, and the Death of Good King Henrie the Sixt*, E2r.
27. Shakespeare, *Comedies, Histories and Tragedies*, q2v.
28. Martin, *William Shakespeare* Henry VI, Part Three, 5.1.81–2.
29. Cox and Rasmussen, *William Shakespeare* King Henry VI Part 3, 5.1.81–2.
30. Ibid., p. 175.
31. William Shakespeare and George Wilkins, *[Pericles] The Late, and Much Admired Play Called Pericles, Prince of Tyre*, STC 22334 BEPD 284a (Q1) (London: [William White and Thomas Creede] for Henry Gosson, 1609).
32. George Wilkins, *The Painfull Adventures of Pericles Prince of Tyre*, STC 25638.5 (London: T[homas] P[urfoot] for Nat[haniel] Butter, 1608).
33. MacDonald P. Jackson, *Defining Shakespeare:* Pericles *as Test Case* (Oxford: Oxford University Press, 2003).
34. John Klause, "Rhyme and the Authorship of *Pericles*," *Notes and Queries*, 255 (2010): 395–400.
35. Joseph A. Dane, "Bibliographical Note on George Wilkins, [Author] of the *Pericles*," *Notes and Queries*, 255 (2010): 401–3.
36. Stanley Wells and Gary Taylor et al., *William Shakespeare: A Textual Companion* (Oxford: Oxford University Press, 1987), p. 59.
37. Suzanne Gossett, ed., *Pericles*, The Arden Shakespeare (London: Thomson Learning, 2004), p. xvii.
38. Wells et al., *William Shakespeare: A Textual Companion*, pp. 556–92.
39. Roger Warren, ed., *Pericles, Prince of Tyre*, The Oxford Shakespeare (Oxford: Oxford University Press, 2004), p. 80.
40. Ibid., p. 80.
41. Ibid., p. 3.
42. Claire Preston, "The Emblematic Structure of *Pericles*," *Word and Image*, 8.1 (1992): 21–38.
43. Duke of Rutland, *The Manuscripts of His Grace the Duke of Rutland, G. C. B., Preserved at Belvoir Castle*, vol. 4, 5 vols. (London: Historical Manuscripts Commission, 1905), p. 494.

44. Michael Leslie, "The Dialogue between Bodies and Souls: Pictures and Poesy in the English Renaissance," *Word and Image*, 1 (1985): 16–30; 24.
45. Inga-Stina Ewbank, "'These Pretty Devices': A Study of Masques in Plays," in *A Book of Masques in Honour of Allardyce Nicoll*, ed. T. J. B. Spencer and Stanley Wells (Cambridge: Cambridge University Press, 1967): pp. 405–48; 429.
46. Thomas Middleton, *Your Fiue Gallants*, STC 17907 BEPD 266a (London: [George Eld] for Richard Bonian, [1608]).
47. Shakespeare and Wilkins, *[Pericles] The Late, and Much Admired Play Called Pericles, Prince of Tyre*, G4v.
48. Gossett, *Pericles*, p. 48.
49. Ibid., p. 52.
50. Ibid., p. 54.
51. Suzanne Gossett, "'To Foster is Not Always to Preserve': Feminist Inflections in Editing *Pericles*," in *In Arden: Editing Shakespeare: Essays in Honour of Richard Proudfoot*, ed. Ann Thompson and Gordon McMullan, The Arden Shakespeare (London: Thomson Learning, 2003), pp. 65–80; 67.
52. Ibid., p. 68.
53. Egan, *The Struggle for Shakespeare's Text*, pp. 30–37.
54. R. B. McKerrow, *Prolegomena for the Oxford Shakespeare: A Study in Editorial Method* (Oxford: Clarendon Press, 1939), p. 7.
55. Egan, *The Struggle for Shakespeare's Text*, pp. 44–7.
56. W. W. Greg, "The Rationale of Copy-text," *Studies in Bibliography*, 3 (1950–1): 19–36, 28.
57. Egan, *The Struggle for Shakespeare's Text*, pp. 153–8, 162–6, 190–206.
58. Ibid., pp. 190–96, 264–5, 267–70.
59. William Shakespeare, *Romeo and Juliet*, ed. Jill L. Levenson, The Oxford Shakespeare (Oxford: Oxford University Press, 2000).
60. William Shakespeare, *Hamlet*, ed. Ann Thompson and Neil Taylor, The Arden Shakespeare (London: Thomson Learning, 2006); William Shakespeare, *Hamlet: The Texts of 1603 and 1623*, ed. Ann Thompson and Neil Taylor, The Arden Shakespeare (London: Thomson Learning, 2006).
61. Paul Werstine, "The Textual Mystery of *Hamlet*," *Shakespeare Quarterly*, 39 (1988): 1–26, 3–6.

3
Shakespeare Dwelling: *Pericles* and the Affordances of Action

Julia Reinhard Lupton

Near the end of *Pericles*, Marina founds a community of women dedicated to needlework, the performing arts, and the practice of eloquence and virtue, an establishment modeled at least in part, as Randall Martin has argued, on the house-churches of Priscilla and Acquila in Ephesus and Corinth.[1] Marina has instituted what contemporary DIY (do-it-yourself) artisans call "a church of craft": "an environment where any and all acts of making have value to our humanness."[2] Although the DIY movement has been co-opted by corporate interests happy to hawk yarn to hipsters as well as housewives, the return to traditional handicrafts in the digital age has also cultivated heightened forms of attention to the environment, labor, beauty, and waste; incubated patterns of enskillment that emphasize peer-to-peer education; and fostered acts of communication that recast crafters as authors and activists (or "Craftivists"). As the phrase "church of craft" indicates and as Marina's own congregational efforts manifest, a political-theological element infuses these communities, insofar as acts of assembly lead members to build relationships to each other within larger seasonal patterns of renewal and rebirth, to engage in forms of gift-giving that emphasize social and environmental justice, and to reopen an archive of skills and recipes that often bear the impress of mythographic motifs and liturgical forms.

In my reading of *Pericles*, I take the phrase "the urgency of the now" to refer to the present time of performance, and hence to drama's constitutive commitment to transformation through theatrical making, active audition, and hermeneutic reencounter. I also read the phrase as a formula for the messianic "time that remains" that Giorgio Agamben recovers from St. Paul in order to conceive of the *kairos* or occasion of action in the moment in response to the prospect of imminent structural transformation.[3] To be absorbed in artisanal activity is to be caught up in the now of making; to be attuned to the social dimensions of that activity is to draw an urgency, a creative orientation toward the future, out of the forms of attention, concentration, and repair that craftwork inculcates in its practitioners.[4] Using Hannah Arendt (on natality and action), the Italian autonomists (on affective labor), and design theory (on affordances), I read *Pericles* as a consideration of the capacities of artisanal efforts to generate political speech out of political-theological and biopolitical forms of life, a becoming-dramatic of skilled routines that I gather under the canopy of "dwelling." Placing architecture, landscaping, and interior décor alongside cooking, housekeeping, and husbandry, dwelling assembles in one milieu the many arts of formal and vernacular design that together establish and curate human location. Dwelling implies a living that is never simply bare, dedicated to the self-disclosure brought about by substantial speech as well as the acknowledgment of our participation in larger economies and ecologies of existence. *Situating us environmentally* and *siting us architecturally*, dwelling infuses the relentless present tense of life routines with the opportunity to acknowledge, reframe, and recraft our embeddness in and exposure to our own creatureliness. Following Eric Santner, I understand creatureliness not as sheer exile in vitality, but as our constitutive prematurity and incompleteness as persons and hence our inventive dependence on linguistic, social, and biotechnical forms of sheltering that themselves provide the locus for new forms of intersubjective self-disclosure.[5]

Does Shakespeare dwell in the past or the present? In his essay "The Digital Touch: Craft-Work as Immaterial Labour and Ontological Accumulation," Jack Bratich describes DIY movements as a return to pre-modern forms of craft in reaction to, but also often deploying, post-Fordist forms of digital design and communication. Key to his analysis is the idea of affective labor, which includes domesticity, the hospitality and service industries, medical care, and entertainment; in short, any employment that *expends* affect in order to *produce* affect in others. Following Michael Hardt, Bratich argues that affective labor characterized the artisanal and domestic arts of early modernity, lost prestige in the industrial period, and has returned as a major component of communicative capitalism.[6] We might speak here of an AFFECTIVE LABOR$_1$ and an AFFECTIVE LABOR$_2$, the first belonging to the time of Shakespeare and the second to our own moment. This doubling of epochs invites a reading of artisanal and domestic place-making in Shakespeare that would be both historical and Presentist, at once attuned to rhythms of craft on and around Shakespeare's stage and geared toward DIY design in the digital age. The shoreline industries, coastal clinics, leafy shelters, and floating hospitals of *Pericles* afford the delivery of powerful emotional charges both among characters and for the audience, with implications for theatre itself as a distinctive form of affective labor. *Pericles*, I argue, can help us mount an account of action that at once brings the human into being as process and question in the tradition of Arendt, while also attending to the manner in which human actions issue out of and respond to object, affect, and resource flows.

The affordances of action

In *The Human Condition*, Hannah Arendt divides the *vita activa* into three spheres of human exertion: *labor* comprises the repetitive energies required to meet the needs of life; *work* fashions a common world out of artifacts of some duration; and *action* concerns the plurality of human beings as creatures who inadvertently reveal themselves through the contingencies of speech. She links all three to what she calls natality, or the condition of being born:

> All three activities [labor, work, and action] and their corresponding conditions [life, worldliness, and plurality] are intimately connected with the most general condition of human existence: birth and death, natality and mortality. Labor assures not only individual survival, but the life of the species. Work and its product, the human artifact, bestow a certain permanence and durability upon the futility of mortal life and the fleeting character of human time. Action, in so far as it engages in founding and preserving political bodies, creates the condition for remembrance, that is, for history.[7]

Labor can mean parturition as well as employment, and much labor in the *oikos* involves the forms of care that attend human birthing.

Yet, birth is also involved in the creation of artifacts and in the new relationships and chains of events that action in its contingency introduces into the world. "Action," Arendt writes, "has the closest connection with the human condition of natality; the new beginning inherent in birth can make itself felt in the world only because the newcomer possesses the capacity of beginning something new, that is, of acting."[8]

Although Arendt distinguishes these three aspects of natality in favor of the initiatory character of action, she often acknowledges the extent to which these forms of effortful existence course among and imply each other. Thus, she avers that human deliberation usually involves some objective state of affairs whose management is "overlaid and, as it were, overgrown with an altogether different in-between which consists of words and deeds and owes its origins exclusively to men's acting and speaking directly *to* one another."[9] Here, action grows out of, not in opposition to, skilled activity: when we work at something in concert with other people, we also talk, consider, negotiate, evaluate, plan, and decide. Things and speech are both *inter-ests* and "in-betweens": the first by lying between people as objects of subsistence and exchange; the second by occurring among interlocutors who reveal who they are in part by the way they handle the object world, the way they treat or fail to treat it as a common concern. In an essay on Arendt and architecture, Patchen Markell notes of this passage that it "*performs* the intertwining it describes," manifesting the way in which the effort exerted to resolve a material challenge can result in forms of speech and action that can deliver new subjective capacities.[10]

Shakespearean drama often gravitates around action in the fullest Arendtian sense. The history plays and the great tragedies unfold above all through scenes of contingent and self-constituting speech in the presence of others: the division of kingdoms, the deposition of monarchs, the exchange of insults, the exercise of diplomacy, the choreography of courtship and courtiership, the cursing and blessing of parents and children, the valedictions of lovers.[11] Yet, dramatic action, especially perhaps in the romances, can also grow out of scenes that seem more closely allied with work and labor than with political performance—or at least from the kind of employment that Michael Hardt and the Italian autonomists call "affective labor." Associated with women's work as well as with the service, hospitality, and culture industries, affective labor includes any sustained effort that requires the manifestation and expenditure of the worker's emotional being in order to produce, direct, or manage the experience of others. Because affective labor is inherently social and often accomplished through speech, it can become action in Arendt's sense of a self-disclosing gesture whose unpredictable consequences are potentially context-changing.

For Arendt, drama is the most political form of art because of its deep kinship with action:

> The specific revelatory quality of action and speech, the implicit manifestation of the agent and speaker ... prevails in all arts but is actually appropriate only to the drama, whose very name (from the Greek verb *dran*, "to act") indicates that playacting actually is an imitation of action ... Only the actors and speakers who re-enact the story's plot can convey the full meaning, not so much of the story itself, but of the "heroes" who reveal themselves in it.[12]

If action belongs to *drama* as the mode in which human beings appear to each other through speech, work and labor might belong to *theatre* as the sensuous disposition of bodies, things, and ambience in performance. My aim, however, is not to oppose the dramatic and the theatrical, but rather to account for the manner in which some of the most speech-driven moments in the romances issue from and wheel around efforts of labor, care, and environmental engagement, exertions whose forms of enskillment and absorption reveal themselves as concertedly social and incipiently rhetorical.

The gerundive "dwelling" designates the processual spaces and rhythms that allow affective labor to give birth to action. Thus, Heidegger associates *bauen* (to build) with *bin* and *bist* (to be), and he identifies the boundaries drawn by dwelling as spaces "from which something *begins its presencing.*"[13] The walls of a room echoed in the rectangle of the table at its center, the banked seating around a stage, and the ring of light cast by a campfire are borders designed to solicit those gathered within their pale to appear to each other through acts of deliberation, contest, testimony, and enterprise. Shakespeare's romances, I argue, are among other things phenomenological engagements with *spaces that afford dwelling*, and *dwellings that afford action*. I use "afford" here in the technical sense developed by ecological psychologist James J. Gibson and refined by designers and architects, to describe the way in which objects and environments solicit or enable specific behaviors, postures, and attitudes among those who handle or pass through them.[14] A building affords shelter from the elements and from the gaze of other people; through its organization of space, visibility, and traffic patterns, a building also affords forms of social interaction (debate, service, work, crime, sex, education, entertainment), some intended as part of the building's program and others ad hoc. According to architect-engineers Jonathan Meier and Georges Feidel, the concept of affordance "emphasizes the complementarity of the relationship between environments and their users."[15] They associate the perception of affordances with the joining of form and function in design: when the intended purposes of a thing or location give themselves up to its human enjoyers through an impression of order, utilitarianism turns into aesthetics, and affordance becomes a visual value and artistic property.

Markell's architectural reading of Arendt could be rephrased in the direction of affordances. Citing Arendt on the idea that a thing's excellence involves not only "'mere usefulness'" but "'its adequacy or inadequacy to what it should *look* like,'" Markell concludes that "to attend to a thing's appearance, in other words, is not to turn away from but to enrich the question of what it's good for."[16] A designer working with affordances might say that a space or object that translucently manifests its own ends moves beyond instrumentality and functionalism into a reflection on what *good design* might have to do with the *good life*, which increasingly encompasses sustainability, social justice, mindfulness, and gender happiness.[17] In theatre studies, Evelyn Tribble has used affordances to consider the way in which specific technologies and architectural features of the theatre support the work of actors by offloading some of their cognitive effort onto the work environment of rehearsal and performance. W. B. Worthen has used affordances in order to shift the playtext/performance relationship from a hermeneutic model (in which a particular production "reads" an authorizing text) to a relationship in which the play text "affords" or supports (but does not determine) new stagings solicited by shifting performance conditions.[18] My own use of affordances aims to link the very precise and empirical thinking about affordances mounted by designers like Meier and Feidel and theatre historians like Tribble to the more phenomenological and speculative deployments pursued by Worthen. Moreover, I do this work with an eye to the philosophical and existential blocking of the human condition by Arendt. Finally, I would like to bring Arendt's largely secular and classically political zoning of the human condition into contact with contemporary domestic, artisanal, and ecological movements, whose designs for living link affordances to biopolitical and political-theological routines.

Pericles is a veritable archipelago of scenes of and about affective labor, beginning with the prince's delivery out of the sea into the nets of the busy, talkative fishermen at the ocean's edge, and culminating in Marina's exit from her church of craft onto the floating hospital constituted by Pericles' ship of melancholy. In *Pericles*, the spaces that the play ends up dedicating to dwelling are not the monumental sites of palace or principality, but rather the fundamentally porous locations of ship, shore, and shelter. The precarious character of these locales for dwelling illuminates the proclivity of all human habitats to be retooled and rezoned through acts of use that are also acts of design. Heidegger speaks of dwelling as assembling a four-fold composed of earth, sky, divinities, and mortals. My own four-fold is composed of the on-the-ground affordances of places and things (Gibson, Meier, Tribble), the intersubjective canopy erected by the *vita activa* (Arendt, Kottman, Beckwith), contemporary reflections on dwelling and affective labor (Bratich, Hardt), and the imaginative capacities of dramatic poetry, as what wraps around and runs through these different discourses as an ongoing resource for existential, political, and political-theological wayfinding.

Of natality, nets, and networks

The first great scene in this collaborative text is Pericles' delivery out of shipwreck onto the coast near Pentapolis.[19] Likely written by George Wilkens, Pericles' entry speech is largely drained of Shakespearean particularity, yet nonetheless touches the themes of birth, speech, and environmental immersion that suffuse the larger play as well as the late Shakespearean corpus:

> Alas, the seas hath cast me on the rocks,
> Washed me from shore to shore, and left my breath

Nothing to think on but ensuing death.
Let it suffice the greatness of your powers
To have bereft a prince of all his fortunes,
And having thrown him from your watery grave,
Here to have death in peace is all he'll crave. (5.41–51)

Although Pericles, pale prince of melancholy, associates his ejection from the sea with approaching mortality, the sheer fact of exodus out of the beating water into the nakedness of the dawning day conveys to we who witness him the inkling of a *vita nuova*. Pericles' act of speaking zones the shore as a plateau for self-disclosure as well as survival and the hope of succor.[20] The birth of Pericles out of the anonymity of the sea and into the space of appearance, moreover, is carried by and coincident with the actor's birth into his role out of the buzzing milieu of theatrical labor backstage.[21] The twinned geniture of this single entry (Pericles reborn as man; actor reborn as Pericles) folds Arendt's account of natality as the new beginning made by action into her definition of drama as the mode where action and acting coincide.

It is the fishermen, however, whose salty vernacular most compellingly garners our attention as they enter preparing to fix nets damaged by the storm:

MASTER [*calling*]:	What ho, Pilch!
SECOND FISHERMAN [*calling*]:	Ha, come and bring away the nets.
MASTER [*calling*]:	What, Patchbreech, I say.
	[*Enter a Third Fisherman with nets to dry and repair.*][22]
MASTER:	Look how thou stirr'st now. Come away, or I'll fetch thee with a wanion. (5.52–8)

The fishermen are caught up in what anthropologist of affordances Tim Ingold calls a taskscape: the organizational space composed by the total "pattern of dwelling activities," "the entire ensemble of tasks, in their mutual interlocking," that engages groups of people assembled and occupied by a set of undertakings.[23] In Wilkens's piscatory pastoral, the fishermen respond to the aftermath of tempest in a topography of affordances framed and cultivated by their craft and profession. Relating the men to their environment, the shoreline workplace also associates the laborers with each other: the Master calls to the other fishermen, one of whom, Patchbreech, may be younger than the others; this apprentice to the older men would also likely be an apprentice in the theatrical company.[24] Here, as so often in Shakespearean drama, the *mise-en-scène* of a dramatically imagined locale for labor (ship, shore, great hall, kitchen, graveyard, sheepcote) opens onto the taskscape of the theatre as a collaborative enterprise involving its own patterns of command and enskillment in a specialized space outfitted with unique affordances. If Pericles' entry as a speaking subject manifests the deep link between action, drama, and natality, the fishermen's entry manifests the equally deep link between stage management and the arts of the *oikos*.

Ingold conceives of environments "in terms of *function*, of what it affords to creatures—whether human or non-human—with certain capabilities and projects of action."[25] Action here is intended in a tactile, corporeal, and immediately instrumental direction, like the men's work with their nets or, later in the play, Cerimon's manipulation of heat and linens in order to revive the comatose Thaisa. Such motions would not count as action in Arendt's fuller sense of intersubjective speech, but rather would remain submerged in the more routinized zone of labor and work. Yet, the fishermen's minimal language of call and response flowers into political discourse as they shift from repair of the nets to repair of the social body:

THIRD FISHERMAN: Master, I marvel how the fishes live in the sea.
MASTER: Why, as men do a-land: the great ones eat up the little ones. (5.67–70)

Picturing class inequality using the metaphors at hand, the fishermen are what Antonio Gramsci calls "organic intellectuals," skilled workers who incubate intellectual and political vocabularies out of their artisanal expertise and self-organizing activities. Through their political speech, the fishermen's work with the nets becomes affective labor in the sense suggested by Michael Hardt, writing in the autonomist tradition initiated by Gramsci. In Hardt's account, the fishermen would belong to the first phase of capitalism, "in which agriculture and the extraction of raw materials dominated the economy";[26] a phase, however, in which these industries were still largely managed by skilled workers employed in the development and transmission of their own manual and environmental knowledges. Labor becomes affective labor when, in Hardt's terms, it produces "social networks, forms of community, biopower," visible here in the forms of satiric camaraderie that knit the fishermen together through but also above their employment by the sea.[27]

Writing in the same vein, Jack Bratich argues that craftwork "finds its value in affect, defined primarily as the power to act."[28] Here, action *is* intended in the Arendtian sense, though connected to oikonomic activity in a manner that Arendt does not usually choose to spotlight. The scene with the fishermen instantiates Arendt's account of the "in-between" of political speech emerging out of the "in-between" formed by objective interests; indeed, her image of political speech "overlaid and, as it were, overgrown" with worldly occupation can itself be overlaid on the fishermen's net-work in order to reframe their speech as a form of action, a means of building class solidarity and class consciousness. Considered historically, these fishermen are mending their nets not unlike the way women worked with fabrics: as skilled workers who trained each other and who talked while they sewed, activities organized by Marina into a church of craft more programmatically later in the play.[29] Considered in relation to the present, we might associate both the fishermen's nets and Marina's academy with the present DIY craft revival, which mixes militant nostalgia with extreme technical know-how and peer-to-peer education in such experimental social and aesthetic forms as steam punk, the Maker movement, and Stitchin' Bitches. In both AFFECTIVE LABOR[1] and AFFECTIVE LABOR[2], work with things becomes social work and work with history. Craftivism is action with archives and objects.

In Bratich's autonomist formulation, DIY affinity circles allow us to "rethink the temporality of capitalism by teasing out a labour thread that passes through capitalism without being reduced to it."[30] Knitting communities by knitting things, craftivists accumulate a social surplus that exceeds their capture in capitalist formations; this same surplus also links up disparate moments of time through the restoration of lost knowledges within new regimes of mutual enskillment and environmental recalibration. In the case of *Pericles*, a fishing net runs through it: pliant and portable instruments of capture, entanglement, and hauling that connect men, shore, sea, and city, these webs of resilient transparency are also real and symbolic mediators among the actors assembled in the workplace of the theatre across the epochs of performance.

In Hans Blumenberg's famous analysis of the "shipwreck with spectator" motif, the shore becomes the fold dividing immersion in existence from the possibility of reflection.[31] In the shore as taskscape, however, the shore remains the site of ebb and flow, with the men working its margin ever pulled back into the sea, riding its energy in order to reap its resources, actions that in turn sweep them back into the city and its exchanges in a double apprehension by ecological and economic cycles. What ebbs and flows are the tides of the sea most certainly, but also the waves of labor and affect (what management experts call "workflow"), whose cooperative rhythms spawn more fully formed social actions, including the political speech of the fishermen, their charity toward Pericles, and the partial self-disclosures produced by the shipwrecked prince in response to their ministrations. The taskscape affords an array of actions, from highly focused deployments of effort and skill to more world- and self-building acts of speech, gift, invention, and acknowledgment. Although it is perhaps unavoidable to think of these actions along a spectrum that extends from the manual, embodied and object-oriented endeavor of fishing to the more capacious and contingent speech of strangers on the shore, the Wilkens–Shakespeare taskscape keeps us attentive to the enabling proximity, co-intrication, and environmental situatedness of these actions. In *Pericles*, the shore is defined by patterns of use whose autopoetic choreography remains environmentally responsive and inherently fluid while also critically cognizant of its own capture in the great net of capital.

Investiture and provisioning

These fishers of fish become fishers of men when they catch Pericles' attention with the salt sweep of their discourse, leading him to disclose himself in extremity:

> What I have been, I have forgot to know,
> But what I am, want teaches me to think on:
> A man thronged up with cold, my veins are chill,
> And have no more of life than may suffice
> To give my tongue that heat to ask your help. (5.111–15)

Responding to his plea for assistance, the Master clothes Pericles in a gown and then promises him a menu of meals redolent with its own scenes of affective labor: "Come, thou shalt go home, and we'll have flesh for holidays, fish for fasting-days, and moreo'er puddings and flapjacks, and thou shalt be welcome" (121–3). The Master's promise of hospitality discovers the "urgency of the now" in the home theatre of the festive table, which opens messianic portals among times and spaces through the special affordances of the invitation as speech act, the meal as sumptuary performance, and the liturgical calendar as theo-bio-technology.

Clothing, not feeding, however, turns out to be the central action of Scene 5. "*The other two Fishermen drawing up a net*" recover the armor bequeathed to Pericles by his father.[32] Handing Pericles the beach-combed booty, the Master reminds him of his debt: "Ay, but hark you, my friend, 'twas we that made up this garment through the rough seams of the water. There are certain condolements, certain vails. I hope sir, if you thrive, you'll remember from whence you had this" (186–8). The Master presents the garment as the collaborative creation of the sea and its skilled pliers; the waves of the ocean bear "rough seams" not unlike the exposed junctions of the recovered equipment or the open weave of the fishing fabric in which the armor arrived on shore. Calling forth a key term for all of the late plays, the actors on the shore use the word "provide" to characterize this collective act of costume design. When Pericles declares, "I yet am *unprovided* of a pair of bases" (described by editor Roger Warren as "a kind of skirt, split in two, worn with armour"), the Second Fisherman assures him, "We'll sure *provide*. Thou shalt have my best gown to make thee a pair" (198–202; emphasis added). To provide is to equip, furnish, or outfit; it also means to look to the future (*pro-videre*), its providential assurance shadowed by a sense of provisionality. Although the recovery of the armor from the sea partially rebuilds Pericles' princely identity, the armor itself is rusty, its seams are rough, and the suit lacks key components that must be made up from the wardrobes of the fishermen. These improvised provisions equip Pericles not only with a rough-and-ready costume, but also with an attitude freshly open to occasion and opportunity. When asked if he knows how to fish, Pericles confesses that he has "never practiced it" (107). By the end of the encounter, however, this angler's apprentice has begun to appropriate a style of action that moves ably between material affordances and linguistic capacity.

When Pericles appears at court, Thaisa remarks:

> He seems to be a stranger, but his present is
> A withered branch that's only green at top.
> The motto, *In hac spe vivo*. (6.46–8)

One of the lords comments:

> He well may be a stranger, for he comes
> Into an honoured triumph strangely furnished. (55–6)

Whereas the other knights are properly outfitted with painted shields, Pericles has used his lessons in beach-combing to fashion a make-shift emblem from materials under foot.[33] The lord describes Pericles as "strangely furnished": "furnish" means to equip, provision, or make ready. "Furniture" can refer to equipment for horses, hunters, ships, armies, and banqueting tables as well as houses and churches; that is, to the ensemble of appliances and supplies that equips actors to manage a specialized taskscape. The withered branch and the rusty armor comprise Pericles' chivalric furniture, appareling him for the sumptuary ordeal of pageantry and signifying his situation in a thingly and environmental manner that is quite distinct from the painted shields of the other knights. To speak in contemporary terms: if the iconicity of the other knights places them at the heart of mainstream branding practices, Pericles exercises a more DIY form of marketing in order to enter the society of the spectacle in a manner borrowed from the habits of the fishermen.[34]

The withered branch at once recalls and radically prunes Pericles' earlier image of sovereignty as "the tops of trees / Which fence the roots they grow by" (2.30–31). The figuration of the state as a sylvan political ecology composed of multiple roots, stems, and branches that together form a sheltering canopy of foliage does not yield an image of personal sovereignty as readily as other political-theological metaphors such as the body politic or the ship of state. Combining Macbeth's sere leaf with the insurgent verdancy of Birnam Wood, the margin of green atop Pericles' blasted branch draws a measure of inventiveness from his melancholia's dark roots. Hope (*In hac spe vivo*, "In that hope I live") germinates in and as the provisionality of the play's complex exchanges among objects and worlds. Arendt associates hope with natality, which she ventures to conceive in scriptural terms:

> The miracle that saves the world, the realm of human affairs, from its normal, "natural" ruin is ultimately the fact of natality, in which the faculty of action is ontologically rooted. It is, in other words, the birth of new men and the new beginning, the action they are capable of by virtue of being born. Only the full experience of this capacity can bestow upon human affairs faith and hope, those two essential characteristics of human existence which Greek antiquity ignored altogether, discounting the keeping of faith as a very uncommon and not too important virtue and counting hope among the evils of illusion in Pandora's box. It is this faith in and hope for the world that found perhaps its most glorious and most succinct expression in the few words with which the Gospels announced their "glad tidings": "A child has been born unto us."[35]

Arendt touches here on the world of the romances, infused with messianic impulses that disseminate Christological narratives within a wider Hellenistic and Jewish field of reference.[36] Profferred like the frankincense and myrrh of an epiphany king, Pericles' bit of tufted driftwood symbolizes his rebirth out of the storm, manifests his education in affordances, and initiates a new action, insofar as the gift constitutes a first joist or brace around which a human relationship might begin to be built. As Randall Martin has noted, it is this humble offering, and not the tournament itself, that the authors of the play choose to depict. Presenting the bough to Thaisa with "graceful courtesy" (6.45) elevates the branch into something rich and strange around which a new beginning can be made.[37]

Pericles' capacity for action, which in this instance means movement out of his flight from knowledge and the sexual panic and restless reclusiveness that accompany it, remain perilously imperfect. In the erotically airless scenes at Pentapolis, Pericles is remarkably unassertive as a lover, while in the next tempest and its aftermath he shows himself all too willing to relinquish Thaisa's body to the sea and deliver their baby to foster care. Although his intentions and attitude are radically different from those of Leontes, the consequences of his actions are similar: in both plays, fathers play a causal role in the assumed deaths, extended seclusions, and unexpected reappearances of their wives and daughters. What one hero experiences as suffered disaster is replayed by the second hero as self-authored delusion; in both cases, the father signals his culpability by sinking into a penitential paralysis that can only be lifted by the action of another. At once bad bouquet, walking stick, and wilted priapus, the withered branch becomes a figure of assisted reproduction and indeed assisted living, signifying the tentative character of Pericles' venture into relationships of partnership and dependency. Always a prince of potentiality and never a king of sovereign self-possession, Pericles cannot enter into action on his own; for this he will need Marina, "the child [who] has been born unto us" in this modern nativity play. Yet, the point of the play is not to prop up the phallus in order to revive its damaged potency, but rather to explore forms of weak sovereignty and soft power that might organize action and agency differently. In Tribble's account of work at the Globe, the theatrical taskscape distributes cognition among multiple actors and memory architectures in order to bring off the miracle of live performance. In *Pericles*, the birth of subjectivity out of affordances and into action is parceled out among several generations, genders, spatial dispositions, and social scenes. The work of the play, and of the romances in general, is to acknowledge, through its dramatic episodes, poetic themes, and theatrical processes, the collaborative, creaturely, and networked character of all forms of action and authorship, including their always only partial release from capture in structures of alienation and exploitation.

Messianic Marina

Thus, Pericles' withered branch returns at the end of the play in the form of the ad hoc housing that Marina has constructed for herself and her community of followers at the edge of the sea:

> She in all happy,
> As the fairest of them all, among her fellow maids
> Dwells now i'th'leafy shelter that abuts
> Against the island's side. (21.38–41)

"Leafy shelter" suggests a form of minimal architecture, an enclosure built like a teepee or sukkah out of branches. Letting in the salt air of the sea and exposed to its risks as well as its beauty, Marina's leafy shelter participates in what contemporary designers call "an architecture of flows," which approaches buildings as improvisational elements perched within larger economic and ecological systems.[38] True to her name, Marina has chosen to build her house of flows as close to the sea as possible—and as far from the urban brothel from which she has used her active eloquence to escape. Yet, her establishment remains connected to the city insofar as "her gain / She gives the curséd Bawd" (21.10–11), implying that she remains indentured to her original investor and hence never fully pastoralized or autonomous. Like the fishermen, Marina remains caught up in, but also cognizant of, the economies of exploitation from which her actions give her provisional independence.

Marina's leafy shelter creates the space in which a community of women practice forms of affective labor—needlework, music, dancing, and rhetoric—that are also arts of self-disclosure. Marina has made room in Heidegger's sense: *Raum* is "a place cleared for settlement and lodging ... from which something *begins its presencing.*"[39] Pericles' stunted branch, single and almost bare, has now been multiplied and assembled into a church of craft, transplanting the prince's original image of sylvan sovereignty into a form of architecture that builds itself out of the organic forms and resources of its site. Here and elsewhere, Shakespeare participates in a tradition of thinking within architectural theory that derives primitive buildings from the spatial disposition and growth habits of trees. In this line of thought, all architecture begins as landscape architecture and only later hardens into something more decisively artifactual.[40] The word "academy" itself originally designated "the grove of Akademos," and it is surely an academy that Marina has founded in her frondescent pavilion by the sea. Marina's design mission can be placed in the line of what Susan Fraiman has called "shelter writing," a term she retools from contemporary periodicals, where the phrase describes mainstream home-and-garden articles, in order to capture the more militant and beleaguered writings of "those whose smallest domestic endeavors have become urgent and precious in the wake of dislocation, whether as the result of migration, divorce, poverty, or a stigmatized sexuality."[41] In her negotiations with the bawd Bolt, Marina has asked to be placed "among honest women" (19.240). Although she is often taken to be running a school for noble women, there is no reason not to think that at least some of Marina's followers resemble their leader: refugees from the dispossessing ravages of parental abandonment, foster care, and sex trafficking who seek new forms of collective life as well as oikonomic autonomy through the skills taught in Marina's messianic house of hope. Marina's leafy shelter is an academy, a trade school, and a cottage industry; it is also a sanctuary for the survivors of sexual shipwreck and an architectural testament (not unlike Timon's seaside earthwork[42]) to the tempestuous and exposed character of creaturely life in the age of primitive accumulation.

In her habits of habitation, Marina is the un-Miranda. The contrast between these two romance heroines is visible in their differing orientations within the "shipwreck with spectator" motif, Blumenberg's blueprint for the origins of conceptuality. Miranda, as her name declares, is very much the spectator, watching disaster unfold off shore and going home to a rocky cave recessed into the earth as a natural fortification. Her counterpart, on the other hand, "is called Marina / For [she] was born at sea" (21.145–6); unlike Miranda's cave, the soft and airy structure of Marina's coastal treehouse places her in the closest possible proximity to the ocean and its insurgencies. Marina dedicates her architecture of flows to the condition of permanent sojourning that Blumenberg associates with the sea: "we are always already embarked and on the high seas."[43] "Where do you live?" Pericles asks, and she responds, "Where I am but a stranger. From the deck / You may discern the place" (21.103–5). If she lives, however, as a resident alien in the "now" of existence, her precariousness visualized in the transient character of her dwelling place, she also cultivates in that same site forms of enskillment, place-making, and community that scaffold a resilient future out of the urgencies of the now.

As Randall Martin has demonstrated, Marina's experiments with space begin inside the brothel itself, where she makes the bawdy house into an edifice for edification, in the tradition of St. Paul. In *The Pauline Renaissance*, John Coolidge points out that to edify (from *oikodomeo*, to build a house) is to build up, to use the power of the word to construct the church as community.[44] In the house-churches of Pauline Christianity, domestic settings afforded table fellowship and acts of worship that in turn rezoned the *oikos* as semi-public places of congregation and witnessing. Marina will eventually found her own house-church by the sea, but she already begins that work here in the brothel through her edifying practices. In the extraordinary exchange between Lysimachus and Marina, the governor insists that the space Marina inhabits determines her vocation: "Why, the house you dwell in proclaims you are a creature of sale" (19.82–3). She responds by recalling him to the carnal knowledge manifested by the very fact of his entry into this space: "Do you know this house to be a place of such resort and will come into it?" (19.84–6). "Dwelling" shifts here from mere occupancy and social determinism ("the house you *dwell in* proclaims you...") to a form of dramatic and cognitive engagement in which entries and exits are signifying acts.

Increasingly agitated by her frank and open handling of language as an instrument of truth, Lysimachus dissolves into authoritarian bluster and then ends with an order: "Come, bring me to some private place. Come, come" (19.102). Although his command identifies the room they occupy as a parlor or antechamber, a deeper renovation of space is at work here: Marina's speech, qualifying as action in the Arendtian sense, has rendered the *oikos* into a provisional polis insofar as their exchange prompts each actor to risk self-disclosure. Through her handling of words, Marina has instituted a scene in the sense developed by Paul Kottman: whereas *skena*, he argues, began as an architectural term, it has come to designate both the location of an action and the action itself, "moving from a valence dominated by technical fabrication to a valence that privileges the unpredictable here-and-now interactions of human beings."[45] In this scene of scenes, Lysimachus is aroused by the virtue that Marina's words and comportment manifest, but he is also, far more profoundly, revolted by the person he has revealed himself to be: tyrannous, preemptory, and equivocal; empty, needy, sordid, sorry, and sad. *Come, bring me to some private place*; that is, *lead me away from the terrible visibility opened up by your speech; grant me refuge from the self you have led me to publish.*

If we find Lysimachus an unlikely lover in this scene, he later exercises Arendtian temerity when he actively courts the very woman who has made him reveal the horror of his own frailty: courage, writes Arendt, begins with the act of "leaving one's private place and showing who one is, disclosing and exposing one's self."[46] A public man seeking private pleasures, Lysimachus has discovered in Marina the possibility of new forms of speech that issue from the rezoning of space through the action of eloquence. He is brave enough to want more.

But what might Marina want from Lysimachus? If Pericles' single withered branch in scene 6 indicates among other things his own unease with the sexual story encrypted in incest, the daughter's exit from her little Island of Lesbos does not straighten out the father so much as queer the family further, in order to give it new resilience and scope. The family is more fully reconstituted at the Temple of Diana, itself an assemblage of efforts, affects, objects, images, and cults. Belonging equally to Diana, many-organed goddess of chastity and childbirth, and to Paul, jewgreek apostle of the urgency of the now, the messianic theme park at Ephesus is designed not syncretically so much as existentially in order to supplement the lack of a sexual relationship with alternative layouts for both sovereignty and sexuality. Janet Adelman saw little hope in the play's final tableau: "the 'night-oblations' Pericles promises to pure Diana [5.3.68–70] seem distinctly a substitute for the resumed nightly rituals of marriage ... even the eventual husband of Marina can be introduced only as a frequenter of the brothel."[47] Yet, perhaps these imperfect restitutions, like Pericles' rusty armor, withered branch, and fishnet stockings, can be bid to tell a story in which human inventiveness taps the affordances of the environment in order to give birth to forms of dwelling that might harbor diverse enjoyments, foster forgotten skills, and host unexpected occasions for action.

Markell glosses Arendt on culture as "the activity of attending to, judging, and caring for the 'things of the world' in their appearance."[48] In this most oddly inculcating, cultivating, and curatorial of plays, Marina becomes a priestess of culture in Arendt's exacting sense. If affordances orient us toward objects and environments, drawing us in the direction of actor-network theory, affordance-based design's attention to traffic patterns, work flow, wayfinding, and organizational space restores the human dimension to the scene of dwelling. Affordances emerge in the effluvial backwash between an object-oriented humanism that irrigates environments of use and a human-centered design that pulls everything artifactual and technological back to its ethical and existential horizons.

"Thou shalt be welcome": the Fisherman's offer to Pericles is also an open invitation to us to read the romances as recipes or action scripts for living by design. It is easy to conceive of the crafting revival in the mode of pastoral nostalgia, in which latter-day Marinas recreate in needlepoint a simpler time when production trumped consumption and food was slow. Still, I have tried to show here that the communicative networks, political speech, ad hoc scenographies, and alternative shelter-writing erected in and through the collaborative labor called *Pericles* frame more salutary portals between contemporary and Renaissance experiments in dwelling. Shakespeare can become a present resource not by providing antique templates for literary event planners (though that is fun, too), but by linking embodied routines of craft and care to subjectivizing speech, collective organizing, economic empowerment, and zoning for sanctuary, accomplished across time and space through testimonial acts of reading and performance. The deepest connections between Shakespeare and DIY, I am suggesting, concern not the recovery of a relinquished past but the assembly of a common future, one that unfurls in the messianic urgency of the now.

Notes

1. Randall Martin, "Shakespearean Biography, Biblical Allusion and Early Modern Practices of Reading Scripture," *Shakespeare Survey*, 63 (2011): 222–3.
2. http://churchofcraft.org/our-mission/, accessed June 16, 2012.
3. Giorgo Agamben, *The Time That Remains: A Commentary on the Letter to the Romans* (Stanford, CA: Stanford University Press, 2005).
4. On forms of attention in craft, see for example Michael Polyani, *Personal Knowledge: Towards a Post-Critical Philosophy* (Chicago: University of Chicago Press, 1962); and Richard Sennett, *The Craftsman* (New Haven, CT: Yale University Press, 2008).
5. Eric Santner, *On Creaturely Life* (Chicago: University of Chicago Press, 2006); Julia Lupton, "Creature Caliban," *Shakespeare Quarterly*, 51.1 (Spring 2000): 1–23.
6. Michael Hardt, "Affective Labor," *boundary 2*, 26.2 (Summer 1999): 90. For a critique of affect and communicative capitalism, see Jodi Dean, *Blog Theory: Feedback and Capture in the Circuits of the Drive* (Cambridge: Polity Press, 2010).
7. Hannah Arendt, *The Human Condition* (Chicago: University of Chicago Press, 1958), pp. 8–9.
8. Arendt, *The Human Condition*, p. 9.
9. Ibid., p. 183.
10. Patchen Markell, "Arendt's Work: On the Architecture of *The Human Condition*," *College Literature*, 38.1 (Winter 2001): 32.

11. For an Arendtian reading of action in Shakespeare, see Paul Kottman, *A Politics of the Scene* (Stanford, CA: Stanford University Press, 2008).
12. Arendt, *The Human Condition*, p. 187.
13. Martin Heidegger, "Building Dwelling Thinking," in *Basic Writings* (New York: HarperCollins, 1977), trans. D. Krell, pp. 349, 359.
14. James J. Gibson coined the term in *The Ecological Approach to Visual Perception* (New York: Taylor and Francis, 1986).
15. Jonathan R. A. Maier, Georges M. Faidel, and Dina G. Battisto, "An affordance-based approach to architectural theory, design and practice," *Design Studies*, 30 (2009): 397.
16. Markell, "Arendt's Work," 31–2.
17. See for example the magazine *Good*, dedicated to building alliances among business, ethics, and design. On the phenomenology of spatial experience and questions of gender and sexuality, see Sara Ahmed, *Queer Phenomenology: Orientations, Objects, Others* (Durham, NC: Duke University Press, 2006).
18. Evelyn Tribble, *Cognition in the Globe: Attention and Memory in Shakespeare's Theatre* (New York: Palgrave Macmillan, 2011). On affordances in drama, see also W. B. Worthen, *Drama between Poetry and Performance* (Malden, MA: Wiley-Blackwell, 2010); and Julia Lupton, "Making Room, Affording Hospitality: Environments of Entertainment in *Romeo and Juliet*," *Journal of Medieval and Early Modern Drama*, forthcoming.
19. I follow the current consensus that the play was co-authored by George Wilkins and Shakespeare, with the first ten scenes (or first two acts) largely written by Wilkins and the remainder by Shakespeare. I cite the Oxford edition edited by Roger Warren (Oxford: Oxford University Press, 2003), unless otherwise noted. Following Warren's procedure, scene and line numbers but no act numbers will be cited.
20. On the open, see Giorgio Agamben, *The Open: Man and Animal* (Stanford, CA: Stanford University Press, 2004).
21. I am drawing here on ongoing research by Christopher Wild and Juliana Vögel at the University of Constance on entries and exits in drama. See also Alice Rayner, "Rude Mechanicals and the *Specters of Marx*," *Theatre Journal*, 54 (2002): 535.
22. Warren supplies the stage direction from Wilkins's *Painful Adventures*.
23. Tim Ingold, "The Temporality of the Landscape," *World Archaeology*, 25.2 (October, 1993): 153, 158. I borrow the term "organizational space" from Keller Easterling, *Organization Space: Landscapes, Highways, and Houses in America* (Cambridge, MA: MIT Press, 1999).
24. Warren speculates that the Third Fisherman may have been played by the same boy who will later personate Marina and who may also have been one of the reporters of the defective Q text (Oxford *Pericles*, pp. 789). On apprenticeship in the theatre, see David Kathman, "Grocers, Goldsmiths, and Drapers: Freemen and Apprentices in the ElizabethanTheater," *Shakespeare Quarterly*, 55.1 (Spring 2004): 1–49. On Ingold's taskscape, Shakespeare's Globe, regimes of enskillment, and theatre as workplace, see Tribble, *Cognition in the Globe*, pp. 101–2, 115.

25. Ingold, "The Temporality of the Landscape," 156.
26. Hardt, "Affective Labor," 90.
27. Ibid., 96.
28. Jack Bratich, "The Digital Touch: Craft-work as Immaterial Labour and Ontological Accumulation," *Emphera: Theory and Politics in Organization*, 10.3/4 (2011), pp. 303–18; p. 308.
29. On women and textiles in the Renaissance, see for example Susan Frye, *Pens and Needles: Women's Textualities in Early Modern England* (Philadelphia: University of Pennsylvania Press, 2011).
30. Bratich, "The Digital Touch," p. 303.
31. Hans Blumenberg, *Shipwreck with Spectator: Paradigm of a Metaphor for Existence* (Cambridge, MA: MIT Press, 1997), trans. S. Rendall.
32. For a theatrical reading of Pericles's armor, see Susan Harlan, "'Certain condolements, certain vails': Staging Rusty Armour in Shakespeare's *Pericles*," *Early Theatre*, 11.2 (2008): 129–39.
33. I would like to thank my student Chris Dearner for connecting the fishermen's beach-combing to Pericles's emblem in the following scene. On beach-combing and other maritime labors in Shakespeare, see Steve Mentz, *At the Bottom of Shakespeare's Ocean* (London: Continuum, 2009).
34. On branding and the society of the spectacle considered from an autonomist point of view, see Adam Arvidsson, *Brands: Meaning and Value in Media Culture* (London: Routledge, 2006).
35. Arendt, *Human Condition*, p. 247.
36. Messianic time in the romances, especially *The Winter's Tale*, has become a major motif in recent criticism. On the Paulinism of *Pericles* in particular, see Randall Martin, "Shakespearean Biography," 212–24.
37. Randall Martin, personal communication.
38. Andrew Ballantyne and Christopher L. Smith, *Architecture in the Space of Flows* (London: Routledge, 2011).
39. Heidegger, "Building Dwelling Thinking," p. 2.
40. Landscape architect Diana Balmori cites the frontispiece of Marc-Antoine Laugier's *Essai sur l'Architecture* of 1753, which depicts "columns emerging from the trunks of trees to form a primitive dwelling," in Diana Balmori and Joel Sanders, *Groundwork: Between Landscape and Architecture* (New York: Monacelli Press, 2011), p. 37.
41. Susan Fraiman, "Shelter Writing: Desperate Housekeeping from *Crusoe* to *Queer Eye*," *New Literary History*, 37.2 (Summer 2006): 37.
42. Hugh Grady calls Timon's tomb "a work of environmental art": "*Timon of Athens*: The Dialectic of Usury, Nihilism, and Art," in *A Companion to Shakespeare's Works: The Tragedies*, ed. Richard Dutton and Jean Howard (Malden, MA: Blackwell, 2003), p. 449.
43. Blumenberg, *Shipwreck with Spectator*, p. 19.
44. John S. Coolidge, *The Pauline Renaissance: Puritanism and the Bible* (Oxford: Clarendon Press, 1970), pp. 23–54. For a literary application of Coolidge's account of Pauline edification, see Gregory Kneidel, *Rethinking the Turn to Religion in Early Modern English Literature* (London: Palgrave

Macmillan, 2008). Rebeca Helfer explores the link between edifices and edifications in *Spenser's Ruins and the Art of Recollection* (Toronto: University of Toronto Press, 2013).
45. Paul Kottman, *A Politics of the Scene* (Stanford, CA: Stanford University Press, 2008), p. 10. See also Sarah Beckwith's stunning reading of Marina's use of language in this scene, in *Shakespeare and the Grammar of Forgiveness* (Ithaca, NY: Cornell University Press, 2012), p. 99.
46. Arendt, *The Human* Condition, p. 186.
47. Janet Adelman, *Suffocating Mothers: Fantasies of Maternal Origin in Shakespeare's Plays,* Hamlet *to* The Tempest (London: Routledge, 1992), p. 198.
48. Markell, "Arendt's Work," 32.

4
Performing Place in *The Tempest*
Cary DiPietro

In 2008, Google started rolling out its "Street View" technology in Google Maps and Google Earth, making it possible to navigate through various positions in an "immersive" photographic view of designated streets in the world. The possibilities of disembodied virtual travel enabled by such technology would seem to anticipate what some have described as our transhuman future; that is, when humans will transcend biology and consciousness will be absorbed into virtual environments, a moment that advocates for transhumanism have described optimistically as "the singularity."[1] Far from detaching us from our physical surroundings, however, the technology has raised more immediate concerns about the consequences of increasingly sophisticated imaging technologies for our lived places. These range from concerns voiced in the media about the violation of individual privacy and fears about the exploitation of global imaging by terrorists or foreign governments,[2] to more pragmatic concerns about how such technologies support or mitigate our ethical commitments to the preservation of places of cultural heritage or the integrity of local ecology.[3] What these anxieties about new media suggest is that we are already "transhuman," to mean that our sense of self is interconnected to our experience of lived places from which we cannot simply detach ourselves, at least until the promised singularity, and until that time, our attachments to places will remain plural and complicated—in *trans*ition across person and place. What, then, are the implications of such new media and their ability to create virtual environments for our self-defining attachments to place; that is, to the ways in which our understanding of ourselves and others are shaped by our sense of belonging to particular places in the world?

I want to use this question as a lens through which to consider the performance of place in Shakespeare's play *The Tempest*. If the internet enables "glocalization"—the communication or representation of local places and experiences across global distances—then so has theatre through the modern period played a similar role as a medium through which knowledge of the world and its inhabitants has been constructed and disseminated.[4] This is not to suggest that theatre is "virtual" in the sense of not "physically existing as such but made by software to appear to do so from the point of view of the program or the user" (*OED*, 4.g), because its characters are embodied by real actors who share the space of the theatre with theatregoers and whose performances involve presence, spatial negotiation, and material exchange; rather than virtual reality, a "real virtuality."[5] And yet, this nuanced inversion still depends on a perceptual awareness of the difference between the real and the virtual that is arguably modern, a post-Cartesian subjectivity that is enabled by, among other things, the new spatial organization of the early modern theatre that makes such separation between real and virtual possible. One thinks, by comparison, of medieval cycle and morality plays, in which performance is realized through an allegorical mode that collapses the difference between the real and what is being represented. The performance of the crucifixion of Christ by guild actors in the York cycle performed during the Corpus Christi festival, for example, like the liturgical sacrament of the Eucharist in which Christ's body and blood are made real, is imbued with real presence; and performed by not just any guild members, but the local pinners who make the nails that pin Christ to the cross. In the morality play genre, by comparison, Everyman and Mankind ventriloquize human experience—what it means to be human—for everyone at the performance. The early modern theatre, however, engenders a sense of dissociation between self and other, the result of which is that human experience is refracted or reflected through the performance of otherness in the secular, cosmopolitan, socially diverse, and increasingly global spatial situation of the theatre.[6] Theatre is thus "virtual" in an optical or perceptual rather than a computing sense.

Indeed, what partly characterizes our understanding of this period as liminally modern is not only the extent to which its cultural objects appear to express nascent modern subjectivities, but also the way in which they assimilate or anticipate modern orders of spatial awareness, from Copernican astronomy and early print cartography to Cartesian and Newtonian conceptions of space and time. We might even argue that the unmooring of the modern subject from the pre-modern attachment to local places—the result of urbanization and transnational exchange, among other phenomena we characterize as part of the processes of "modernization"—is coextensive with the supplanting of place by the new consciousness of space and time.[7] Thus, philosophers working within the framework of phenomenology, most notably Martin Heidegger and Maurice Merleau-Ponty, have sought to recover the importance of place, partly by recharacterizing modernity, which is an exclusively temporal marker, as an experience of dis*place*ment.[8] So too it might be argued that the early modern theatre as a kind of "virtual" technology promises the false illusion of nearness to place, and in so doing engenders the sense of dis*place*ment that is characteristic of our own contemporary experience of global new media.

The Tempest constitutes a promising site for the discussion of these issues, no less because of the apparent placeless-ness of the setting. The unnamed island on which the action takes place is located somewhere in the Mediterranean between Tunisia and Italy, and amid the tensions produced by the traffic of political, religious, and commercial exchange between countries around that region; moreover, its allusions to the new world and the literature of early modern travel and exploration situate it in the context of a proto-colonial English expansionism; even more, its Arcadian qualities and visual effects place it alongside the English pastoral and popular court entertainments.[9] To explain the play's social and cultural meanings by "mapping" it, however, might be argued to reproduce the desire to control and impose order on "uncharted territories" in the manner of its implicit colonial, political, and geographical ideologies, subordinating the island's locale to a global positioning system.[10] In contrast, I want to explore the play's ecology, by which I mean the interconnections of humans with their lived environments; specifically, I want to consider how attachments to place are evoked by or through theatrical performance, and whether the consequences of such attachments are positive or negative. On the one hand, we might read the play through the lens of a colonizing territorialism to argue how, for example, Prospero imposes order on the island, constructing and manipulating its ecology to his own ends. Not only does the play enact a fantasy of nature subordinated to human interests, its idealization of nature through pastoral rhetoric and theatrical artifice could be argued to mitigate responsibility for lived ecology. On the other hand, performance engenders felt experiences by audiences in the theatre, so we could argue alternatively that the play's performance of ecology produces felt attachments to place. The performance of the ecology of the island might therefore be used in the context of a global environmentalism to motivate an ethic of responsibility.

In either case, *The Tempest* evokes a sense of place through its highly aestheticized representation of nature. The island provides the only setting for the play, Prospero having been supplanted from Milan by his usurping brother Antonio, living there in exile with his daughter, Miranda; it also provides the setting for a number of spectacular visual effects coordinated by Prospero, such as the opening storm sequence, the disappearing banquet of Act 3, and the ethereal wedding masque of Act 4. These effects were probably influenced to some extent by the visual scenic effects of the Jacobean court masques of Inigo Jones and the technologies being imported from Italy and France, such as perspective-painted scenery, the wing-and-shutter system, and machinery for special effects. However, despite evidence that the play was performed at court on at least two occasions during Shakespeare's lifetime, the first in 1611 (which provides an approximate date for the play), *The Tempest* was most likely written for performance either at the Globe theatre or the indoor Blackfriars, where, in the case of the latter, even though it was indoors, elaborate scenic effects were unlikely to have been used.[11] Indeed, *The Tempest* is characteristic of Shakespeare's earlier plays written before the King's Men acquired Blackfriars in 1608, if not by the extent to which it makes use of visual episodes, then in the way such episodes are mediated through ekphrastic speech. Dramatic spectacle is augmented when characters describe through speech their wonder and amazement, as, for example, when Alonso describes the "strange shapes" that bring in the banquet: "I cannot too much muse. / Such shapes, such gesture, and such sound, expressing— / Although they want the use of tongue—a kind / Of excellent dumb discourse" (3.3.36–9).[12] When Ferdinand, led by Ariel's enchanting song, first eyes Miranda, she is to him a "wonder" (1.2.429)—her name deriving, after all, from the Latin verb *miror*, to wonder—and during the wedding masque in Act 4, he exclaims, "Let me live here ever! / So rare a wondered father and a [wife] / Makes this place paradise" (4.1.122–4).[13] In a moment of ironic reversal near the end of the play, Miranda expresses her own "wonder" (5.1.184) when she meets Alonso and his court, declaring, "O brave new world / That has such people in't" (185–6). Still, it is mainly the visitors to the island who express their wonder and thus augment our own wonder at the island's strange spectacles, some of them seen, some of them only described.

"Wonder," in the sense of an "emotion excited by the perception of something novel and unexpected, or inexplicable" (*OED* 7.a) or "astonishment mingled with perplexity or bewildered curiosity," is a thematic component of Shakespeare's play.[14] Prospero controls the island through the use of his "art"—the word is employed nine times in the play to refer to Prospero's magic—a word that carries multiple senses: "art," in addition to its sense as artifice, is skill "in the practical application of a particular field of knowledge or learning" (*OED*, 1.b), human skill or agency especially as opposed to nature (12), as well as crafty or cunning artfulness (11).[15] Indeed, the play's dramatic irony depends on our knowledge that the storm of the opening scene and the "direful spectacle of the wreck" (1.2.26) have been orchestrated by Prospero to bring his usurpers to the island. Prospero reassures his daughter that, despite her "amazement" (1.2.14) at the suffering she has witnessed, the storm was in fact harmless. The play thus thematizes mastery of the natural world through craft and knowledge. Prospero's knowledge is perhaps derived from the library of volumes Gonzalo provides for him at the moment of his exile from Milan (1.2.166–7); a powerfully symbolic motif in early modern culture generally, the book signals the intersection of such social phenomena as rising literacy, the burgeoning book trade in early modern Europe, cartographic and ethnographic knowledge of the world, and a proto-scientific epistemology that emphasizes visual observation, categorization, and explanation.[16] One thinks, by way of analogy, of contemporaneous curiosity cabinets, or cabinets of wonder, collecting what were seen to be exotic and wonderful objects from around the world arranged for visual observation, but that were also indicative of the early modern accumulation of knowledge and the desire to collect, contain, and classify a growing world of the strange and unknown. As a witness to the play, we are asked to judge or evaluate Prospero's coercions of nature—whether of the magical ecology of the island, or the plight of Caliban or Ariel, which might evoke either our sympathy or curiosity. At the same time, the play's effects depend on the strangeness of the spirits and noises and the aesthetic pleasure they elicit, the island's "Sounds, and sweet airs, that give delight and hurt not" (3.2.139), as described by Caliban. Later in the play, Gonzalo also links the experience of wonder to the island itself, commenting that "All torment, trouble, wonder, and amazement / Inhabits here" (5.1.106–7). Shakespeare thus evokes a sense of place through richly rhetorical language and ekphrastic descriptions, through which our experience of wonder is amplified or "refracted" through that of the characters.

That sense of place is further aestheticized through the well-known conventions of the Elizabethan pastoral, the island recalling the idealized English countryside of Spenser's *Faerie Queene*, borrowing not shepherds but its folklore landscape: Ariel sings of cowslips' bells (5.1.103) and torments Stephano and Trinculo with "pricking gorse and thorns" (4.1.180); in the masque episode, Juno calls on Ceres, goddess of fertility and symbol of nature's fecundity, to preside over an English harvest of wheat, rye, barley, oats, and peas (4.1.60–2). Caliban too describes the fecundity of the island when he offers to act as guide to Stephano and Trinculo: "I'll pluck thee berries, / I'll fish for thee... bring thee where crabs grow... dig thee pignuts, / Show thee the jay's nest, and instruct thee how / To snare the nimble marmoset. I'll bring thee / To clust'ring filberts... and get thee / Young seamews from the rock" (2.2.159–71).[17] Much like the forest outside of Athens in *A Midsummer Night's Dream* or the nominally French Arden in *As You Like It*, the island blends an idealized English landscape with the pan-European neoclassical pastoral. Shakespeare's combination of courtly romance and political treachery also recalls the same in Sidney's *Arcadia*, whose originally Greek place name reflects Sidney's appropriation of both the setting and pastoral conventions of Virgil's *Eclogues*. The King of Naples, Alonso, and his entourage are compelled to the island by the storm that Prospero conjures, and the island provides the setting for their eventual reconciliation, thus fulfilling a pastoral trope by contrasting social corruption with a redemptive natural world. The pastoral rhetoric of a "return to nature" thus sees humans motivated to an ethical reversal by the experience of an uncorrupted, pristine ecology—one whose seeming lack of regard for humanity inspires awe and humility.

Far from being a merely aesthetic celebration of the abiding qualities of nature, however, the English pastoral enables cultural and nationalist ideologies about the place of the English; as in *The Faerie Queene*, in which Queen Elizabeth and Tudor England are allegorized in an epic narrative about England's golden age that never was, the pastoral's idealization of nature elided with nostalgia for the past, the "return" to which affirms the values of an English aristocracy in the present and celebrates Elizabeth as an ideal monarch. The rhetoric of a return to nature was also employed discursively in early modern colonial discourse that described the Americas as a utopian paradise, a virgin land ripe for cultivation; indeed, the word "colony" derives from the Latin *colonia*, to mean "farm" or "landed estate," and its cognate *colonus* to mean "farmer" or "tiller" of land, reflecting the practice of colonial power in the new colonies.[18] The island as a place in *The Tempest* is arguably linked to colonial discourse by way of Shakespeare's use of early modern travel literature and ethnography as source material. Specifically, Shakespeare is thought to have drawn on a letter by William Strachey describing the wreck of his vessel, *The Sea Venture*, off the coast of Bermuda and his eventual arrival at Jamestown in 1609; more demonstrably, Gonzalo's utopian speech in Act 2, in which he muses about an imagined "commonwealth" had he "plantation of this isle" (2.1.149), alludes to Michel de Montaigne's essay "Of the Caniballes," quoting John Florio's 1603 English translation almost verbatim, in which Montaigne contrasts the prelapsarian simplicity of Brazilian natives to the political and social corruption of Europe. Describing his ideal commonwealth, Gonzalo muses: "All things in common nature should produce / Without sweat or endeavour; treason, felony, / Sword, pike, knife, gun, or need of any engine / Would I not have; but nature should bring forth / Of its own kind all foison, all abundance / To feed my innocent people" (2.1.160–5).[19] Given the shared utopianism of Gonzalo and Montaigne, that the island is unnamed by Shakespeare seems a deliberate gesture toward Thomas More and the pun in his *Utopia* (1516) to mean an ideal place (*eu topos*, after the Greek for "good place") and no place (*ou topos*).

Although the allusion to Montaigne implicates the play in the rhetoric of early modern colonialism—of the exploitation of natural resources and the "cannibals" and Calibans, who might claim some indigenous attachment to them—the play as a whole cultivates an awareness of the simplicity of such rhetoric. In the episode with Gonzalo in Act 2, this is achieved by the dialogue between Antonio and Sebastian, who deflate Gonzalo's fantasy of a prelapsarian paradise by pointing out its logical inconsistencies: that nature would provide without human labor, but it would be planted; that Gonzalo would govern it but would not be king; that "innocent" men and women without occupation or clothing would be idle "whores and knaves" (2.1.167). Their cynicism is perhaps motivated by the stories of the struggling colony at Jamestown in Virginia whose charter was established in 1606, and of descriptions of the precariousness of life in the new world where nature could be hostile, if not lethal; but in the context of an emergent awareness of global ecology, their dialogue provides a view of the complexity of human interaction with the environment that deflates Gonzalo's simplistic idealism.

In terms of its own representation of place, the play invites us to think in similar terms: that its evocation of place, however idealized, is unreal, not a place, like the conjured banquet of Act 3, a parody of the "foison" of nature imagined by Gonzalo, or the wedding masque of Act 4, which Prospero assures the "dismayed" (4.1.147) and "moved" (146) Ferdinand is nothing more than "the baseless fabric of a vision" (151): "the cloud-capped towers, the gorgeous palaces, / The solemn temples, the great globe itself" (152–3), Prospero explains, shall dissolve, though it is unclear whether he refers to places represented in the masque—perhaps only "shown" through his ekphrastic description—or to the real towers and palaces we see just outside of the Globe in early modern London and its environs. Indeed, in a moment that both instantiates and simultaneously challenges the distinction between the virtual and the real, Prospero compares the illusory quality of theatrical artifice to the "insubstantial pageant" (155) of our own subjective experience of the world: "We are such stuff / As dreams are made on, and our little life / Is rounded with a sleep" (156–8). And so, in a self-consciously theatrical gesture, Prospero detaches our existence from our physical surroundings and consciousness is absorbed into a singularity with aesthetic artifice, early modern virtual reality.

Prospero's metaphor, however, is not wholly benign. He invokes a conventionally humanist view of existence evacuated of inherent meaning—it is a "baseless fabric"—and this implicitly justifies his exercise of power over the island's life. He controls the play's pastoral economy by directing his spirits as actors in exchange for his own return to Milan, and the comedy concludes with his restoration to power. As an early or proto-modern archetype, Prospero "tends to his garden," cultivating order out of political and social disorder, the eponymous "tempest." The play's evocation of the sublime qualities of nature—heightened by the ekphrastic rhetoric of wonder and the hyperbole of the pastoral—comes to seem more exploitative, a fantasy of environmental control expressed in the metaphorical equation of nature with art. Indeed, Prospero's "art"—a word that resonates with early modern alchemy and the occult—begins to sound dangerously hubristic when set against more contemporary forms of environmental engineering such as fracking and concerns about commercial farming, climate change, genetically modified foods, and nuclear catastrophe. Throughout the play, the island's ecology is rhetorically embellished in ways that both heighten the pleasure we might derive from the representation of place while at the same time drawing attention to the artifice and the fantasy of human mastery. In the speech in Act 3 I quoted earlier, Caliban tells Stephano and Trinculo not to be afraid of the tabor and pipe music being played unseen by Ariel: "Be not afeard. The isle is full of noises, / Sounds and sweet airs that give delight and hurt not" (3.2.135–6). The aesthetic pleasures of the island's sights and sounds, as Caliban explains, cause him to become sleepy, leading to their metaphoric equation with dreams: "and then in dreaming," Caliban tells them, recalling his own experience, "The clouds, methought, would open and show riches / Ready to drop upon me, that when I waked / I cried to dream again" (140–3). The magical promise of the island is too good to be true.

In *Sense of Place and Sense of Planet*, Ursula Heise argues that there is a rhetoric of what she calls "spiritualist immersion in place" in contemporary arguments for the preservation of the environment.[20] The commonly evoked trope of the "blue planet" is predicated on the same dichotomy of an idealized natural state of local ecology in conflict with a corrupting human influence. Thus, both Renaissance pastoralism and many strains of contemporary environmentalism share in an aesthetic of the natural sublime; humans are motivated to an ethical reversal by experiencing the awe of an uncorrupted, pristine nature. For Heise, in the case of environmentalism, an essentialist concept of place is problematic because it relies on the "assumption that genuine ethical commitments can only grow out of the lived immediacies of the local," an assumption captured by the well-known coinage "Think globally, act locally."[21] The problem is that local actions are inadequate: global-scale problems require not only a global response, but an awareness of the different kinds of action required in different places to meet the needs of different groups of people. In fact, Heise uses Google Earth metaphorically to describe an alternative model that takes into account the various cultural contexts and political commitments of communities of people in a complex network of global ecological relationships, an approach that values "the abstract and highly mediated kinds of knowledge and experience that lend equal or greater support to a grasp of biospheric connectedness."[22] By comparison, a rhetoric of the local compels us to act by constructing affective attachments to place that subordinate global concerns for ecology to our own limited experience of the local. Heise thus uses a poststructuralist epistemology to critique the "ethic of proximity" in contemporary environmental movements, a fetish of the local arousing affective attachments to place that obviate the more complex biospheric relationships of global ecology.

In a similar manner, we might argue that the aestheticized representation of nature in *The Tempest* idealizes ecology in a way that obviates the complexities of lived global ecologies, effectively colonizing them. In making her case, Heise turns to the work of the social theorist Henri Lefebvre, whose spatial theory provides one way of thinking through the dichotomy between place and space implicit in this argument; that is, between the aesthetic or "virtual" representation of place and the social space of performance in the theatre. For Lefebvre, space is a social production in which subjectivity is constituted through what he calls spatial practices. Space is not an objective or empty canister that gets filled up with material, but rather it comes into being by way of a "register of the perceived," to mean, rather than a passive visual-spatial reception, the more active projection onto a spatial field of the material expression of social relations, "of all aspects, elements and moments of social practice."[23] Thinking through this lens, we might consider how the theatre is a space of social production, arranged spatially according to networks of exchange relations such as how much one is able to afford for admission or according to spatial hierarchies of rank and status. Epistemologically, scenic representations of place, both ekphrastic and visual, might be seen to accord with a notion of theatrical space as social production; in more prosaic terms, one of the ways by which theatre situates people spatially is by constructing knowledge of the world and mapping it through representational practices. There is, unfortunately, no easy way to explain specifically aesthetic representations of place in Lefebvre's typology of space because they are not "lived" in quite the same way. In his tripartite schematic, where spatial practice is the first order, "representations of space" are the conceived or conceptual abstractions "that may inform the actual configuration of such spatial practices, for example, Cartesian geography, linear perspective,"[24] and so on; and "spaces of representation" refer to the lived moments of space, where space is appropriated by the imagination, overlaying "physical space, making symbolic use of its objects."[25] By "representation," Lefebvre appears to intend not quite the sense of mimetic "copy," but something more like "imprint," the superimposition on spatial fields of social relationships and human psychology.

Nonetheless, Lefebvre's spatial theory offers a compelling way for thinking about representations of place in *The Tempest*, to the extent that its own represented places "colonize" both theatrical space through rhetorical artifice and lived space through the metaphor that equates artifice with our experience of the world. If place is subordinated to space in Lefebvre's typology, the point we might derive is that representational practices are coextensive with the spatial practices of theatre and, in fact, these cannot be separated out: the characters are embodied by actors, scenic settings are situated spatially in early modern London, and so on. This is exemplified in the play's final speech, when Prospero asks us directly to release him from his "bands"—to mean his exile on the island and, simultaneously, his role as an actor—with the help of our "good hands" (Epilogue 9–10). The imbrication of the three orders of space is an important part of Lefebvre's argument. In other words, space cannot be understood without considering the interconnected nature of what we perceive as cognitional individuals, what we conceive as social subjects, and how we "live" space. In the case of the play, we might argue that its "representations of space" subordinate a sense of scenic place by "imprinting" or imposing order on theatrical space, colonizing it through artifice. In other words, our sense of wonder is produced by the power of representation to transform theatrical space into the "baseless fabric of a vision."

Lefebvre's typology of space provides a great explanatory model for the theatre as social production, but it nevertheless diminishes the unique character of the aesthetic—for example, the power of performance to evoke a sense of place—as yet another instance of socio-spatial exchange. There is no space for thinking about how performance as a unique form of cultural communication moves beyond epistemology by, for example, developing our felt attachments to character and setting; or perhaps we should say that the felt experience of performance has no *place* in the spatial practice of theatre. In the case of *The Tempest*, its pastoralism arouses nostalgia insofar as the rhetorical descriptions of the island rely on playgoers' own experiences of English nature, whether they recall recent experiences, or, as in the case of Shakespeare as a migrant displaced to London, the pastures of his youth in Warwickshire. Moreover, such felt attachments to place evoked by the play necessarily motivate an ethic of ecological responsibility precisely because nature is idealized; mimetically, the island represents not how the world is, but how it might be.[26] This is the point that Heise leaves out of her criticism of the ethic of proximity in global environmentalism: that although the rhetoric of the local obviates an awareness of biospheric connectedness, felt attachments to place are what motivate ethical commitments of responsibility, even if such commitments come in the form of problematically pastoral models of stewardship that, in a global context, are "cultivated" or come with an idealized understanding of ecological relationships. That is to say, representational practices play a key role in cultivating in us those felt commitments to the environment.

What I want to do here is conjoin an epistemological understanding of theatrical space—which is both valuable and necessary—with an ontological understanding of place and, specifically, an argument that the performance of place is in fact inseparable from the "ground" of our experience in the theatre. This ontological ground is not a locale per se, not the terra firma on which the theatre structure is built or on which we stand or sit. As theorists working in the field of phenomenology such as Edward Casey and, more recently, Jeff

Malpas have argued, "place" is the condition that makes our experience possible. Indeed, the binary between place and spatial awareness is a false one because they are inseparable, the one impossible to conceive without the other.[27] The structure of spatial experience is given in and through place. Malpas thus argues: "The way in which human identity might be tied to place is thus merely indicative of the fundamental character of our engagement with the world—of all our encounters with persons and things—as 'taking place' in place" (15). He uses the Heideggerian phrase "being-in-the-world" to explain how place provides the *a priori* ground of experience: even while our perceptual experience of the world shapes our understanding of subjective space, it cannot come into being without first being emplaced in what Malpas calls "objective space."[28] Place might thus be understood neither "in terms merely of some narrow sense of spatio-temporal location, nor as some sort of subjective construct, but rather that wherein the sort of being that is characteristically human has its ground. So far as the idea of experience is concerned... the structure and possibility of experience... is inseparable from an understanding and appreciation of the concept of place."[29]

Performance is undeniably socially constituted, but the felt experience of performance is arguably irreducible to an ungrounded epistemology. Performance, we say, is something that "happens," in time—it is momentary, ephemeral—but it also "takes place." One of the ways in which performance therefore acquires force is through its power to effect our attachments to places in the world.[30] The distinction between the real and the virtual, between the space of the theatre and the aesthetic representation of place, breaks down when we think not in terms of how performance obtains to a concept of the real and thus acquires force, but instead in terms of how performance effects felt attachments to place that provide the constitutive ground of our experience. Think, by way of analogy, of your own experience of Google Earth: what is the first thing you do? You seek out your own place in the world because you are attached to it. Your awareness of it as representation does not diminish that attachment, but rather makes it more complex by allowing you to situate your place in the world. Moreover, your engagement involves an interactive performance not unlike performance in the theatre, one that positions you in multiple places at once (at your computer, in a city, in a country, on the globe), or in relation to your multiple place attachments.

In terms of the theatre, the terms *locus* and *platea*—sometimes used to delineate location and place, especially in discussions of medieval performance—might help us to navigate the plurality of such felt attachments, if only as a conceptual starting point, one whose binary problematically reinforces the notion of reality versus virtuality. On the surface, they conveniently describe the difference between the bounded location of the dramatic action produced by the rhetorical and visual effects of scenic time and place, the *locus*, and the place where the performances takes place, the *platea*. These are not objective or empty spaces on the stage or in the theatre, but are rather modes of performance determining and determined by our sense of place, as the example of the epilogue reminds us: Prospero need only "step out" of the scenic location of the island metaphorically to address the audience, and he keeps, as it were, one foot in the fictive setting as he prepares to return to Naples. The overlapping place-ness of *locus* and *platea* extends to the play's many moments of self-conscious theatricality. We might go so far as to argue that it is our ability to draw connections between the place-world of the play and our own experience of place that makes it meaningful for us; which is not to say that the performance of place elides with the local or locale, but that we can effectively occupy more than one place at the same time, and that we can bring our felt attachments to place to bear on a more epistemological understanding of other places, and vice versa.

Shakespeare's play is finally somewhat ambivalent about the pastoral model of stewardship it offers, on the one hand rewarding Prospero with a comic conclusion while, on the other, providing indirect and sometimes not so subtle critiques of his power, all the while celebrating the magical appeal of the island's sounds and sweet airs. At the same time, Shakespeare repeatedly reminds his audience of the theatrical artifice of the world it stages, that the island occupies a lived space in the theatre, and that its inhabitants are embodied by living actors who share that space with theatregoers. It stages a theatrical fantasy, a nostalgic "return" to a pastoral ideal, albeit through an impermanent aesthetic, in the space of early modern London. The implications of this return to nature are felt no less urgently for us than they were by theatregoers in the early seventeenth century, many of whom, like Shakespeare, migrated from the countryside to the urban landscape of an ever-expanding metropolis. Although there are significant differences between Elizabethan attitudes toward, for example, land stewardship, agricultural cultivation and colonization, and our own concerns with ecology and the dangers posed by neoliberal capitalism and agribusiness, nevertheless, the play acquires meaning, both then and now, by intersecting the felt attachments to place that it effects through performance with the cognitive dissonance of its aesthetic artifice in the space of theatre. In its evocation of the place of the island—through theatrical effect and ekphrastic description—the play compels us to recall our own felt experiences of being in the world, our memories of the awe and "magic" of nature, and positions them in the intersubjective space of the theatre.

Heidegger has in mind this notion of what he calls "being-in-the-world," our boundedness to place, when he describes the sense of placeless-ness engendered by new information technologies—in his case, film and radio—and their ability to collapse the distances of space and time. Google Earth certainly seems to exemplify the diminution of place: when we zoom out from our own local "street view," we end up somewhere in space looking down on our blue planet. However, far from lessening our felt commitment to place by zooming out from it, the technology provides the virtual network of information, the baseless fabric that allows us to place our own experience of the world in an intersubjective system of global ecological relationships. The theatre arguably enables a similar negotiation between epistemology and ontology, providing a ground for an understanding of our lived experience in terms of felt commitments to place, but in relation to larger, global epistemologies. On the one hand, we can critique *The Tempest* for the way in which its implicit cultural and political discourses are spatialized in the imaginative geography of the setting: the island's ecology and its inhabitants are exploited to achieve the play's comic conclusion, its nature subordinated to the social institutions of law, government, and the family to which its European characters return. Yet, on the other hand, an alternative understanding of the performance of place as the ontological ground of our experience of the world might lead us to a different understanding of its ecology in terms of felt commitment and responsibility, the theatre a place that allows us to zoom in and out of its English, Mediterranean, and New World contexts without diminishing our experience of its place in performance.

Notes

1. For a brief summary of "transhumanism" (sometimes called "posthumanism"), see, for example, Mark Walker, "Ship of Fools: Why Transhumanism Is the Best Bet to Prevent the Extinction of Civilization," *H+: Transhumanism and Its Critics* (Philadelphia: Metanexus Institute, 2011), pp. 94–111; and in literary studies, for a view critical of transhumanism, see Katherine Hayles, *How We Became Posthuman: Virtual Bodies in Cybernetics, Literature and Informatics* (Chicago: University of Chicago Press, 1999), esp. Chapter 1, pp. 1–24. She also responds in *H+ Transhumanism and Its Critics* in her essay "Wrestling with Transhumanism," pp. 215–26. The application of the mathematical term "singularity" to transhumanism has been popularized by the transhumanism advocate Ray Kurzweil. See, for example, Kurzweil, *The Singularity Is Near: When Humans Transcend Biology* (New York: Viking Penguin, 2005).
2. While Google has shown some sensitivity to privacy concerns raised in numerous countries, especially in the United States and the United Kingdom, by implementing computer programs that automatically blur out, for example, faces and license plates, the company has had greater difficulty bringing the technology to countries with heightened security concerns such as Israel. In "Privacy, Reconsidered: New Representations, Data Practices, and the Geoweb," Sarah Elwood and Agnieszka Leszczynski identify Google Street View technology among a number of technologies in the "geoweb" or geospatial web, meaning Web 2.0 frameworks and practices, especially those that emphasize user interactivity, which typically involve the "'geotagging' of online content, or the assignation of place names, latitude/longitude coordinates, or any other locational information to text, images, videos, or other Web content" (p. 6). These technologies, they argue, demand the reconceptualization of privacy, in part because they facilitate identification and disclosure of personal information more immediately and with less abstraction. *Geoforum*, 42.1, pp. 6–15.
3. Jeff Malpas, whose work is discussed at greater length below, considers the possibilities and limits of new media in relation to cultural heritage in "New Media, Cultural Heritage and the Sense of Place: Mapping the Conceptual Ground," *International Journal of Heritage Studies*, 14.3, pp. 197–209. On the relationship between global technology and local ecology, see Ursula K. Heise, *Sense of Place and Sense of Planet: The Environmental Imagination of the Global* (Oxford: Oxford University Press, 2008), esp. Chapter 1, pp. 17–68.
4. The *OED* provides a different definition of "glocalization" by tracking movement from the global to the local: "The action, process, or fact of making something both global and local; spec. the adaptation of global influences or business strategies in accordance with local conditions; global localization." "glocalization, n.," *The Oxford English Dictionary*, 3rd edn., December 2009; online version March 2012.

5. "virtual, adj. (and n.)," *The Oxford English Dictionary*, 2nd edn., 1989; online version March 2012. The term "real virtuality" was suggested by Steven Mullaney in his oral commentary on a number of papers that applied the term "virtual reality" to theatre, including an earlier version of this chapter, at panel sessions organized for the Renaissance Society of America meeting in May 2011 in the special topic "Theatre and the Reformation of Space in Early Modern Europe," sponsored by the Making Publics project (MAPS), McGill University.
6. Among their many reforms, English Protestant ideologues, especially from the mid-seventeenth century, rejected the doctrine of the eucharistic real presence as heretically iconic, Christ's body in fact spiritual or virtual rather than materially present in the Eucharist. The *OED* cites Jeremy Taylor's 1653 *A controversial treatise on the real presence and spirituall of Christ in the blessed sacrament: proved against the doctrine of transubstantiation* as an instance of "virtual" to mean that which "is so in essence or effect, although not formally or actually" (4.a): quoting Taylor, "they [Catholics] say [Christ] is taken by the mouth, and that the spiritual and the virtual taking him in virtue or effect is not sufficient, though done also."
7. Edward Casey provides a fulsome discussion of the hegemony of space–time thinking in modern philosophy in the first chapter of *Getting Back into Place: Toward a Renewed Understanding of the Place-World* (Bloomington, IN: Indiana University Press, 1993); he moves from Galileo to Descartes to Kant, first to consider the primacy of chronological order or duration in the conceptual relationship between consciousness and the lived world, and then, through Henri Bergson, to consider the "spatialization" of time as a linear progression. "The crux of the problem," he argues, "is that time is conceived in such a way that everything else is made subjacent to it, beginning with place and ending with space" (p. 8).
8. Heidegger is important to both Casey and Malpas in their attempts to reclaim place as the primary ground of experience. Heise, in *Sense of Place* (p. 35), identifies Heidegger's essay "Bauen Wohnmen Denken" (Building Dwelling Thinking, 1951) and Merleau-Ponty's *Le visible et l'invisible* (The Visible and the Invisible, 1961) as works in the European phenomenological tradition that critique the displacement of place in modern philosophy.
9. Much criticism of the play has thus been concerned with the problem of "locating" the play ideologically in relation to contemporary travel narratives and colonial discourse. See, for example, the essays collected by Peter Hulme and William H. Sherman in *"The Tempest" and Its Travels* (Philadelphia: University of Pennsylvania Press, 2000). Patrick M. Murphy reviews the diverse variety of discussions of the play in its geographical and historical contexts in "Interpreting *The Tempest*: A History of Its Readings," in *The Tempest: Critical Essays*, ed. Patrick Murphy (New York: Routledge, 2001), pp. 3–72. Although more than ten years old, the essay provides an extensive bibliography of secondary readings.

10. In his discussion of "Alien Habitats in *The Tempest*," Geraldo de Sousa defines "habitat" after the Latin *habitare*, used originally in Latin books to describe flora and fauna in natural places of growth, to denote the "complex ecological relations of all living organisms to their physical surroundings, habits, and modes of life" (p. 439); in Murphy, *The Tempest*, pp. 439–62. He uses the figure of alien habitats to consider the play's representation of place in relation to the emergent colonial practice of logging, especially of redwood in Brazil, and rising concerns in the early seventeenth century about deforestation in England.
11. Virginia Mason Vaughan in her Arden edition (London: Thomson Learning, 2005), pp. 6–7, briefly puts forward this view, citing E. K. Chambers, *William Shakespeare: A Study of Facts and Problems*, 2 vols. (Oxford, 1930), vol. 1, p. 489; Stephen Orgel, in the single-volume Oxford edition (Oxford: Oxford University Press, 1998), provides a more detailed discussion, pp. 1–3, concluding that the play was not written for court nor produced as a masque (p. 2).
12. All textual references to Shakespeare's play are made to *The Oxford Shakespeare: The Complete Works, Second Edition*, ed. John Jowett, William Montgomery, Gary Taylor, and Stanley Wells (Oxford: Clarendon Press, 2005).
13. I have followed Orgel's single-volume Oxford in adopting the reading "wife" rather than "wise" on the assumption that it is the compositor's misreading of "f" for a long s in the authorial copy, or possibly the breaking apart of the "f" in the course of printing the Folio. In either case, the association of Miranda with "wonder" is established by her name and for Ferdinand to refer to her as wife after the symbolic ceremony of the masque is more than fitting given the play's comic structure.
14. "wonder, n.," *Oxford English Dictionary*, 2nd edn., 1989; online version March 2012.
15. "art, n.," *Oxford English Dictionary*, 3rd edn., September 2008; online version December 2011. An entry for this word was first included in *New English Dictionary* (1885).
16. The pairing of Renaissance empiricism with the occult, a proto-science with magical art, in the material object of the book is exploited beautifully by Peter Greenaway in his 1992 film *Prospero's Books* (UK).
17. The "pignut" is a groundnut resembling the chestnut and sometimes eaten as a wild root vegetable. The marmoset is, of course, native to South America rather than Europe, though the term was often applied to any small monkey (see *OED*, "marmoset, n."). Oxford, following Theobald's suggestion, substitutes "seamew" for the Folio's "scamel," ostensibly a printer's error, to refer to the common gull. In "Alien Habitats," De Sousa argues alternatively that, especially from the perspective of the visitors, "this island is a harsh environment, whose natural resources are either depleted or hard to find" (p. 448).
18. "colony, n.," *Oxford English Dictionary*, 2nd edn., 1989; online version March 2012.

19. Extracts of these two sources are reproduced in appendix in both Vaughan's Arden and Orgel's Oxford edition.
20. p. 41.
21. Ibid., p. 41.
22. Ibid., p. 62.
23. Henri Lefebvre, *The Production of Space* [1974], trans. Donald Nicholson-Smith (Oxford: Blackwell, 1991), p. 15. Christian Schmid explains: "In concrete terms, one could think of networks of interaction and communication as they arise in everyday life (e.g., daily connection of residence and workplace) or in the production process (production and exchange relations)." "Henri Lefebvre's Theory of the Production of Space: Towards a Three-Dimensional Dialectic," in *Space, Difference, Everyday Life: Reading Henri Lefebvre*, ed. Kanishka Goonewardena, Stefan Kipfer, Richard Milgrom, and Christian Schmid (New York: Routledge, 2008), pp. 27–45; p. 36.
24. Victor Burgin, *In/Different Spaces: Place and Memory in Visual Culture* (Berkeley, CA: University of California Press, 1996), p. 27.
25. Lefebvre, *The Production of Space*, p. 39.
26. Hugh Grady provides a similar though much more nuanced explanation of the significance of aesthetic utopianism in *Shakespeare and Impure Aesthetics* (Cambridge: Cambridge University Press, 2009). He uses Adorno's *Aesthetic Theory* to argue that art's "impurity" enables a negative dialectical critique, the fact of its social and economic determination coupled with its status as a passive or nonthreatening reflection of the real world—not disinterested, but disengaged. See Chapter 1, esp. p. 29.
27. Malpas, for example, rejects the post-Cartesian notion that space is physical extension (*res extensa*) and that place is some location subject to sensibility (*res cogitans*). He therefore rejects the restricted sense of place as socially or mentally constructed.
28. The distinction between what he calls objective and subjective space is developed in Chapter 2 of *Place and Experience*, pp. 44–71. Casey, by comparison, works within the Cartesian notion of spatial extension by thinking primarily in terms of place as the body's emplacement in space and its "arc of reachability." Like Malpas, he similarly reads place as, in Kantian terms, an a priori intuition, but relocates it "resolutely in the body" rather than in the mind: place is "'the first of all things' because we know it from the very beginning. But we know it thus only because our bodies have always already, i.e., a priori, given us access to it" (p. 110).
29. Malpas, *Place and Experience*, p. 33.
30. I borrow the term "force" from W. B. Worthen, *Shakespeare and the Force of Modern Performance* (Cambridge: Cambridge University Press, 2003), p. 9. Worthen defines performative force by drawing on the revisions by Derrida and Butler of Austin's notion of performative utterances. Following Butler, Worthen argues that theatre is a "citational" practice that, rather than citing the dramatic text in a repetitive or hollow way, instead reiterates "regimes of performance": "Plays become meaningful

in the theatre through the disciplined application of conventionalized practices—acting, directing, scenography—that transform writing into something with performative force" (10). Worthen moves in the right direction by empowering performance as an affective force, but his argument still depends on an epistemological distinction between the real and the virtual.

5
Green Economics and the English Renaissance: From Capital to the Commons

Charles Whitney

> Why does there appear to be no one to blame for the ongoing destruction of the economy, society and environment? The government, banks, experts, and regulators have all claimed innocence, while taxpayers have had to speculate on their futures. It is time to point the finger: it is the discipline of economics that has brought about this state of affairs. From business to the media to academia, economists now run the world. —Arjun Appadurai[1]

> Systems of common ownership, of negotiation and sharing of resources within communities—systems which existed in our economic past—are providing inspiration for those who are starting on the journey towards a sustainable economic future. —Molly Scott Cato[2]

I do not think that economists run the world, but they do work for and guide those who run much of it. Economic theory as well as production is centrally involved in the ecological degradation that has exploded along with post-Second World War capitalist globalization. However, although comparatively low on mainstream political priority lists, especially in the United States, this apparently relentless environmental decline is an important factor helping to stimulate a range of promising, ecologically aware approaches to economic theory and practice worldwide. In the United States this phenomenon, influenced in part by similar developments in the United Kingdom, has been called the New Economics Movement, whose goal is, in boilerplate, "to transform our fossil fuel-powered, finance-bloated, inegalitarian economy into one that is resilient, just, and sustainable in the environmental and economic transition given true urgency by climate change."[3] Compatible initiatives exist in other countries, with those in developing nations often focusing more explicitly on opposition to neoliberal globalization. All challenge some axioms of what is variously termed mainstream, orthodox, or neoclassical economics: the grow-or-die imperative, reduction of the human to *homo economicus*, and emphasis on money, debt, private property, and domination of the economy by the market. That domination includes a corporate approach to sustainability whose focus is increasingly perceived to aim primarily at sustaining the corporation.[4] The notorious slipperiness of the word "sustainability" signals a more extensive process of blending, compromise, or greenwashing in the adoption of environmental goals.

The recognition that human beings have already affected the environment to the point that the planet has entered a threatening new geological period, the Anthropocene, is a related factor underscoring the need for the reconsideration of dominant economic assumptions that appear to be having increasingly devastating effects. That recognition is also stimulating new research and reconsideration of the human record in all its aspects,[5] including of course the study of sixteenth- and seventeenth-century England, where the influence of ecocriticism continues to grow. England came to be an early center of capitalist development in that period, and here I consider how ecological and economic approaches to Renaissance literature and early modern culture and society might be usefully equipped with the insights of green economics, considered as an integral part of the new directions in economic thought and practice referenced above. Given the threats we now face as well as the insights they have helped stimulate, can green economics inflect our understanding of the nature and significance of early modern England's transition to capitalism, one so historically relevant to our own? And could any valid new inflection help to underscore, clarify, or address our present problems?

As my epigraph by green economist Molly Scott Cato suggests, significant aspects of her orientation parallel some features of early modern economic attitudes and institutions. That recourse to the past is often integral to the presentation of an alternative economic or political perspective, as in Sir Thomas More's *Utopia* or William Morris's *News from Nowhere*. For its part, ecocriticism has revealed many relatively eco-friendly attitudes and practices in the early modern (usually pre-Restoration) period that were later eclipsed. Even the oppressive gradations of the Elizabethan world picture, as Gabriel Egan's *Green Shakespeare* shows, feature a holistic awareness of reciprocal dependencies that suggests an ecological awareness; a recent collection also later referenced here is *The Indistinct Human in Renaissance Literature*,[6] which explores a resourceful flexibility subsequently obscured. Here, my somewhat conjectural evaluation of the relevance of early modern economic attitudes and practices, especially so-called common-field agriculture and Shakespeare's treatment of commons enclosure in *As You Like It*, will involve a certain amount of reverse mirroring, duly qualified by acknowledgment of the hard and subservient lives of most English copyholders, cottagers, and hired farm workers. For the proposition seems compelling that after much delay in addressing climate change and other environmental problems as well as the social injustices resulting (not to mention those integral to our economic system), some of what was becoming culturally residual then in relation to the capitalist dominant needs to become culturally emergent now, in some new form, in relation to that same dominant. That is the position I am urging here. To the degree that is true, opportunities may exist for supplementing the current emphasis on the rise of market relations in economic criticism of Renaissance literature with an emphasis on the nature and importance of the alternative economic relations existing at that time.

In the dimensions of both economics and ecology, the topic of the commons relates past and present powerfully, not primarily because it provides a basis for analogies, but because in various senses the commons has been the target of continuous assault in modern history.[7] Commons rights and their denial through enclosure remained for centuries in England—and still are today in many parts of the world—central issues as private property, market relations, and globalization continued to advance, although those issues have often been oversimplified and romanticized. Today, perhaps hundreds of millions of people are sustained by membership in traditional agrarian or forest commons. The sense of community and the shared resources therein provide a subsistence basis that can compensate for joblessness or exploitative labor—or relieve one from the necessity of such labor. However, lacking outright ownership, users of such commons are often vulnerable to eviction, as in today's global wave of real-estate speculation.[8] In a larger sense, "the commons" includes an indefinitely large list of cultural and natural entities that are typically possessed by no one, from dances, languages, and traditional crop breeds to the Earth's atmosphere and oceans; the commodification of some of these appropriates them from the commons to the private sphere. Hence, protecting the environment from damage by private use or appropriation means essentially protecting a commons shared by the inhabitants of Earth from enclosure.[9]

Twenty years ago, Richard Wilson revealed the surprising importance of embattled common-field agriculture to Shakespeare's festive comedy *As You Like It* (1599).[10] The play confirms the new, culturally residual, and politically weaker status of commons rights by registering the crucial decline of property owners' support for them during the 1590s. The opposing sympathies and interests represented in the moment of *As You Like It* can be paired in a reverse mirror with those of our time: market fundamentalism and relentless globalization on the one hand, and worldwide resistance and exploration of alternatives on the other, especially in the wake of the worldwide financial crisis and recession. Both are crisis moments, speaking broadly, that exhibit similar features, both ecological (overpopulation, increased food insecurity, and bad weather) and economic (enclosures of commons and mass protests over widening immiseration and economic inequality).

By "green economics" I do not mean to refer specifically to the views of any green political party or to the subdiscipline of that name, although my main source, Cato, is a party member and a green economist. To my understanding "green economics" has a more general use, referring to the practical applications of a core set of principles, some of which are adopted from the relatively well-defined discipline of ecological economics. First, the economy is not separate from the environment, but rather a subset of the earth's ecosystems, the energy and resources of which are finite. From this perspective, the source of economic value ultimately resides not in land, labor, or the process of exchange itself, but rather in the Earth's ecosystems. In the long run, the Earth and its ecological systems are the source and the limit of economic value, despite human effort and technical or financial ingenuity. And the run has been long.

Second, economics is not a value-free science, for the total well-being of ecosystems—animals, plants, and the environments that sustain us—is an end in itself. From this holistic viewpoint, quantifying the costs and benefits of new products, policies, or applications, as mainstream economics' cost–benefit analysis seeks to do, is either impossible or unreliable. The principle of the greatest good for the greatest number in such analysis is also questionable, because in practice it often discriminates against the poor and the nonhuman.[11] The green variety is a form of political and moral economics.[12]

Green economics explores the implications of these principles in pursuing social as well as environmental justice. Cato's view is that the dominance the capitalist market now enjoys is "environmentally obsolete."[13] A plurality of ways of provisioning is required, in which the market is merely a part. The goal is a just, steady-state, or no-growth economy that encourages technological development without increasing consumption or reducing biodiversity. That defines a valid sense of "sustainability." Grass-roots movements leading to sweeping political reforms would be required for a shift toward measures like local and regional production based on commons rights and for-benefit and cooperative enterprises in addition to property ownership, inclusion of environmental costs ("externalities") in pricing along with government subvention of those costs, work-time reduction and the development of more labor-intensive work to reduce gross domestic product (GDP), and discouragement of the consumer society and encouragement of a convivial one. "Permaculture" is the technological ideal, in which ecosystems are preserved and waste from one process always becomes raw material for another. Many such proposals seem to have a secondary implication: as alien as some of them seem with respect to what we still imagine to be our world, they might suit us well when adverse environmental conditions disrupt that world in the future—when travel and trade, for instance, become more difficult, expensive, and dangerous.[14]

So defined, green economics supplies important themes for the so-called new economics, the various separate applications of which may lay a groundwork for large changes in economic production and organization "when the right political moment occurs," as economist Gar Alperovitz puts it below, a moment that could coincide with those above-mentioned grass-roots movements. The phrase itself happens to label a British and a US foundation: the new economics foundation (*sic*) and New Economics Institute respectively. Both are dedicated to research, planning, and policy; the latter is more directly focused on promoting solutions to climate crisis, while the former also offers a range of practical tools and services to businesses and communities. At the new economics foundation (nef), household and community, where women's participation is usually primary, are recognized as the cores of economic activity. Decentralization and a diversity of private and cooperative companies are ideal. GDP growth is condemned either as a measure of well-being or as an economic goal; nef introduced the Happy Planet Index, now one of many alternative measures. Whether the issue is how to keep money circulating locally rather than departing for financial centers, or how to control carbon emissions worldwide, the emphasis is on reembedding distinctively economic matters into their broader contexts of political, social, ecological, ethical, and spiritual life.[15]

Alperovitz describes the "New Economics Movement" in a range of US initiatives. It is

> a far-ranging coming together of organizations, projects, activists, theorists and ordinary citizens committed to rebuilding the American political-economic system from the ground up.
>
> The broad goal is democratized ownership of the economy for the "99 percent" in an ecologically sustainable and participatory community-building fashion. The name of the game is practical work in the here and now—and a hands-on process that is also informed by big picture theory and in-depth knowledge.
>
> Thousands of real world projects—from solar-powered businesses to worker-owned cooperatives and state-owned banks—are underway across the country. Many are self-consciously understood as attempts to develop working prototypes in state and local "laboratories of democracy" that may be applied at regional and national scale when the right political moment occurs.[16]

Among other examples cited here are B corporations chartered to subordinate profit to public service, community land trusts, social enterprises geared to service before profit, legislation requiring private banks to address community needs, local currencies, and 11,000 employee-owned companies. Then there are activist campaigns and organizations, such as those aiming to end corporate personhood.

And traditional concerns like credit unions, municipally owned utilities, and other publicly owned enterprises actually play a huge role in the US economy.

In the developing world, let me add, food sovereignty or the right to a secure source of food is a major focus, given the widespread perception that "industrial agrifood is tragically one of the planet's major drivers of global poverty and environmental destruction."[17] Organizations ranging from the once-armed Zapatistas to Via Campesina and Brazil's Landless Rural Workers' Movement (MST) oppose neoliberal globalization and work for environmental justice, and many have links with counterparts in the developed world.[18] And with hundreds of self-regulating, common-pool economic systems existing and under development around the world, the new economics movement in the sense of pragmatic and sustainable alternatives to neoliberal globalization is global.[19]

Besides their ecological commitments and nonmarket aspects, the fundamental distinction between neoclassical economics and the economic orientations of most of the above seems to be that between, on the one hand, the economy as a distinct sphere—a "science"—in which self-interested, private individuals and firms pursue profit (their self-serving goals hopefully becoming transformed into public benefits) and, on the other hand, the economy as a means of serving the well-being of humans and the environments we inhabit. There is a major caveat here, however: Alperovitz's new-economics businesses exist in an old-economics environment, one with the remarkable capitalist ability to adapt. The many thousands of worker-owned companies in the United States and elsewhere have widely divergent organizations, and some are constituted this way for the tax breaks. (There are tax breaks!) Alperovitz includes the area of green finance in his survey, meaning financial instruments that trade stocks in pollution credits, such as the cap-and-trade system. The vulnerability of this approach to co-optation by becoming primarily a source of revenue for governments and a source of profits for investors undermines its credibility. As for the common-pool resource concerns in developing countries that I have noted, when is such an organization a true commons, and when is it merely another way to organize work groups for more efficient exploitation?[20]

Caveats aside, the above distinction between neoclassical and new economics has an analogue in sixteenth-century England, where it was most explicitly framed by the so-called Commonwealthmen of mid-century as that between acting either for the sake of the "commonwealth" or in pursuit of "commodity"; that is, private benefit.[21] The anxious surmise that hovered throughout the century was, and again today is, widespread: it might be lethal to assume that private vices can reliably be channeled into public virtues. The Commonwealthmen moralists (Robert Crowley, Hugh Latimer, Thomas Becon, and Thomas Lever) were Lutheran ministers and social critics who responded to the rise of market-oriented acquisitiveness and opposed the depopulating enclosure of common land, stressing the reciprocal duties of all members of society to labor for the general welfare.[22] Their outspoken conservatism never questioned the rank-ordered, profoundly unequal social system, but they took an economic position in support of the commons system that was at the same time political, moral, and religious. Their emphasis on the socio-economic duties of monarchs and persons in authority provided the basis for John Ponet's argument for the right of revolt.[23] A related work of political economics, Thomas Smith's more measured and influential *Discourse on the Commonweal of This Realm of England* (written in 1549), also opposed enclosure. As the commons system suffered pressure from depopulating enclosure, it came to signify a set of moral regards, convictions, dispositions, or sensibilities that were shared by the great majority of society at that time, and were enshrined in law. These dispositions centered on the value of the common good, of which the commons system was a prime expression. Today, for many, economics has once again become political and moral economics.

Common-field agriculture remained widespread in most parts of early sixteenth-century England,[24] and was the most prominent among common-pool resources that also included fisheries, fens, and purlieus, all of which were to varying degrees administered by those who actually utilized them. This agricultural system, though, might almost as well be called private-field agriculture, because it was a mixture of both, and the extent of a family's private plot was a great factor in its relative well-being. Participants ran from from well-to-do copyholders to the poorest of farm laborers with tiny or no plots of their own. "Private" plots were not actually owned outright, but rented from the landlord, who also owned the common fields and equipped his tenants with a separate set of regulations, manorial ones. Common rights, private plots or laboring income, and local markets at which livestock could be sold served complementary functions and together provided, weather permitting, a living at subsistence level or higher.[25]

The common land itself offered first and foremost grazing, along with a range of other benefits not limited to fire materials (wood, furze, bracken), wood for pens, animal bedding, ash for soap, thatch for roofs, coverings for harvested crops and vegetables, and rushes for baskets, mats, hats, chair seats, toys, bedding, netting in plastered walls, wrapping for cheese, and lighting. The nature of rights varied: they could be authorized for such provisions as coal, stone, loam for bricks, nuts, fishing, game, and so on.[26] Even for the hired hand and his family, as historian Alan Everitt puts it, common

> rights alone added a few simple graces to an otherwise bare existence, and bred in the labourer a sense of home and independence. For the cottager with ample common rights, there was profound truth in Sir Henry Wotton's dictum:
>
> > How happy is he born and taught
> > That serveth not another's will.[27]

Here, Everitt precisely identifies the paradoxical relationship between mere "subsistence" and what has become the contemporary goal of many farmers, pastoralists, and fisherfolk today, "food sovereignty." Begun by Via Campesina in 1966, this worldwide movement aims to protect and expand local, sustainable production and independence from export-based industrial agriculture. Sometimes, then and now, bare life and the sovereign are not far apart.

The English system was far from a straightforward commons system and hardly exemplifies the full range of commons benefits that green economists envision for some democratic, convivial, and sustainable commons of the future. Nevertheless, it includes enough ingredients and has gained enough interest over time to make it once again a compelling reference point for recasting kingdoms into other molds. If this is what could be done under the conditions of the time, what could be achieved now? The constraints of a commons system that includes paying landlords are obvious. With regard to the prime green directives of degrowth and sustainability, this system's record is mixed. The rural English population increased over centuries—slowly and intermittently, to be sure—by spreading to unutilized areas, causing considerable ecological impact, until it ran short of land in the sixteenth century. At that point, continued population pressure overcame the system's built-in limitations on growth, and became a major cause of the enclosure movement, the depopulating effects of which immiserated so many.

However, in another respect—resource use—this system is a model, for the prime directive is always to preserve the commons' ability to furnish its plenty without stint. It is a matter of survival that neighborhood be maintained, that, for instance, one not overburden the common fields with more livestock than they can support. Many "inhibitory"[28] rules of that kind, as Cato calls them, also tended to slow human population expansion by making sure that no family overused common resources. These rules are why Garrett Hardin's famous thesis concerning the "tragedy of the commons" is wrong.[29]

Biodiversity is an essential aspect of environmental preservation. If a corporation invented a way to absorb all the carbon dioxide that the Amazon forest does, would anyone say let's cut that forest and raise cattle? (In fact, this is being done now without that invention.) Biodiversity was a significant issue in both the 1607 Midlands Rising against enclosures and the sustained early seventeenth-century resistance to the enclosure and drainage of common-pool fens. To ruin an ecosystem to focus on one or a small number of its resources (pasturage, oil seeds) seemed anathema.[30]

These protests against over-specialization may indicate some sense of the commons as what would be called today an ecocentric commonwealth of nature that includes human and nonhuman, as "a level of organization of human society that includes the nonhuman," as G. Snyder puts it.[31] Unlike a single farm under private ownership, the whole point was to develop among those who had commons privileges a kind of polity, one that extended to the well-being of plants and animals on whom one's life depended. Such a primarily self-provisioning environment may reinforce a respectful stewardship of nature, if not the sense of the sacred, quasi-divine power of the natural world and its seasonal cycles that some environmentalists stress.[32] In such a polity, human nature itself might indeed be considered rather "indistinct," and "coextensive" with "non-human living things," potentially joining other examples of early modern representations of the indistinct human featured in the collection mentioned above.[33]

The rich popular culture and festivity of early modern England had much of their roots in rural tradition. The convivial celebration of seasonal rites affirmed an ethic of creatureliness and cycles, of death and new life, of limits and endurance. The human–humus nexus that Margreta de Grazia explores in *Hamlet*, for instance, affirms and celebrates with the help of a gravemaker a carnivalesque natural cycle in which humans become loam some time after becoming food for worms.[34] That ethic was ingrained in the mutually agreed, seasonally appropriate rules of inhibition on which commons management depended, which were the basis of its level of sustainability. As work was often communal, so were those celebrations. Of rural Maygames and other festive traditions, Everitt remarks, "Unlike the leisure pastimes of today, the recreations of Tudor and Stuart labourers were not merely a means of escape: they formed a kind of inherited art of ritual, centering around their daily occupations, and based upon the ordinary sights and sounds of the village."[35]

Along the same lines, green economists stress the importance of "convivial" labor as opposed to industrial productivity, and find it in rural tradition. Ivan Illich's definition is invoked: "the autonomous and creative intercourse among persons, and the intercourse of persons with their environment... I consider conviviality to be individual freedom realized in personal interdependence and, as such, an intrinsic ethical value."[36] Here, the economic sphere is experienced as embedded in the larger affective life, distinguishing this kind of work experience from the selling of one's labor, though the distinction goes beyond that. This disposition toward cooperation in preserving a natural environment and its biodiversity day by day resonates deeply with many greens, because in the first place much more of it would seem to be required as soon as possible to ameliorate the damage humans have done to the global commons. However, when "the discipline of sharing things fairly with one's neighbors was relaxed," remarks historian Joan Thirsk on the demise of the commons system, "[t]his was the great revolution in men's lives, greater than all the economic changes following enclosure."[37]

Here, in conclusion to the discussion of the commons system, are two pertinent observations concerning enclosure of the global commons today in the sense of commodification. Many kinds of seeds for crops have been bred over generations by farmers, from India to the Amazon. Making minor genetic modifications, agribusinesses patent the breeds, thereby gaining the exclusive right to sell them. The breeds have been essentially pirated from the commons and transferred to the private sphere.[38] Similarly, the debate over how to reduce carbon emissions and hence global warming also involves an issue of enclosure. The debate, Cato points out, "is polarized between those who seek to commodify the atmosphere and create a pseudo-market to trade the right to pollute it, and those who see it as a commons that should be protected through socially determined and socially just agreements."[39] The market approach requires that private individuals profit from selling something they have legally acquired as their property, the right to pollute our air. This approach, the cap-and-trade system or the financialization of nature, is gaining ground. The outcome of that debate might produce changes even more significant than the one Thirsk elucidates.

Karl Marx traced the beginnings of capitalism to the enclosure movement, which provided surplus labor. Were a neoclassical economist to make enclosure equally central, her version of modern history might run like this: in England a labor-intensive commons system yielding modest profits for owners gave way to a more efficient system in which workers selling their labor could make large profits for entrepreneurs, especially in the wool industry, launching our affluent, exciting, democratic, and populous world. A green economist might put things this way: the forcible dismantling of a relatively sustainable and in not insignificant ways democratic commons system may have opened the way for some wonderful things, but also for systemic misery, and it has now launched the Anthropocene period, when the degree of liberty in a society can be gauged roughly by its ability to burn carbon and thereby contribute to the eventual loss of all the good things the dismantling achieved. An indication of "systemic misery" would be that Cato can describe the effects of both the early enclosures and India's so-called Green Revolution with the same words: "huge social upheaval and destruction of social systems" and "displacement, urbanization, unemployment, population increase and malnutrition."[40] For maximum productivity does not necessarily equal maximum efficiency when the "externalities" often elided by neoclassical economics are brought in. In *Utopia*, More's Ralph Hythloday explains how post-enclosure productivity can be counter-productive, as sheep eat up England by producing the externalities of vagrancy, crime, and crime's fatal punishment, factors not reflected in the price of wool.

In the course of the sixteenth century, up to the time of *As You Like It* at its end, the sensibilities that referred economic questions to moral imperatives about society and the commonwealth were challenged by the rise of wage labor and novel economic opportunities created by a dynamic market economy. Nevertheless, these sensibilities remained important even as London teemed with the fenced-out masterless as well as with some of their tricked-out former masters and mistresses, and as the theatre found its place in the exciting, disturbing, liberating, and oppressive market world.

The performance of enmity and exile in *As You Like It*, Wilson shows, figuratively addresses enclosure, with the fenced-out side gaining the play's full sympathy. Orlando and Adam, Rosalind and Celia, and Duke Senior and his followers retrace the footsteps of many dispossessed peasants to the Forest of "Arden," literally the Ardennes in France but figuratively Arden in England, a well-known refuge. Orlando's antagonist brother Oliver rehearses the "Elizabethan success story of the rise of the gentry by engrossing and enclosure at the expense of evicted relatives and tenants"[41] (engrossment involved consolidating an estate by evicting small farmers within it, sometimes family members). Forced out, Orlando contemplates becoming a criminal as those thrown off the land were reputed to do, and the willing exile of his companion Adam from his hateful master after a lifetime of service resembles the situation of the dispossessed as well. Orlando's physical threats against his brother and later aggressive demand for food reference food riots. In the forest, the shepherd Corin's opportunist, absentee master is selling his land in London, where financiers profited most from engrossment and enclosure. In these ways the play gestures toward a moral economics, suggesting that enclosure, despite being profitable, often involves selfish calculation with no regard for justice.

The popular-festive aspects of the play, Wilson shows, also support anti-enclosure sentiment, though from a certain distance. Popular resistance to enclosures often involved protests inflected by festive traditions, and the play associates the forest exiles with the Robin Hood tradition, which "upholds the collective values of the poor against the 'ambition' of the rich."[42] Popular-festive protests could include cross-dressed men, she-males well represented in the play: first by Rosalind's Ganymede disguise complete with boar spear, and second, with the gender impersonation reversed, when Ganymede impersonates Rosalind. Blackface such as Celia adopts was also a feature of protests. The play's stag-horn ritual celebrating the deer slayer is also based on popular protests against enclosures, given that deer, as the quarries of the privileged, were not only poached but sometimes targeted in protest. However, though in a nice reversal one putative encloser, Duke Frederick, retires as a penitent hermit in the forest, the play neither carries its spotty, anti-enclosure level of meaning to a conclusion, nor do its elements of festive protest themselves directly pillory enclosure. The principal characters return to their courts as winners, shorn of figurative nuance, the play "neutralizing the rites of collective action."[43]

Recent events and the state of the enclosure debate in the late 1590s clarify the play's treatment. To explain them, let me restate at a little more length that only some of the enclosures that had always been mandated by landlords or by those who held common rights themselves were under attack; the objectionable ones—objectionable even though overpopulation was a root cause of enclosure—produced depopulation, throwing people off the land, in most cases because the enclosure would convert arable land to pasture. Now, on the one hand, in the second half of the century popular protest and moral considerations had eventually forced the government to regulate the enclosure process, making it somewhat fairer, though the poorer sort remained the chief sufferers. And the profit that could be gained through enclosure and conversion to pasturage convinced some better-off peasants and many people of means that it was in balance good for them and possibly good for the country. So in 1594, Parliament rescinded some anti-enclosure laws. On the other hand, right after that legislative move the century's worst dearth gripped the countryside for several years, and for many eviction was added to near-famine conditions. The 1596 Oxfordshire revolt was one consequence, and another was Parliament's 1597 reaction to fears of famine and unrest: revival of some of the anti-enclosure laws, after considerable debate.[44] In this context, as Wilson argues, though the play shows sympathy for victims of enclosure, it does reflect a moment when the political nation had lost a certain amount of resolve to continue opposing enclosure. Something else on the horizon was much more interesting.

That moment matches the one that many see today, in the reverse mirror. We struggle with different views on the place of morality in economics, differences pertaining for instance to social inequality and to the increasingly interconnected global marketplace's impact on the environmental commons. That struggle takes place in a comparable atmosphere of apprehension, frustration, and irresolution as the environment suffers, food prices and income inequality rise, weather suddenly morphs into a strange and hideous adversary, and world population grows further beyond the planet's capacity. Joshua Clover recently defined the present historical moment as a significant economic inflection point in two relevant respects. First, the financial crisis and the continuing decline in the aggregate rate of profit in business and finance since about 1973 demonstrate the limits of the value created through the "post-structural" model of economic exchange; that is, through the only seemingly magical circulation of capital in financial instruments, as well as through the communication-based labor of the service economy. Second, in his concluding sentences Clover seems to envision the end not only of US financial hegemony but of capitalism itself. He observes that "given capital's need to expand and the world-system's material limits," capitalism's hegemony may face "a flight to something else entirely."[45] Green economics locates value in ecosystems, not exchanges, and is all about working within the Earth's "material limits" in response to the present economic assault. If it is a marginal force almost everywhere, many of the principles guiding it are not. They supply seeds for "something else."

So *As You Like It* frames this tentatively hopeful but still rather dismal economic, reverse analogy between past and present. Yet it is a remarkably cheery sort of play. It is actually a comedy firmly centered on the wooing of one Rosalind. Is there not anything in that to sweeten a topical economic meditation? It seems to me that if there were, it would lie in the lovers, who are on Wilson's and my readings figuratively evicted from the land by grasping landlords. In bringing Orlando's fantasy of a love relationship down to earth, Rosalind adapts the festive elements that the play links to commoning in order to envision and negotiate life in a new world. Rosalind's sublime banter does not figure in Wilson's reading or in recent ecocritical ones. Still, the adaptation I refer to is effected primarily through Rosalind's determined campaign, posing as the she-male Ganymede who in turn poses as her, to identify marriage between herself and Orlando as beastly, insisting on the creatureliness of marriage partners by continually resorting to animal metaphors that strike at the distinction between human and animal mating and relationship. Touchstone's quips and the stag-horn ritual, where man and beast become one, play complementary roles for this hilarious campaign, which draws on traditional topsy-turvy, debasing, carnivalesque reversals such as were nurtured in convivial rural meetings, among other places.[46] However, Rosalind's initiative also draws in the play's suggestion that Arden is a sort of "republic of nature," as Todd Borlik puts it,[47] a place not of high and low ones but of "co-mates and brothers,"[48] and a place where deer are called "burghers" (2.1.23) and "citizens" (2.1.58), deer whose killing is lamented and who weep tears.

Rosalind's dispossessed condition is ironically referenced in an animal simile when she as Ganymede alleges to Orlando that she is a native of the forest, as native "as the cony that you see dwell where she is kindled" (3.2.345–6). To dwell where one was born is to be very much of a place, to have a tie only loosened with difficulty; if dislodged, one takes along the mode of being learned in that place. As instanced below, Rosalind as (figurative) dispossessed common-dweller migrant brings forward into her new condition an iteration of the common as that commonwealth of human and nonhuman discussed above, supplying an ecocentric awareness of the indistinct nature of the human in its semiotic as well as material relationship with the beastly. This rich strand in the play, as Gabriel Egan says, also includes a humbling sense of limits, of the "vulnerability to predation"[49] in multiple senses. The hunter who wears deerskin and horns in the stag-horn scene (4.3) looks like Actaeon and his horns signify cuckolding. That is part of the common truth Rosalind carries into the "wide world" (1.3.39) beyond the common and the understanding of which she demands in a partner.

In Act 4, Scene 1, Celia marries Ganymede and Orlando in a mock ceremony. In her "holiday humor" (4.1.73) ready for wooing, Ganymede's Rosalind offers the married condition as a carnivalized chain of being that joins mad beasts, joins heavenly–beastly, androgynous cock-pigeon/parrot/ape/monkey/hyena with her poetical–beastly, cuckold-destined snail/hen. Ganymede:

> I will be more jealous of thee than a Barbary cock-pigeon over his hen, more clamorous than a parrot against rain, more newfangled

than an ape, more giddy in my desires than a monkey. I will weep for nothing, like Diana in the fountain, and that when you are disposed to be merry. I will laugh like an hyena, and that when thou art inclined to sleep. (157–64)

If she thinks Orlando good, she will have "twenty such" (124), and she approves the snail as a wooer because he comes with a house and "brings his destiny with him," "horns," thereby arriving "armed with his fortune" to forestall "the slander of his wife" (61, 65–6).

Earlier, the fool Touchstone helpfully mocked Orlando's Petrarchan verses for Rosalind, mocking that involved hart, hind, cat, grain harvest, nut, and the rose and its prick (3.2.101–12). Rosalind thrilled to hear Celia read Orlando's *opus magnus* ("How should this a desert be...," 3.2.127–56), but saw the need to reverse his rank-ordered cosmos. In that cosmos a "heavenly synod" (3.2.152) commanded nature to infuse all the greatest women's graces or parts into a single body, Rosalind's, Orlando hoping to serve her. Rosalind therefore invokes the antidote, the Pythagorean metempsychosis that jumbles the orthodox chain of being: "I was never so berhymed since Pythagoras' time that I was an Irish rat, which I can hardly remember" (3.2.180–82).

The other two relationships of love in the play also undergo beastly metamorphosis: Rosalind and Celia are "Juno's swans" (1.3.78), who marry for life, and Rosalind likens Oliver and Celia's abrupt engagement to "the fight of two rams" (5.2.32). As for the banished lords and their followers, life in the Forest of Arden resembles that of a hired hand in a successful common, or commonwealth of nature, one that affords him a subsistence existence, and yet paradoxically a food-sovereign one in the sense of being able to provision himself without having to do the bidding of another in order to eat. All sing,

> Who doth ambition shun
> And loves to live i' th' sun,
> Seeking the food he eats
> And pleased with what he gets,
> Come hither... (2.5.36–9)

Though it reflects a moment of transition concerning a specific, major economic issue of its time—enclosure—*As You Like It* not only takes sides against the wrong kind of enclosure, but affirms aspects of the commons experience, of a discursive tradition that was becoming residual but that could enrich the still-evolving cultural and economic terrain of its moment. The sophisticated fun that Robert Watson has shown this play has with the period's anxieties about identifying what is authentically natural[50] owes a great deal to the festive wisdom of this popular context. Perhaps an aspect of Shakespeare's poetic power could be linked to capital's mobility in infinite exchange, but Rosalind proves her mate according to the convivial powers of a traditional discourse revamped. And that involves an admiring affirmation of those powers, rather than an enclosing of them, by a playwright who knew a good deal about farming.[51]

In the reverse mirror, this play points us toward a political and moral notion of economics as pursuit of the common good. By alluding to hard economic conditions produced by enclosure that had become worsened by the terrible weather of the 1590s, it registers the crucial role extreme weather could play in forcing reconsideration of economic, political, and environmental assumptions. Its green world, moreover, is a place of refuge from economic disruption, as was the real Forest of Arden at the time. In the play, the creation of that world by the desperate, the disaffected, and the enterprising supplies an alternative base that breaks the resolve of figurative enclosers Frederick and Oliver. The happy ending results from the moral transformations of those enclosers, motivated by the loss of Frederick's daughter and heir, and at least partly by the erosion of Oliver's commitment to the hard new ways given his rough treatment at the hands of a Frederick made desperate by his loss. In the reverse mirror, then, the phenomenon of Arden gestures toward the potential of our emerging politically, morally, and ecologically aware economics, though its carnivalesque discourse may not be clearly visible, at least yet. The play underscores that this emerging constellation today is shaped partly from or is analogous to traditional sources prominently on display in the English Renaissance, especially those connected to the commons system.

The matter of the commons is by no means the only one that can illustrate how much the new economics relates to economic attitudes in the Renaissance. Of course, the convivial, community-focused, and moral economic assumptions that remained strong in that period were implicitly related to a religious worldview irrelevant in many ways in today's multicultural and globalized setting. However, recontextualized, certain quaint notions that shaped a good deal of Renaissance literature might take on new significance in relation to green economics and to our environmental challenges more generally: that this world is somehow broken, systematically unjust, deeply misguided, and due for a gigantic comeuppance, that a just world lies somewhere else, and that one should live for and in the sight of that world.

In closing, I want to touch on something more specific: usury. Like forced enclosure, usury transgressed or rendered moot traditional arrangements based on mutual trust and social obligation. Charging legally binding interest on money loaned is a far cry from making sure that the common field from which one extracts provisions remains in good enough condition to restore itself so that others can use its increase later. As market relations developed in the latter half of the sixteenth century, the demand for investment money naturally increased, yet dependence on lending money at interest came to seem a great moral issue in England, and of course became a major theme in the plays of Shakespeare and other dramatists. *Homo economicus* was being born then, but David Hawkes has shown how much living humans were horrified and thought it monstrous.[52] Many who found themselves practicing usury nevertheless thought usury wrong. What did landowners do when victimized by usurers and their own insatiable pursuit of commodities? Some were forced to sell their lands, leaving their commoning tenants on the highway to drink the green mantle of the standing pool.

In their critique of contemporary banking, Boyle and Simms of the new economics foundation single out debt as the key aspect of our dominant economic system that must be altered to achieve a sustainable economy based on general well-being or the common good. In Britain and the United States, over 97 percent of money is created through private banks issuing loans. The need to pay back loans with interest is the principal engine that makes the economy grow, whether the growth is actually beneficial rather than harmful to the well-being of the general—and increasingly it is not, they say, and should be curbed. There is a disturbing, insatiable quality to the economic model we generally take for granted when one looks at it that way. As Hawkes demonstrates, English people of Shakespeare's time would have sensed the creepy much more quickly than most of us, and yet we are now finding a new affinity with their attitudes.

The point is not that one should join a global eco-village collective, but that, given our knowledge of how the globalization juggernaut seems to be working out and of the threats posed by our environmental crisis, our picture of this economically and literarily crucial time and place deserves reconsideration. In an important sense, the world to which it gave birth is no longer our world. Something with similarities to the economy that became residual then needs to become more dominant now. That involves thinking and reading recursively, from capital to commons, or to a plurality where nothing is dominant. Was the commons system inefficiently labor intensive? Globalization's efficient operations have created more workers than there are jobs. In 2002, the world's top 200 corporations generated 28 percent of world GDP with a good deal less than 1 percent of the workers of the world, 0.82 percent.[53] That is labor sketchy. On the other hand, the whirligig of time has recently brought us Tim Jackson's projections of a future no-growth economy, a key component being labor-intensive, low-emissions, "community-based social enterprises."[54]

Notes

1. Arjun Appadurai, conference opening remarks, The Bruce Initiative on Rethinking Capitalism, University of California, Santa Cruz, April 26, 2012. For generously reading and commenting on a preliminary version of this article, I would like to thank Steve Mentz, Gabriel Egan, Ewan Fernie, and Charlotte Scott; thanks as well to the perceptive guidance of the editors Hugh Grady and Cary DiPietro, and to Amy Woodward for research assistance.
2. Molly Scott Cato, *Environment and Economy* (Routledge: Abingdon, 2011).
3. Abby Scher, "Greetings from the New Economy," *Dollars and Sense*, August 4, 2012, accessed online through Common Dreams, August 4, 2012.
4. Stacy Alaimo, "Sustainable This, Sustainable That: New Materialisms, Posthumanism, and Unknown Futures," *PMLA*, 127:3 (May 2012): 558–64 (see also other articles in this issue); Leerom Medovoi, "A Contribution to the Critique of Political Ecology: Sustainability as Disavowal," *New Formations*, 69 (Summer 2010): 129–45.
5. Dipesh Chakrabarty, "The Climate of History: Four Theses," *Critical Inquiry*, 35 (Winter, 2009): 197–222.
6. Gabriel Egan, *Green Shakespeare: From Ecopolitics to Ecocriticism* (Abingdon: Routledge, 2006); Jean E. Feerick and Vin Narduzzi, *The Indistinct Human in Renaissance Literature* (Houndmills: Palgrave Macmillan, 2012).

7. Ashley Dawson, "Introduction: New Enclosures," *Imperial Ecologies, New Formations*, 69 (2010): 8–22.
8. Common Dreams staff, "Wild, Wild West Mentality Pervasive as Global Land-Grab Continues: FAO Chief Says Private Investors Threaten Food Sovereignty of the World's Poorest," October 29, 2012.
9. See for instance David Bollier, *Silent Theft: The Private Plunder of Our Common Wealth* (New York: Routledge, 2002); Michael Hardt and Antonio Negri, *Commonwealth* (Cambridge, MA: Harvard University Press, 2011).
10. Richard Wilson, "'Like the Old Robin Hood': *As You Like It* and the Enclosure Riots," *Shakespeare Quarterly*, 43:1 (Spring 1992): 1–19.
11. Herman Daly, "Steady-State Economics: A New Paradigm," *New Literary History*, 24 (1993): 811–16; Herman E. Daly and Joshua Farley, *Ecological Economics: Principles and Applications* (Washington, D.C.: Island Press, 2004); Peter A. Victor, "Ecological Economics and Economic Growth," *Annals of the New York Academy of Science*, 1185 (2010): 237–45; Molly Scott Cato, *Green Economics: An Introduction to Theory, Policy, and Practice* (London: Earthscan, 2009).
12. Michel Serres, *The Natural Contract*, trans. Elizabeth MacArthur and William Paulson (Ann Arbor: University of Michigan Press, 1995) develops a foundational argument for the extension of rights to broad aspects of the nonhuman world.
13. Cato, *Environment and Economy*, p. 219.
14. Bill McKibben, *Eaarth! Making a Life on a Tough New Planet* (New York: St. Martin's Griffin, 2010).
15. David Boyle and Andrew Simms, *The New Economics: A Bigger Picture* (London: Earthscan, 2009).
16. Gar Alperovitz, "The Rise of the New Economy Movement," May 20, 2012, accessed online through Alternet, October 13, 2012. See also Alperovitz, "The New-Economy Movement," *The Nation*, June 13, 2011; Alperovitz, *America Beyond Capitalism: Reclaiming our Wealth, Our Liberty, and Our Democracy*, 2nd edn. (Boston, MA: Democracy Collaborative Press and Dollars and Sense, 2011); Marjorie Kelly, *Owning Our Future: The Emerging Ownership Revolution* (San Francisco: Berrett-Koehler, 2012); E. F. Schumacher, *Small Is Beautiful: Economics as if People Mattered*, 3rd edn. (New York: Harper, 2010); Elinor Ostrom, *Governing the Commons: The Evolution of Institutions for Collective Action* (Cambridge: Cambridge University Press, 1990).
17. Eric Holt-Giménez and Raj Patel, *Food Rebellions! Crisis and the Hunger for Justice* (Oakland, CA: Food First Books, 2009), p. 3.
18. Dawson, "Introduction: New Enclosures," pp. 14–16.
19. Jeffrey Juris, *Networking Futures: The Movements against Corporate Globalization* (Durham, NC: Duke University Press, 2008).
20. George Caffentzis, "The Future of 'the Commons': Neoliberalism's 'Plan B' or the Original Disaccumulation of Capital?" *New Formations*, 69 (Summer 2010): 23–41.
21. Keith Wrightson, *Earthly Necessities: Economic Lives in Early Modern Britain* (New Haven, CT: Yale University Press, 2000), pp. 153–4.

22. Neal Wood, *Foundations of Political Economy: Some Early Tudor Views on State and Society* (Berkeley: University of California Press, 1994), pp. 155–90; Ellen Meiksins Wood and Neal Wood, *The Trumpet of Sedition: Political Theory and the Rise of Capitalism, 1509–1688* (New York: New York University Press, 1997), pp. 27–42.
23. Wood and Wood, *The Trumpet of Sedition*, p. 51.
24. Wrightson, *Earthly Necessities*, p. 77.
25. Ibid., 51–3.
26. Cato, *Environment and Economy*, pp. 220–21; Alan Everitt, "Farm Labourers," *The Agrarian History of England and Wales*, vol. 4, ed. Joan Thirsk (Cambridge: Cambridge University Press, 1967), pp. 404–5.
27. Everitt, "Farm Labourers," p. 406.
28. Cato, *Environment and Economy*, p. 219.
29. For an insightful and pertinent critique of Hardin's thesis, see pp. 44–52 in Crystal Bartolovich, "A Natural History of Food Riots," *Imperial Ecologies, New Formations*, 69 (2010): 42–61.
30. Ken Hiltner, *What Else Is Pastoral? Renaissance Literature and the Environment* (Ithaca, NY: Cornell University Press, 2010), pp. 133–5, 138–41.
31. Quoted in Cato, *Environment and Economy*, p. 220.
32. Ibid., p. 219.
33. Jean E. Feerick and Vin Narduzzi, *The Indistinct Human*, p. 5.
34. Margreta de Grazia, *Hamlet without Hamlet* (Cambridge: Cambridge University Press, 2007).
35. Everitt, "Farm Labourers," p. 458.
36. Quoted in Cato, *Environment and Economy*, pp. 96–7.
37. Joan Thirsk, "Enclosing and Engrossing," *The Agrarian History of England and Wales*, vol. 4, ed. Joan Thirsk (Cambridge: Cambridge University Press, 1967), p. 255. See Crystal Bartolovich, "'Travailing' Theory': Global Flows of Labor and the Enclosure of the Subject," in *A Companion to the Global Renaissance: English Literature and Culture in the Age of Expansion*, ed. Jyotsna G. Singh (Oxford: Wiley-Blackwell, 2009), pp. 51–66.
38. Vandana Shiva, *Biopiracy: The Plunder of Nature and Knowledge* (Boston: South End Press, 1990).
39. Cato, *Environment and Economy*, p. 225.
40. Ibid., p. 223.
41. Wilson, "'Like the Old Robin Hood,'" p. 5.
42. Ibid., p. 7.
43. Ibid., p. 16. Wilson goes on to argue that the play supports King James's patronizing *noblesse oblige* policy toward victims of enclosure. My view is that while the play can be read to open up a number of social issues, including that of ameliorating the ill effects of enclosure, it does not generally advocate positions clearly. However, it does clearly express sympathy for the victims of enclosure-related injustice.
44. Thirsk, "Enclosing and Engrossing," pp. 206–9, 226–31, 254–5.
45. Joshua Clover, "Value / Theory / Crisis," *PMLA*, 127:1 (January 2012): 107–13.

46. See Robert Weimann, *Shakespeare and the Popular Tradition in the Theater: Studies in the Social Dimension of Dramatic Form and Function* (Baltimore, MD: Johns Hopkins University Press, 1978); Michael D. Bristol, *Carnival and Theater: Plebeian Culture and the Structure of Authority in Renaissance England* (New York: Routledge, 1989).
47. Todd Borlik, *Ecocriticism and Early Modern Literature: Green Pastures* (Abingdon: Routledge, 2011), pp. 180–83.
48. William Shakespeare, *As You Like It* in *The Norton Shakespeare: Based on the Oxford Edition*, ed. Stephen Greenblatt et al., 2nd edn. (New York: W. W. Norton, 2008), 2.2.1. All further references are to this edition.
49. Gabriel Egan, *Green Shakespeare*, p. 103.
50. Robert N. Watson, *Back to Nature: The Green and the Real in the Late Renaissance* (Philadelphia: University of Pennsylvania Press, 2006).
51. Robert F. G. Spier and Donald K. Anderson, Jr., "Shakespeare and Farming: The Bard and Tusser," *Agricultural History*, 59:3 (July 1985): 448–61.
52. David Hawkes, *The Culture of Usury in Renaissance England* (New York: Palgrave Macmillan), 2010.
53. "Key Facts" about "Multinational Corporations," *Share the World's Resources* (STWR), online, accessed October 30, 2012.
54. Tim Jackson, *Prosperity without Growth: Economics for a Finite Planet* (London: Earthscan, 2009), p. 130.

6
"Consuming means, soon preys upon itself": Political Expedience and Environmental Degradation in *Richard II*

Lynne Bruckner

The pattern of political leaders selling out the environment for political expedience is so excruciatingly familiar and predictable that it contributes to the plotline of a major Hollywood film (*The American President*, 1995). Even those politicians who run on an environmental platform, it appears, are required by economic and/or political pressure to exploit the biotic world. While President Barack Obama's arrival in the White House initially fostered optimism for environmental advocates, the President's decision to embrace nuclear power, offshore oil drilling, and "clean" coal as keystones of his energy policy quickly cooled their enthusiasm.[1] Similarly, despite being flanked by his introduction to the 1992 edition of *Silent Spring* and the release of (the problematic, yet highly significant) *An Inconvenient Truth* (2006), Al Gore's tenure as Vice President failed to advance ecologically sound practices, though he attempted (yet failed) to get the Kyoto Protocol through Senate. It would appear that anyone in or next to the Oval Office is unlikely to enact significant environmental change, unless such change leads to further global degradation (cf. George W.).[2] Shakespeare's *Richard II* provides a thoughtful meditation on land use and rule. While stewardship of the earth was understood differently in the era, the play nonetheless underscores how political leadership encourages and perhaps requires the misuse and exploitation of the natural world. It is only when out of power that Bolingbroke and Richard connect to (and value intrinsically) the earth. The further Richard is from the crown, the more he aligns himself with the land as a living entity. Such affiliation with the ecological world is essential if humans, especially those in power, are to do more than give mere lip service to environmental stewardship.

For anyone concerned with the health of the planet, it is difficult to consider the recent US elections without considering the United States' ongoing and excessive reliance on fossil fuels. Obama attempted to jump-start innovations in renewable energy when he arrived in office; in recent months, however, the President has fast-tracked both hydraulic fracturing (fracking) and the southernmost part of the Keystone pipeline, which will carry highly corrosive oil from Canada's tar sands to the Gulf Coast, though he is insisting that the northernmost part be rerouted. Virtually hog-tied by the economic legacy left to him by the GOP,[3] the financial and political force of the oil and drilling industry, the drilling rhetoric of the Republican Party, and a dire need to create more jobs, Obama showcased his support of fracking in his 2012 Presidential Address, stating, "we have a supply of natural gas that can last America nearly 100 years... this will support more than 600,000 jobs by the end of the decade." Recent campaign speeches continue to indicate his support of environmentally questionable methods for procuring fossil fuels. We cannot, however, simply fault Obama. His options are restricted not only by beltway politics, but also by the desires and demands of citizens of the United States, who are rarely willing to give up the convenience that comes with relying on carbon-based energy. As Greg Garrard notes, ecocritics need to contend with

> the way environmental values and concerns can be professed and felt deeply by people without decisively changing those people's behavior, and the way this personal inconsistency is mirrored by that of politicians who express belief in the terrible danger of global warming but do not take action as if they really believed.[4]

However remote it might appear, all of us who rely on fossil fuels are complicit with environmental degradation and the attendant harm it enacts on other life forms. The seeming remoteness between our own actions and the health of the planet—our own bodies and the living world—is a concern for many ecocritics. Not surprisingly, then, many ecocritics find that a Presentist approach is essential. Richard Kerridge, in an essay on *Macbeth*, writes, "The sense of emergency with which ecocritics must read belongs peculiarly to our own time. ... To read ecocritically is therefore to read from an extremely specific present." And the short answer to Sharon O'Dair's self-posed question, "Is It Shakespearean Ecocriticism if It Isn't Presentist?," is a resounding "no."[5]

Stewardship

Richard II was understood as a play about politics in the Elizabethan era, and it resonates politically for readers today. While multiple factors drive Richard's failures as king, the issues that concern this chapter are his profligate use of state funds, the expense of war, and the consequent need to treat the earth as an economic resource, rather than a resource to be protected. As the play underscores, a good leader is a good steward of the land, though care of the land in the early modern era was not synonymous with our current notion of stewardship. In the twenty-first century our ecological responsibilities include guarding against further losses in biodiversity; defending wild places, green spaces, aquifers, watersheds, and the ocean; protecting threatened (really all) species of fauna and flora; maintaining and restoring ecosystems, habitats, and travel corridors; trimming our carbon emissions, checking our consumerist habits, and curbing the assumption that we deserve to live highly convenient lives. In the Renaissance, however, good environmental stewardship focused largely on trimming, checking, and curbing nature itself. For early moderns, "a tamed, inhabited, and productive landscape *was* beautiful."[6] As Keith Thomas writes, "agricultural improvement and exploitation were not just economically desirable; they were moral imperatives."[7] While certain kinds of "improvement" were controversial, especially with the rise of enclosure and market-driven crop production, a cultivated, productive landscape was the aesthetic and cultural ideal.

This aesthetic was underwritten by a Christian ethos. Gardening, as it was the one form of labor that occurred before the fall, held out the possibility of returning to a "state of pre-lapsarian grace by the cultivation of the soil."[8] For Amy Tigner, "The larger philosophical ideology of the period... equates the perfect political state to a pre-lapsarian Edenic state and the king to Adam, who must be the steward enabling the profitable plants to flourish and grow in the garden."[9] Gardens, and enclosed gardens in particular, were material figures for the ideal of Eden—an ideal that the nation as a whole sought to achieve. Located in direct opposition to Richard's disordered and fallen England, such is the garden depicted in Act 3, Scene 4 of the play.

Modeling the ideals of good stewardship, the garden scene yokes responsible management of the natural world to responsible management of the nation. Scholarship has long read the scene as an allegory for good government and an explicit critique of King Richard's failures of leadership. Ecocritics (for whom materiality generally takes precedence over metaphor) have emphasized that the scene depicts in very specific terms an early modern garden. In their reading of the Gardener's statement—"O, what pity is it / That he [Richard] had not so trimm'd and dressed his land / As we this garden!" (3.4.56-8)[10]— Rebecca Laroche and Jen Munroe find that "he calls to our attention not the fact that Richard (or anyone else for that matter) neglected imagining England in metaphoric terms as a garden but rather that Richard would have ruled the kingdom better had he taken a cue from those who work outside with the land."[11] For the Gardener and his men, tending the land is predominantly a matter of positive discipline—tying back what has gone wild, pruning what grows too quickly, eradicating weeds, and killing caterpillars.

> Go, bind thou up yon dangling apricots,
> Which, like unruly children, make their sire
> Stoop with oppression of their prodigal weight:
> Give some supportance to the bending twigs.
> Go thou, and like an executioner,
> Cut off the heads of too fast-growing sprays,
> That look too lofty in our commonwealth.
> All must be even in our government.
> You thus employ'd, I will go root away
> The noisome weeds, which without profit suck
> The soil's fertility from wholesome flowers. (3.4.30–40)

While words like "executioner," "commonwealth," and "government" make clear the allegory, the practices in which the Gardener and his men engage also line up with husbandry manuals of the era. The Gardener's directive to bind the "apricots" that are like "unruly children" fits neatly with a parallel drawn by Thomas: "it was widely held that most children would need to be beaten and repressed. Timber trees, correspondingly, were to be pollarded (i.e., beheaded), lopped or shredded."[12] While recent scholars have qualified Lawrence Stone's assumptions about the subhuman status of early modern children, such treatment was often viewed as good nurture. Multiple passages from Thomas Tusser's immensely popular *Five Hundreth Points of Good Husbandry* (1573) underscore the importance of a "trim" and tidy garden:

> Newe set do ask watring, with pot or with dish
> newe sowne do not so, if ye do as I wish.
> through cunning w^t dybble, rake, mattock & spade:
> by line & be leauel, trim garden is made.[13]

A farmer himself, Tusser underscores the importance of straight and level rows; he suggests with enthusiasm multiple tools for manipulating soil and growing things. Similarly, in the second part of his *Gardener's Labyrinth* (1577), Thomas Hill indicates the diligence and force required for growing hearty plants:

> I purpose to vtter ... the Phisicke benefites to eache Hearbe I adde, wyth other matters profitable, to the ende the owner or Gardener may with better good will be moued to bestowe an earnest care and diligence aboute the often remouing, as well of daintie floures as Hearbes, with the clipping, pressing down, breaking away, and cutting off the endes of rootes, that these may growe thicker and bigger both in Hearbe and roote.[14]

Hill's goal is to "move" the owner or Gardener to "an earnest care and diligence" when it comes to herbs and flowers. Right care includes removing, clipping, pressing down, breaking, and cutting various parts of the plants to ensure their health. Such language resonates with the binding, cutting, and rooting away performed in the garden of *Richard II*, illuminating the degree to which the scene powerfully references the materiality of a sixteenth-century garden (provided the manuals are descriptive as well as prescriptive). The physical descriptions of maintaining a garden ground the play in the living world, connecting the treatment of land and flora to royal decisions and policies.

The garden scene is one of the seven major additions to the play, suggesting *Richard II*'s investment in land and living things. It is likely that Shakespeare and/or many in his audience knew of Tusser's *Five Hundreth Points of Good Husbandry*—a book that A. L. Rowse dubs "the most popular countryman's book of the day."[15] Moreover, as a quick examination of the Agas Map of London shows, there were many gardens within the city limits.[16] It is almost certain that a majority of Shakespeare's audience, even those who didn't have country houses or small summerhouses on the outskirts of the city,[17] were familiar with gardening and the work it entailed. Market gardening was quickly developing in the areas around London, especially with the importation of new gardening techniques from the Low Countries in the 1590s.[18] Innovative practices are evidenced in the gardening scene; training trees against walls was relatively new, and apricots were only introduced to England in the mid-1500s.[19] The importance of productive gardening techniques, I suspect, would have reverberated significantly for audiences in the 1590s.

A nexus of materiality and allegory, the garden evinces comparisons between the physical act of gardening and larger issues of land management and politics. It is, as Heidi Scott notes, "a microcosm of Richard's isle"—and for Shakespeare's audience, of Elizabeth's isle as well.[20] The years between 1593 and 1597 were a time of extraordinarily poor harvests and famine, as the "1590s marked the beginnings of the apogee of the Little Ice Age."[21] Making matters worse, the Parliament of 1593, in light of the "great plenty and cheapness of grain," elected to discontinue the statutes against the conversion of arable land to pasture, exacerbating the crop yield in the fall of 1594.[22] Famine had also been a problem in the mid and late 1580s; flour prices rose by 65 percent in 1585–6. The sustained dearth of the 1590s, however, was far worse, with flour prices nearly tripling from 1593 to 1597.[23] Scarcity and want, moreover, were amplified in years of war; "the crown's armies and people competed for food or other consumables in the 1590s."[24] It is difficult not to believe that the original audience for *Richard II* (c. 1595) connected the garden scene to failures of stewardship.

(D)earth

Scholars have noted the importance of land/earth both in Shakespeare's plays more broadly and in *Richard II* specifically. Frederick Waage, in "Shakespeare Unearthed," asserts that "Elizabethan and Jacobean writers on agriculture were very sensitive to the issues involved in soil amendment, and, as in so many of Shakespeare's references, to the effects of neglect and stewardship." Waage goes on to note the "proto-ecological perceptions expressed through [Shakespeare's] references to 'earth,' and 'soil.'"[25] Richard Altick's well-known "Symphonic Imagery in *Richard II*" traces the symbolic imbrication of "earth-ground-land" (among other image clusters), with a particular focus on English earth.[26] For Altick, these related words serve four primary symbolic purposes: to represent the English nation; to evoke Englishmen's shame and disgrace for failing to care for the land; to stand for the vanity and frailty of human life; and to suggest the untended garden, the latter being emblematic of the declining English realm. What did not concern Altick, and what deeply concerns me, is the tension *Richard II* outlines between the conditions of national leadership (being king) and the act of stewardship for the land (in material rather than symbolic terms). While the play underscores in both Gaunt's "scepter'd isle" speech and the garden scene that good rule is a matter of good stewardship over nation *and* nature, the two kings in the play commodify the earth when in positions of power, though it is Richard's financial exploitation of the land that is writ large in the play. Only when alienated from power do Richard and Bolingbroke locate a more affiliated and thus reciprocal relationship to the soil. In Richard's case, such reciprocity locates the human body as part of a larger natural system, offering a perspective more likely to evince sound stewardship.

Gaunt's "scepter'd isle" speech inaugurates the play's ruminations over Richard's abuse of the land. The speech also presents the island as an ecological and geographical fantasy, constructing England as an untouched gem, inviolable by its enemies (war and disease). Although finally a critique of state corruption and Richard's profligate abuse of the land and national coffers, the speech describes England as a "precious stone set in the silver sea" (2.1.46). This image suggests (fantasizes) that the island is impenetrable, perfect, and whole. Claiming that the sea serves the island in "the office of a wall, / Or as a moat defensive to a house / Against the envy of less happier lands," Gaunt works to establish England as a chosen "other Eden" that cannot be defiled—at least not externally (2.1.47–9, 42). Gaunt's perspective on England's "natural" protection is (and was) a myth, not only in terms of the history of the British Isles, but also in terms of ecological realities; an island can no more be sealed off from biotic influence than can the human body.[27]

While Gaunt's depiction of England is highly problematic in its Edenic insularity, the "scepter'd isle" speech simultaneously offers an important pre-Cartesian sensibility: one that understands the earth as living, lively, and nonmechanistic. Nature has "built" this fortress "for herself"; the sea "serves" the nation; the shore "beats back" the siege (2.1.43, 47, 62). Referring not only to "this earth of majesty" (2.1.41), but also to "this blessed plot, this earth, this realm, this England, / This nurse," the passage assigns a level of agency to the earth itself. A "teeming womb of royal kings" (2.1.50–51), it is filled with vitality. While contested (and largely eradicated) by the rise of science, the notion of a living earth was still a habit of mind in the sixteenth century. In many ways, *Richard II* rests on an epistemological cusp—straddling the notion that the earth is/is not living. As Carolyn Merchant has amply shown, the latter mode—viewing the earth as inert—licenses unchecked exploitation of the natural world.[28]

Gaunt rarely uses the word "land" in this speech; "land" is less lively than "earth," and it connotes use value ("arable land") and/or ownership. Tellingly, the one line in which "land" does occur (and twice) is as Gaunt makes the transition between the ideal of England and its/her degradation by Richard.

> This land of such dear souls, this dear dear land,
> Dear for her reputation through the world,
> Is now leased out—I die pronouncing it—
> Like to a tenement or pelting farm. (2.1.57–60)

The pun on "dear" signals not only the land's status as beloved, but also its economic value, that which makes it subject to abuse. Indeed, having lived too high on the courtly hog, Richard is forced to put the realm to farm in order to pay for the war in Ireland. Exploiting the earth for immediate cash in hand, Richard gives others (his favorites) the right to "to extort taxes on their own behalf."[29] The king makes inappropriate use of the nation's land, thus distancing himself from the earth. As Gaunt underscores, Richard diminishes the living earth, reducing it to a tenement or smallholding, mere land. It becomes a source of direct revenue, no longer a source of life and certainly not "alive" in itself.

Once Richard enters the scene, Gaunt confronts him with the truth: "Thy deathbed is no lesser than thy land, / Wherein thou liest in reputation sick" (2.1.95–6), drawing a parallel between the body of the king and the waste of the land. The ailing Duke of Lancaster attempts to show Richard not only his error in judgment, but also his misapprehension of the earth. Harping on the word "land," Gaunt insists to Richard that his well-being and that of the earth are one and the same: "Thy waste is no whit lesser than thy land" (2.1.103). As he makes this point, Gaunt's (Shakespeare's) linguistic choices indicate that to value the earth in purely economic terms is to reduce it to land. Such thinking has consequences:

> It were a shame to let this *land* by lease.
> But, for thy world, enjoying but this *land*,
> Is it not more than shame to shame it so?
> *Landlord* of England art thou now, not king.
> (2.1.110–13, emphasis mine)

Nowhere in this exchange with Richard does Gaunt refer to the earth or its fecundity; nowhere does he depict the king as anything other than ill. Richard's economic exploitation of the land was likely to generate condemnation from the play's sixteenth-century audience as well. As William O. Scott finds, the very idea of leasing "might well have aroused controversial associations, quite apart from what Gaunt makes of it."[30] While Gaunt's error is imagining a pristine England that never was, Richard's is far more destructive: he has rendered the living earth inert.

Gaunt believed that "though Richard my life's counsel would not hear, / My death's sad tale may yet undeaf his ear" (2.1.15–16), but Richard cannot or will not hear his uncle's stern words. As York notes, Richard is only open to "flattering sounds" (2.1.17) that play to his narcissism, the "vanity" that is "buzzed into his ears" (2.1.24, 26); "All in vain comes counsel to his ear" (2.1.4). It is only in Act 3, Scene 2 that Richard becomes a king who is prepared to hear difficult truths, stating "Mine ear is open and my heart prepared" (3.2.89). The figure of Richard's ear serves as an indicator of his relationship to the world beyond his own self-interest. Only after his ear (read body) is open to the biotic world, only after he is brought down to earth, does Richard move beyond what Donna Haraway terms "human exceptionalism"—exceptionalism heightened by his sense of divine right.[31]

Waste—"uncultivated country," *OED, 1a*, noun

For not tending to England as does a careful gardener his plot of land, Richard has "suffered this disordered spring"; he is "the wasteful King" (3.4.49, 56), who in wasting the earth is wasting himself. As scholars of land law have found, "waste" is a signal term in the play. Focusing on the "doctrine of waste," Dennis Klinck reads Richard as both landlord and wasting tenant.[32] In somewhat reductive terms, Richard is the "landlord" of the realm as he has farmed it out for taxation by others, yet also, as he "holds" the realm (and the body politic) for the next ruler, he is a tenant. Stemming from the medieval era but still very much in play in the Renaissance, this doctrine holds that farmers (or lessees)—not tax farmers in this case—"during their terms, shall not make waste, sale, nor exile of house, woods, and men, nor of any thing belonging to the tenements that they have to ferm [sic]."[33] Violations of this doctrine were used to oust tenants; if Richard, too, is a wasting tenant, he, too, is liable "to lose the thing he has wasted."[34] Significantly, waste can occur as a matter of action (disparking Bolingbroke's parks) or neglect (failures of stewardship). It is useful to remember, moreover, that "seigniorial rights stemming from the land—rights associated with being king—did *not* mean the land was the king's 'own.'"[35] In short, Richard has the right to collect fees from Bolingbroke's land, but not the use of the land itself.

In ecological terms, and especially with an eye toward early modern deforestation, the violation of Bolingbroke's property rights is one of Richard's most egregious acts. Richard blatantly abuses his royal privilege and sets in motion his own demise by denying Bolingbroke his lawful inheritance: "we seize into our hands / His plate, his goods, his money, and his lands" (2.1.210–11). The king's disregard for Bolingbroke's rights galvanizes the resistance against him; Ross expresses outrage that Richard "hath not money for these Irish wars, / His burdenous taxations notwithstanding, / But by the robbing of the banished Duke" (2.1.260–62). The Earl of Northumberland asserts that Richard has made England this "declining land" (2.1.241). Richard violates the rights of his subjects and compromises natural resources in the service of a war he cannot afford. It hardly needs to be said that the connection between environmental degradation and war is both longstanding and ongoing.[36]

Richard's agents (Bushy and Green) are the ones who actually compromise Bolingbroke's property. Unfolding to Bushy and Green "some causes" of their deaths, Bolingbroke states, "...you have fed upon my signories, / Disparked my parks and felled my forest woods" (3.1.22–3). While not specified in the play, "disparking" would be a matter using Bolingbroke's parks for activities other than protecting deer for the hunt; here, images of (war-related?) forest industries such as ironworks might course through the minds of Shakespeare's London audience. The charge of illicitly felling timber would be a sharp sting for early moderns, as deforestation was perceived as a severe problem.[37] Not unlike Richard, Elizabeth "readily sold off timber from royal forests to finance military projects such as the Irish war."[38] As both Jeffrey Theis and Vin Nardizzi discuss, the degree of deforestation in Renaissance England has been debated, and it is likely that the crisis was more local than widespread. Shortages in wood were probably felt acutely in "urban centers and... those regions where the iron and shipbuilding industries depended on an abundant supply of wood and timber."[39] Certainly, England's project of nation-building required timber for ships and iron forges.[40]

It is difficult not to see points of intersection between Richard and Elizabeth's land and timber management, even if the connections are framed obliquely. The ongoing debt under Elizabeth, a result of inflation outpacing rents on crown land, led to granting entrepreneurs "space in the forests in return for immediate cash."[41] Throughout her reign and particularly during times of war, Elizabeth also sold extensive portions of crown land. For example, the *Calendar of State Papers Domestic* provides the "account of the clear yearly value of all the lands sold by Her Majesty's Commissioners, and money received or expected for the same, from 14 November 1589 to 20 November 1590." Adjusted for inflation, the figure would be roughly £50,522,000 or $79,026,512.[42] It is not irrelevant that in the same month payment was made to the Navy Treasurer "for clothing for foot bands in the Netherlands."[43] The sale of crown lands facilitated not only the move to agrarian capitalism, but also "the enclosure of both common and demesne land."[44] The play connects war, national debt, faulty land management, deforestation, and displacement; it is very likely that such linkages would have spiked a response in early modern audiences, not to mention those in our own era.

Getting Down to Earth in *Richard II*

Richard's fall from power is directly tied to his failure to tend to the earth. The imagery of rise and fall structures the play, with Richard getting ever closer to the biotic world. For Bolingbroke, as for Richard, loss motivates an assessment of what he values. The future king—generally seen by scholars as a man of physical action—is most eloquent and reflective when Richard banishes him from England. In this moment of departure, we glimpse a richer understanding of his dependence on the earth:

> Then England's ground, farewell. Sweet soil, adieu,
> My mother and my nurse that bears me yet!
> Where'er I wander, boast of this I can:
> Though banished, yet a trueborn Englishman. (1.3.269–72)

Bolingbroke directly addresses England's "sweet soil," and the lines imply that he touches the earth in this moment.[45] He speaks intimately of England's ground as the source of his life and sustenance, introducing the familiar construction of the earth as mother, one repeated later by both John of Gaunt and Richard (2.1.51, 3.2.8). Once he returns to England, however, Bolingbroke's focus is on the land as hereditary property: "My Lord I answer to 'Lancaster', / And I am come to seek that name in England" (2.3.70–71). As Bolingbroke moves toward kingship, his identity depends primarily on what he owns and controls, the land being the most valuable asset. Making his move to reclaim his property (and perhaps the crown), he promises material rewards to those who take his part. He states to Percy (Hotspur), "And as my fortune ripens with thy love, / It shall be still thy true love's recompense, / My heart this covenant makes; my hand thus seals it" (2.3.48–50). And he repeats this promise to Northumberland: "All my treasury / Is yet but unfelt thanks, which, more enriched, / Shall be your love and labour's recompense" (2.3.60–62). Finally, late in the play, he states to Hotspur: "We thank thee, gentle Percy, for thy pains, / And to thy worth will add right worthy gains" (5.6.11–12). Such promises will exact a price on both the new king and the earth, as indicated in *Henry IV, Part I*. Indeed, what better image for intruding on the ecological world than Hotspur's plan to straighten the winding Trent on the land apportioned between him, Mortimer, and Glyndwr (3.1.95–102).

While Bolingbroke's "rising" narrative encapsulates the spatially organized relationship between power and earth, Richard's follows the inverse pattern. The play's eponymous king initially exploits the land as an economic asset, but with the loss of power he moves beyond this narrow perspective. Beginning in Act 3, Scene 2, Richard seeks affiliation with the English earth. Unlike Bolingbroke, Richard expresses profound emotion when he returns to England from Ireland: "I weep for joy / To stand upon my kingdom once again" (3.2.4–5). Touching the earth (a gesture that recalls Bolingbroke's earlier "sweet soil" speech), Richard speaks directly to the land: "Dear earth, I do salute thee with my hand" (3.2.6, 11). He meets with it: "greet I thee my earth," substituting "my" for his earlier "our." Instead of emphasizing his royal possession of the land, Richard casts his relationship to the land in more intimate and feminized terms:

> As a long-parted mother with her child
> Plays fondly with her tears, and smiles in meeting,
> So weeping, smiling, greet I thee my earth,
> And do thee favors with my royal hands. (3.2.8–11).

In contrast to Bolingbroke who sees the earth as nurturer (his "mother" and "nurse"), Richard assumes a maternal relationship to the land. In addition to casting himself as loving mother, Richard expresses the complexity of his emotions, "weeping, smiling." Significantly, his tears (like the open ear) indicate a more permeable body, a moment where internal and external worlds meet. He still locates himself as king (doing "favors" with his "royal" hands), yet he is touching the earth, addressing and opening himself to it. His handling of the earth reinscribes his earlier decision to "seize" Bolingbroke's land and align it with chattel (2.1.210–11). Here, he describes an intimate and complex relationship to a living earth. Richard is both the earth's "mother" and its "sovereign." The earth is dependent on him like a "child," yet his power is waning (more than he knows), and he must look to the earth to "throw death upon thy sovereign's enemies" (3.2.22). No longer land, the earth is assigned agency; Richard and the earth form an assemblage of living entities. While Richard still sees the earth as in his service, the economically defined distance between king and land has collapsed.

Throughout this scene, Richard experiences and constructs the earth as "feeling," rather than inert. He speaks to the earth, conjuring it to protect him against his foes:

> Feed not thy sovereign's foe, my gentle earth,
> Nor with thy sweets comfort his ravenous sense;
> But let thy spiders that suck up thy venom
> And heavy-gaited toads lie in their way,
> Doing annoyance to the treacherous feet
> Which with usurping steps do trample thee.
> Yield stinging nettles to mine enemies,
> And when they from thy bosom pluck a flower
> Guard it, I pray thee, with a lurking adder,
> Whose double tongue may with a mortal touch
> Throw death upon thy sovereign's enemies. —
> Mock not my senseless conjuration, lords.
> This earth shall have a feeling... (3.2.12–24)

Gabriel Egan has noted that this passage indicates an "earthly sympathy with human affairs."[46] Richard hails his "gentle earth" in tones that are far from commanding—"I pray thee," with the familiar "thee" indicating an intimate connection. The earth in this passage is filled with vitality and, with its references to snakes, the passage gestures toward spontaneous generation.[47] While some scholars find that this moment exemplifies Richard's medieval sensibility (that God and earth will support his divine right), we might also note his prescience. Soil is full of life; a "spoonful of healthy soil contains millions of beneficial microscopic organisms of various kinds that perform vital 'functions'... These organisms include beneficial species of bacteria, fungi, protozoa, microarthopods and nematodes."[48] Richard's sense of the earth as living and teeming with life forms is, at a microscopic level, entirely in sync with current science.

As Richard's fortunes continue to decline, he grows closer to the ground materially and figuratively; such closeness is accompanied by tears, his eyes a portal to the body. He wants to "talk of graves"—to "make dust our paper, and with rainy eyes / Write sorrow on the bosom of the earth" (3.2.141–3). At times, body and soil converge;

Richard laments that he has nothing "but death, / And that small model of the barren earth / Which serves as paste and cover to our bones" (3.2.148–50). Here, "that small model" suggests both a "microcosm (the body)" *and* "enveloping shape (the grave)."[49] If the earth cannot defend him against his foes, it will register his grief and serve as his grave. Richard seeks direct contact with the earth: "let us sit upon the ground, / And tell sad stories of the death of kings" (3.2.151–2). While there is certainly an element of self-pity in Richard's description of the fate of kings, he also comments on the frailty of human life and the impermanent, insubstantial nature of royal power.

Richard consistently links himself to the earth through his tears. In addition to writing "sorrow on the bosom of the earth" (3.2.143), he imaginatively proposes:

> shall we play the wantons with our woes,
> And make some pretty match with shedding tears;
> As thus to drop them still upon one place
> Till they have fretted us a pair of graves
> Within the earth, and therein laid? "There lies
> Two kinsmen digged their graves with weeping eyes." (3.3.163–8)

Here, the image of weeping "still upon one place" to fret "a pair of graves" suggests a fusion of earth, tears, and body—a blending that disallows those notions of exploitation Richard endorsed earlier in the play, as the human body is now affiliated with the earth, even if only discursively.

The play offers other images of human/nature hybridization; plants and humans repeatedly mix. The Duchess of York asks Aumerle, "Who are the violets now" (5.2.46) and his father exhorts him to "bear you well in this new spring of time, / lest you be cropped" (5.2.50–51). Consider Aumerle's lines after his father discovers he is party to a traitorous plot. Kneeling in front of Bolingbroke, he swears:

> For ever may my knees grow to the earth,
> My tongue cleave to the roof within my mouth,
> Unless a pardon ere I rise or speak. (5.3.29–31)

Jean Feerick has written brilliantly of this moment: "Aumerle here imagines himself as a rooted plant, welcoming the loss of the distinguishing marks of his humanity—articulate speech and mobility—as the price of his treachery."[50] The king similarly becomes a plant when the queen, speaking of Richard in the Tower, urges that her ladies "not see / My fair rose wither" (5.1.7–8), but then recants and asks them to look up so they "in pity may dissolve to dew / and wash him fresh again" (5.1.9–10). Remarking on the hydraulics of loss and sorrow manifested in his crown's descent, Richard, too, wants to dissolve into water. While Bolingbroke's crown is "dancing in the air," Richard's is "that bucket down and full of tears am I" (4.1.176, 178). Willing a dissolution of self, he wishes he were "a mockery king of snow... / To melt myself away in water-drops!" (4.1.250, 252).

The notion that the human and the natural world are blended or connected through liquid (tears or blood) is substantiated by the larger context of the play. Consider the Duchess of Gloucester's appeal to Gaunt, as she urges him to avenge her husband's death: "Edward's seven sons... / Were as seven vials of his sacred blood, / Or seven fair branches springing from one root" (1.2.11–13); the imbrication of tree and blood persists for 13 lines more. The signifying chain of body, liquid (tears/blood), earth persists throughout the play, but tears and earth are most frequently attached to Richard. And it is through his tears that he makes his way to the earth, though this blending is only finalized in blood.

My thinking here is strongly influenced by Gail Kern Paster's work, particularly her reading of Spenser's Amavia in Book II of *The Faerie Queene*. As Paster explains, "Slowly bleeding out, Amavia's body becomes a feature of the landscape in a process of dissolution that is clearly reciprocal." Amavia's blood, "deepened by grief," is absorbed by the ground: "Thus insanguinated, the ground expresses human blood's analogical relation to rivers and streams; it recalls blood's place in bodily topography as the body's liquid source of nourishment as well as its current of feeling and consciousness."[51] While tears mark out Richard's fluidity with the earth, the play also traffics in connectivity through blood and streams. In the closing acts of the play, tears are the signifier for Richard, while Bolingbroke is marked by blood (though he is not alone in this).

In some ways, the spreading of blood speaks to a positive merging of the human and the natural. As Linda Woodbridge notes, "several passages [in Richard II] recall *sparagmos*, dismemberment and sprinkling the earth with blood for fertility: 'Ten thousand bloody crowns

/ ...[shall] bedew / Her pastures' grass with faithful English blood' (III.iii.96–100)."[52] Blood does work to fuse the human and the biotic world, forging a cycle of growth. And significantly, both blood and brine were used as soil amendments in the era.[53] Nonetheless, blood is a more ambiguous signifier, as it derives not from sadness borne but death. The Bishop of Carlisle prophesizes a violent future under King Henry, stating, "The blood of English shall manure the ground" (4.1.128).[54] The end of the play underscores the troubling quality of bonding the human to the natural through blood. For the most significant manuring in the play is that which comes from Richard's body. In his last lines, the fallen king states,

> Exton, thy fierce hand
> With the King's blood stained the King's own land.
> Mount, mount, my soul; thy seat is up on high,
> Whilst my gross flesh sinks downward, here to die. (5.5.109–12)

Despite his profligate and irresponsible rule, and despite his abuse of the land, Richard fuses with the biotic world through his tears, and finally his blood, for "the King's blood" has "stained the King's own land." Richard's "gross flesh" will sink further into the earth, simultaneously condemning and fertilizing King Henry's rule, which will grow plant-like from Richard's blood.

> Lords, I protest my soul is full of woe
> That blood should sprinkle me to make me grow.
> ... Grace my mourning here
> In weeping after this untimely bier. (5.6.45–6, 51–2)

The new king recognizes fully the problem of a reign built on blood, and he is now in possession not only of Richard's realm, but his tears as well. Yet the audience knows that such affect and knowledge will never pay his debts. For those, he will inevitably turn to his land.

Then *and* Now

Most citizens of the United States view state and national lands as a public trust; many assume that our state forests and our national parks are safe from corporate incursions. While drilling has been occurring on state and federal lands for over 50 years, hydraulic fracturing is a far more invasive process. A single well requires clear-cutting the forest to create a well pad of five to fifteen acres. Each wastewater pool is three to five acres and around twenty feet deep. Most wells are drilled to a depth of roughly 7,000 feet and from there the drilling is continued horizontally for up to two miles. Up to seven million pressurized gallons of "slick water" (water mixed with proprietary toxic chemicals) are injected into each well. Around one third of that water will come to the surface; the flowback contains the "proprietary" chemicals as well as immensely briny foundation waters, which have been deep in the earth for over 300 million years. At this time, there is no safe protocol for disposal of the wastewater; current practices include sinking the water into even deeper injection wells (which appears to cause earthquakes) and spreading the toxic water on roads for de-icing or dust control.[55] Fracking is exempt from the Safe Drinking Water Act. While methane gas does burn cleanly, in its raw form it is a "far more potent greenhouse gas than carbon dioxide"; up to eight percent of the gas is released during the collection process."[56] At this time, there are roughly 49,000 leases covering 38 million acres of federal and tribal land; these "leases currently contain 90,000 drill holes and see about 3,400 new wells drilled per year—90% of which use fracking."[57] In Pennsylvania, roughly 140,000 acres of state forest land—some of which is in old-growth forest—have been leased, for Marcellus pads.[58]

It is painfully difficult to stomach fracking at any level, but fracking in state forests and national parks is a violation of a public trust, a violation that cannot be readily reversed, if at all. Documentary filmmaker Ken Burns has written about his film, "The National Parks: America's Best Idea," a six-episode, Emmy Award-winning PBS series. He states, "we are all co-owners of some of the most moving places on Earth." Burns goes on to insist, "That's what the national parks do. They perform a kind of open-heart surgery on us, permitting us more room in our hearts for the love of these places, for the love of our country, for the love of our family."[59] While Burns might sound a bit like a twenty-first-century Gaunt, his recognition of the visceral, bodily openness (even if *he* intends it metaphorically) evinced by our national parks (and state forests) resonates in important ways. Material, bodily connections to the earth are urgent now, particularly as a very hostile form of surgery—butchery is a better term—is occurring on our public lands as I write.

Richard II evinces how the living earth too often is held hostage to a combination of financial mandates and politics as usual. In the very way that *Richard II* may have sparked political concerns about land management and forests for Elizabethans, the play can readily evoke similar concerns in a contemporary audience. Richard's failure to make appropriate use of national land along with his violation of Bolingbroke's property, especially the felling of his forests, is analogous in too many ways to current environmental incursions on our federal and state lands. If we do not come to understand (and get those in office to understand) that our survival depends on our affiliation with the natural world, if we continue to lay waste to the earth even as we generate more waste, we will indeed be consumed by our "consuming means."[60]

Notes

1. John Broder, "Environmental Advocates Are Cooling on Obama," *New York Times*, 17 February 2010.
2. The "Halliburton Loophole" provides a fine example of the sort of "protections" generated under George W. Bush: "Since 2005 (at the urging of then Vice President Dick Cheney, whose former company Halliburton is a major player in the fracking boom), drilling companies have been exempt from safe drinking water statutes and hence not required to list the chemicals they push down wells" (McKibben). On fracking, see Bill McKibben, "Why Not Frack?," *New York Times Review of Books*, 8 March 2012; Edward Humes, "Fractured Lives: Detritus of Pennsylvania's Shale Gas Boom," *Sierra Magazine*, July/August 2012.
3. The "Grand Old Party," the Republican Party.
4. Greg Garrard, *Teaching Ecocriticism and Green Cultural Studies* (London: Palgrave Macmillan, 2012), p. 13.
5. Richard Kerridge, "An Ecocritic's *Macbeth*" and Sharon O'Dair, "Is It Ecocritical if It Isn't Presentist?," both in *Ecocritical Shakespeare*, ed. Lynne Bruckner and Dan Brayton (Burlington: Ashgate, 2011), pp. 193–4 and 71, respectively. More recently, O'Dair finds that historicists can contribute "to present ecological action." See "'To fright the animals and to kill them up': Shakespeare and Ecology," *Shakespeare Studies* 39 (2011): 24–83, esp. 75. My chapter follows Cary DiPietro and Hugh Grady, who dismantle the Presentist–historicist dichotomy, arguing that "the act of interpreting Shakespeare always involves multiple pasts and a changing, developing present." See "Presentism, Anachronism and the Case of *Titus Andronicus*," *Shakespeare*, 8 (2012): 44–73, esp. 45.
6. Keith Thomas, *Man and the Natural World* (Oxford: Oxford University Press, 1983), p. 255.
7. Ibid., p. 254.
8. Ibid., p. 236.

9. Amy Tigner, *Literature and the Renaissance Garden from Elizabeth I to Charles II: England's Paradise* (Farnham: Ashgate Press, 2012), p. 85.
10. For this and all citations to Shakespeare's plays, see *The Norton Shakespeare*, ed. Stephen Greenblatt, Walter Cohen, Jean E. Howard, and Katharine Eisaman Maus (New York: W. W. Norton, 1997).
11. Rebecca Laroche and Jen Munroe, "On a Bank of Rue: Ecofeminist Inquiry and the Garden of *Richard II*," forthcoming in *Shakespeare Studies*, special issue "Food and Identity."
12. Thomas, *Natural*, p. 220.
13. Thomas Tusser, *Fiue hundreth points of good husbandry*, 1573, p. 44^v.
14. Thomas Hill, *The gardeners labyrinth*, 1577, p. 4^v.
15. A. L. Rowse, *The England of Elizabeth: The Structure of Society* (New York: Macmillan, 1960), p. 100.
16. See, for example, section C7 of the online map of London provided by the University of Victoria, *The Map of Early Modern London*, ed. Janelle Jensted. Thanks to Jen Munroe for pointing me to this resource.
17. Thomas, *Natural*, p. 248.
18. Joan Thirsk, *The Agrarian History of England and Wales*, vol. 4, *1500–1640*, ed. Joan Thirsk (Cambridge: Cambridge University Press, 1967), pp. 195–6.
19. *The Arden Edition of King Richard II*, ed. Peter Ure (Cambridge, MA: Harvard University Press, 1956), p.119n29. On apricots, see Thirsk, *Agrarian History*, p. 196.
20. Heidi Scott, "Ecological Microcosms Envisioned in Shakespeare's *Richard II*," *The Explicator*, 67.4 (2009): 267–71, esp. p. 267.
21. Brian Fagan, *The Little Ice Age: How Climate Made History 1300–1850* (New York: Basic Books, 2000), p. 103.
22. Thirsk, *Agrarian History*, p. 228.
23. Steve Rappaport, *Worlds within Worlds: Structures of Life in Sixteenth-Century London* (Cambridge: Cambridge University Press, 1989), p. 136–7.
24. Ibid., p. 136.
25. Fred Waage, "Shakespeare Unearth'd," *ISLE*, 12.2 (2005): 139–64, esp. 146. On earth in *Richard II* specificically, see Jean E. Feerick, "Groveling with Earth in Kyd and Shakespeare's Historical Tragedies," in *The Indistinct Human in Renaissance Literature*, ed. Jean E. Feerick and Vin Nardizzi (Basingstoke: Palgrave Macmillan, 2012), pp. 231–52.
26. Richard Altick, "Symphonic Imagery in *Richard II*," *PMLA*, 62.2 (1947): 339–65, esp. 341–4.
27. Here I draw from my "Teaching Shakespeare in the Ecotone" in Bruckner and Brayton, *Ecocritical Shakespeare*, pp. 223–4.
28. Carolyn Merchant, *The Death of Nature: Women, Ecology and the Scientific Revolution* (San Francisco: Harper & Row, 1983).
29. *King Richard II, updated edition*, ed. Andrew Gurr (Cambridge: Cambridge University Press, 2003), p. 93n45.
30. Scott outlines how opportunistic landlords used a variety of methods to convert relatively secure copyholds to less secure leases, which could lead

to enclosure. William O. Scott, "Landholding, Leasing, and Inheritance in *Richard II*," *Studies in English Literature*, 42.2 (2002): 275–92, esp. 278–9.
31. Haraway's notion of human exceptionalism "is the premise that humanity alone is not a spatial and temporal web of interspecies dependencies." Donna J. Haraway, *When Species Meet* (Minneapolis: University of Minnesota Press, 2007), p. 11.
32. On land law and *Richard II* see James E. Berg, "'This Dear, Dear Land': Dearth and the Fantasy of Land-Grab in *Richard II* and *Henry IV*," *English Literary Renaissance*, 29.2 (1999): 225–45; Dennis R. Klinck, "Shakespeare's Richard II as Landlord and Wasting Tenant," *College Literature*, 25.1 (1998): 21–34; and Scott, "Landholding." On enclosure, see James R. Siemon, "Landlord Not King: Agrarian Change and Interarticulation," in *Enclosure Acts: Sexuality, Property, and Culture in Early Modern England*, ed. Richard Burt and John Michael Archer (Ithaca, NY: Cornell University Press, 1994), pp. 17–33.
33. *Statute of Marlbridge*, qtd. in Klinck, "Landlord," p. 24.
34. Ibid., pp. 23, 31.
35. Berg, "Landgrab," pp. 229–30.
36. Currently, the Pentagon is the "biggest consumer of fossil fuels in the world." John Gartner, "US Military Not Retreating on Clean Energy," *Forbes*, 11 May 2012.
37. As Jeffrey Theis writes, "sometimes whether or not a people correctly perceive their times is less important than what their perceptions… tell us about their era, for perceptions, not empirical rationalism, typically govern human actions." *Writing the Forest in Early Modern England: A Sylvan Pastoral Nation* (Pittsburgh, NJ: Duquesne University Press, 2009), pp. 16–17.
38. Ibid., p. 52.
39. Vin Nardizzi, *Wooden Os: Shakespeare's Theatres and England's Trees* (Toronto: University of Toronto Press, 2013).
40. Simon Shama, *Landscape and Memory* (New York: Vintage Books, 1995), p. 154.
41. Ibid., p. 155.
42. *Calendar of State Papers Domestic, Elizabeth (1591–1594)*, p. 9. The figure detailed in the entry is "total 126,305*l*. 0s 5 ¼d."
43. Ibid., p. 13.
44. Scott, "Landholding," p. 279.
45. In the 1978 Derek Jacobi production, Bolingbroke squats down to touch and handle a piece of earth.
46. Gabriel Egan, *Green Shakespeare* (New York: Routledge, 2006), p. 82.
47. Ed Geisweidt notes "the pervasive belief that serpents could be generated spontaneously." "'The Nobleness of Life': Spontaneous Generation and Excremental Life in *Antony and Cleopatra*" in Bruckner and Brayton, *Ecocritical Shakespeare*, p. 96.
48. See Michael Martin Melendrez, "Soil Ecology and the Soil Food Web," *Soil Secrets*, 1974, revised 2003, www.soilsecrets.com.

49. See *Norton Shakespeare*, p. 454n6.
50. Jean Feerick, "Groveling," p. 242.
51. Gail Kern Paster, "Becoming the Landscape: The Ecology of the Passions in the Legend of Temperance," *Environment and Embodiment in Early Modern England*, ed. Mary Floyd-Wilson and Garrett A. Sullivan, Jr. (Basingstoke: Palgrave Macmillan, 2007), p. 142.
52. Linda Woodbridge, *The Scythe of Saturn: Shakespeare and Magical Thinking* (Urbana: University of Illinois Press, 1994), pp. 193–4.
53. In his adaptation of Conradus Heresbachius's husbandry manual, for example, Googe writes, "Some would have radishes watred and nourished with salt waters: being sodden, they come to be very sweete." Googe, Barnabe. *Four books of husbandry*, p. 58^r.
54. Woodbridge asserts, "the magic doesn't work: the blood manuring the ground is an image of civil war." Woodbridge, *Scythe*, p. 194.
55. "Five Primary Disposal Methods for Fracking Wastewater Fail to Protect Public Health and Environment," *National Resources Defense Council*, 9 May 2012. Also see McKibben, "Why Not Frack?"
56. Humes, "Fractured."
57. Christopher Helman, "New Federal Fracking Rules Look Reasonable: Enviros Not Satisfied," *Forbes*, 5 April 2012.
58. Scott Detrow, "Can Pennsylvania's State Forests Survive Additional Marcellus Shale Drilling?," *StateImpact: a reporting project of local public media and npr*, 12 September 2011.
59. Ken Burns, "National Parks Feed America's Soul," *USA Today*, 22 May 2012, p. 1A.
60. My sincere thanks to Margaret Whitford for her splendid 2004 term paper on earthly imagery in *Richard II*. Her perceptive reading of the play percolates through this chapter. Thanks are also due to Jeffrey Theis for his comments on an early draft.

7
"What light through yonder window speaks?": The Nature Theater of Oklahoma *Romeo and Juliet* and the Cult(ure) of Shakespeare

W. B. Worthen

> Where exactly does one want to draw the line separating performance from adaptation? Do such performances "really" constitute Shakespeare's plays?
> —Margaret Jane Kidnie, "Where Is *Hamlet*?"

> So he went to marching up and down, thinking—and frowning, horrible, every now and then; then he would hoist up his eyebrows; next he would squeeze his hand on his forehead and stagger back and kind of moan; next he would sigh, and next he'd let on to drop a tear. It was beautiful to see him. By and by he got it. He told us to give attention. Then he strikes a most noble attitude, with one leg shoved forwards, and his arms stretched away up, and his head tilted back, looking up at the sky—and then he begins to rip and rave and grit his teeth—and after that, all through his speech, he howled, and spread around, and swelled up his chest, and just knocked the spots out of any acting ever *I* see before. —Huck Finn on the Duke of Bilgewater, Mark Twain, *Huckleberry Finn*[1]

For all its power in articulating the notion of a "literary dramatist," the "return of the author" in contemporary Shakespeare criticism extends what Michael Bristol calls "the incessant border disputes, skirmishes, and raids carried out between advocates of performance-oriented interpretation and the practitioners of more strictly and textually-based hermeneutic procedures." For Bristol, the "largely trivial character of this debate" has largely to do with its focus on "precedence and the allocation of authority" in an economy in which "precedence" has long been guaranteed: the assertion of the literary character of Shakespeare's writing as motivating the force of "interpretive" performance is a nearly frictionless position both in contemporary Shakespeare scholarship and throughout the popular understanding of Shakespeare performance.[2] The notion that performance has to be displaced for the author to "return" to literary studies might be paired with a pendant question: has the author ever really left the apparently unruly precincts of Shakespearean performance?

The Nature Theater of Oklahoma *Romeo and Juliet* may not seem to address the positioning of Shakespeare on the disciplinary landscape, where the plays mark still-vexed institutional and theoretical contentions in literary, theatrical, and performance studies. Shakespeare's play figures largely in the performance, but very few lines of *Romeo and Juliet* are actually spoken; when they are, they are routinely spoken as quotations, usually misremembered quotations at that. Rather than undertaking a merely fashionable "deconstruction" of "the presence of Shakespeare's most famous love tragedy in the contemporary Western cultural unconscious" (as Rachel Anderson-Rabern suggests), the Nature Theater—which is not from Oklahoma, but takes its name from the theatre featured in Franz Kafka's unfinished novel *Amerika*—de-dramatizes the performance of *Romeo and Juliet*, using the peculiar "scenic *écriture*" of performance as a mode of inquiry into the status of "Shakespeare as literary dramatist" in contemporary American culture.[3] Attending to the cultural work performed by the specter of the literary dramatist, and by the theatre conceived as an act of authorial inscription and interpretation, the Nature Theater of Oklahoma *Romeo and Juliet* stages an inquiry into the figuration of Shakespeare *now*.

The performance falls into three parts. In the first part, two actors take turns telling the story of *Romeo and Juliet* as recalled by eight different people, interviewed by the company's co-artistic director Pavol

Liška via telephone. The actors do not impersonate and individuate these subjects; that is, they do not enact realistic, individuated portrayals of Linda Cooper, Teresa Gridley, or the other interview subjects (who are unidentified in performance), in the way Anna Deavere Smith impersonates Angela Davis or Lance Armstrong, registering the codedness of their vocal, gestural address in a meticulous act of *Verfremdung*. Instead, the actors are marked by costume, diction, gesture, and movement as "actors," performing each of the transcribed and edited monologues—which they hear on stage through unconcealed earbuds—in the same rather exaggerated manner, purposely recalling the imagined conventions of the nineteenth-century American stage.[4] Following the eighth monologue, "Anne" (Gridley) and "Bobby" (Robert M. Johanson)—identified in the script, the theatre program, and the DVD credits, but unnamed in the performance—speak to one another, taking up an informal meditation on love, neediness, acting, and the challenge of performing Shakespeare today. Finally, "Bobby" climactically confesses that he has never read *Romeo and Juliet*: blackout. Applause, lights up, curtain calls. Blackout again, this time followed by the two actors reading the balcony scene over the sound system. Lights up on the empty stage, applause.

For Huck Finn, the Duke "just knocked the spots out of any acting ever *I* see before," and the eight monologues, four by "Anne," four by "Bobby," are assertively American in their performance and cultural texture. Like Twain's novel, they deploy familiar phrases of contemporary American speech to lay claim to a democratic, demotic Shakespeare. In "American," Shakespeare is imprecise ("There's somethin' about somebody kissing somebody with poison on their lips, and that—"), repetitive, slangy, cool rather than learned (the Capulet family are "Sort of the hipsters of the town"), often crude ("Romeo's still got a—Raging hard-on—For Juliet"), and full of ums, ands, ahhs.[5] Though each monologue tells the entire story of *Romeo and Juliet*, they're arranged asymptotically, curving increasingly close to, but never fully capturing, the narrative and tonal vector of Shakespeare's script. Not surprisingly, what remains in memory are the play's key scenes: the Capulet ball and the meeting of the lovers; the balcony scene; a contrived plot involving poison and feigned death; the lovers' final meeting in the tomb. Some respondents recall the Nurse (often identified as a maid), others Paris, the Friar, the apothecary, Tybalt, and/or the "guy with a very—Flourishy name like—Like—uh… EURISTHEPISS!" (90). Some are more focused on whether or when or how often Romeo and Juliet have sex; some remain baffled by the logic of the poison intrigue. Yet even when reduced to mere narrative, to plot, *Romeo and Juliet* is remembered as an intrinsically verbal organism, its action bound to specific lines of dialogue, regained through a manifest effort of memorial reconstruction:

> What light—
> Through yonder window
> Speaks?
> It is the East!
> And Juliet is the West! (84)

How does this *Romeo and Juliet* understand Shakespeare at the intersection between literary drama and the embodied work of performance? The dramatic action of Shakespeare's writing is (literally) recalled to the stage, but does not determine the process, the texture so to speak, of the event. This *Romeo and Juliet* alienates the "plot" of Shakespeare's play, which is represented at the confluence of individual memory and sustaining social institutions: literature, the schools, the stage. So, too, the performance—underlined as historical burlesque—is also alienated from a conventional understanding of its dramatic function, "interpreting" dramatic language. Taking up Lawrence Levine's complaint that "historians and critics" have "arbitrarily separated the 'action and oratory' of Shakespeare's plays from the 'dramatic and poetic artistry' with which they were, in reality, so intricately connected" in the nineteenth century, the Nature Theater *Romeo and Juliet* meditates on the historical institutions of Shakespeare performance as a means for the transmission of that artistry.[6]

Romeo and Juliet locates the encounter with Shakespeare as contact narrative: Shakespeare in school. Though it might seem, as Karinne Keithley remarks, to "catalog an utter failure of literary education," it would be fairer to say that *Romeo and Juliet* charts the fortunes of the "all-but-compulsory exposure" to Shakespeare in American secondary education, a Shakespeare conceived less in terms of a specifically "literary" or "theatrical" pedagogy than more broadly as "the locus of pedagogical experience for Americans."[7] The essentially "popular" nineteenth-century Shakespeare—widely performed, routinely excerpted, extensively burlesqued, sharing the bill with music, skits, acrobats, and animal acts—celebrated by Lawrence Levine (and more recently by the National Endowment for the Arts' *Shakespeare in American Communities* project) has been succeeded, Denise Albanese argues, not by the elite, academic, "highbrow" Shakespeare of academic scholarship, but by a Shakespeare retailed through "the *culture of mass education,* an institution whose production began... with the rising to prominence of industrialized capitalism at the turn of the twentieth century," and bears with it the social and cultural impulses of its inception.[8] As Joseph Quincy Adams pointed out at the Folger Shakespeare Library in 1932, public education expanded just as "the forces of immigration became a menace to the preservation of our long-established English civilization," situating Shakespeare as "the cornerstone of cultural discipline," as indeed "the chief object of their [students'] study and veneration."[9] Evoking anxieties about the impact of immigration in the United States, Adams's still-familiar rhetoric pinpoints the stress line running through Shakespeare's alleged function in the culture of American teaching. Shakespeare is certainly good for (disciplining, legitimizing, humanizing, homogenizing, globalizing) *us,* but are *we* good enough for Shakespeare?

The celebration of school Shakespeare as an instrument of potentially transformative class ambition structuring mass education cannot, however, overcome the inherent mystification of the project, at least according to *Romeo and Juliet*'s characters: "I don't know why, but this is the first Shakespeare you read, generally"; it is "the überplay for high school, And then once you hit college—It becomes *Hamlet*" (85, 86). School assimilates and disciplines its potentially distracted and rebellious flock to the Shakespeare curriculum, leading it for some reason, "I don't know why," from *Romeo and Juliet* to *Hamlet* and then... out—out of school, out of Shakespeare. While several of the respondents remember reading the play, they don't seem to "remember reading it" with, say, veneration, or even much interest. For one woman, it is not reading *Romeo and Juliet* but watching another girl reading it in gym class that lives in memory ("I think I fell in love with HER a little.... I remember being really impressed—By her!"); in the end, reading the play did not have "much of an effect on me" (87–8). Perhaps surprisingly, the Nature Theater's experimental performance asserts Shakespeare as a literary event, an event of reading; and yet, the purposes and pleasures of that performance are finally as fugitive as its words.

The Nature Theater's "in your own words" *Romeo and Juliet* stages an ambivalent regard for the literary drama. Performing the playwright's distinctive medium—words, language, "literature"—as beyond reach, reading, comprehension, *Romeo and Juliet* evokes a pervasive—if pervasively disowned—genre of instructional performance: the translation to an idiomatic Shakespeare as a means of preserving any Shakespeare at all. We are a long way, now, from New Criticism's heresy of paraphrase: as the *Teacher's Guide* to the National Endowment for the Arts' *Shakespeare in American Communities* suggests, contemporary "study and veneration" of Shakespeare require a contemporary lexicon: in one assignment, students should "write their own versions" of selected Shakespeare monologues, "modernizing the diction and the situation, but preserving the structure, themes, and emotions" of the original.[10] Of course, the verbal "modernizing"—"repurposing" is Thomas Cartelli's apt term—of Shakespeare's plays dates back nearly to Shakespeare's day, taking in cultural landmarks from Nahum Tate's *King Lear*, to the Lambs' *Tales from Shakespeare*, to the highly edited and emended text of Laurence Olivier's film *Hamlet*, to popular burlesques from Twain to *Gilligan's Island*, and of course to enterprising editions like the *No Fear Shakespeare*: "THE PLAY *PLUS* A TRANSLATION ANYONE CAN UNDERSTAND."[11] The Nature Theater of Oklahoma *Romeo and Juliet* addresses the desire to preserve Shakespeare as a "cornerstone of cultural discipline," while also performing what Cartelli has called "the rapidly diminishing legibility of 'original-language Shakespeare.'"[12]

Despite its "slant" Shakespearean theatricality, in the Nature Theater *Romeo and Juliet*, Shakespeare is, finally, book learning. Performance helps several of the informants recall the events of *Romeo and Juliet*—one person remembers "more from *West Side Story*"—but such memories are illicit: the musical is "just—BASED—on it. It's not anything exactly like" (80). And while the vernacular may be a way to Shakespeare, in these accounts performance only points to the absence of authentic engagement with "Shakespeare," to what is not there rather than to what is:

> And you know what's sad is that I read it in high school,
> And really what I'm remembering is the movie!
>
> Which one?
> The Leonardo DiCaprio... Claire Danes movie!
> 1999 or something?

It's really sad that I'm basing my information on that—
But—
There you go. (85)

There you go: the "work" that should live in the book and volume of the brain has been swept away by the trivial recordings of performance, a sadly inferior version of the "information" of the play, hardly anything at all. As "information," *Romeo and Juliet* appears to degrade when moved from its generative medium (print) to another (performance), and most of the monologues struggle to return the author to his proper prominence through quotation. The Nature Theater of Oklahoma stages *Romeo and Juliet* as loss, as lost writing, a phantom document in the personal history of reading. When Romeo "serenades her. While she's—up. On her balcony," the trick of memory may not be the misremembered serenade, but the betrayal of poetic purity by the misleading purposes of performance itself: "(Or maybe that's just for—like theater purposes. I'm not really sure about that.)." Faced with performance "information," there's only one thing left to do: "Jeez! Now you got— I'm gonna have to go back and READ it!" (89, 77).

The Nature Theater *Romeo and Juliet* positions the play as a "public object" and, while Shakespeare's function across a range of differential cultural and social hierarchies is both "more elusive and more pervasive" than a highbrow/lowbrow paradigm might suggest, hierarchies of value nonetheless persist.[13] *Romeo and Juliet* suggests that the purchase of *West Side Story* or Baz Luhrmann's aggressively titled *William Shakespeare's Romeo + Juliet* or any "theater purposes" on our memory, or on *Romeo and Juliet*, is a melancholic one, the introjection of loss, an unhealing wound, the scar left when the true artwork is withdrawn. *Romeo and Juliet* and Shakespeare are sites of shaming failure: the failure of the memory to store a culturally licensed narrative more completely, with more accurate quotation from the text. Although reading the words requires their translation to a legible scene in which they might have conceivable performative force, the book—not the stage or the screen—is the source of Shakespearean mastery.[14]

Thematically, the Nature Theater *Romeo and Juliet* richly explores the complex cultural division of modern Shakespeare—authorial text versus deauthorizing performance. And, as *The Murder of Gonzago*

Figure 7.1 Robert M. Johanson and Anne Gridley rehearsing the Nature Theatre of Oklahoma *Romeo and Juliet*. In this photograph, both the footlights and the prompter's box are still under construction. Design by Peter Nigrini

reminds us, nothing looks more like theatre than obsolete conventions of performance: while the dialogue of this *Romeo and Juliet* emphasizes the irrecoverable absence of the text, the performance renders a decisively "Shakespearean" mode of performance perhaps all too present. Recalling Twain's mockery in *Huckleberry Finn*, in *Romeo and Juliet* a grandiose theatricality displaces and replaces Shakespeare's dialogue. The two actors—Anne Gridley costumed in an ill-fitting, peach-colored, empire-waisted frock, with a plastic coronet of garland and flowers; Robert M. Johanson Hamlet-like, faded black or brown tights, sleeveless, frilly black doublet, street shoes adorned with large, fake buckles—each strike poses reminiscent of the high rhetorical style of the nineteenth-century stage, often with little regard to the words they are actually speaking.[15] An oversized attitude of supplication—arms raised to the heavens, face clenched with outsized passion—is as likely to embody "Ummm" as any of Shakespeare's scripted words. The gestures are large, sweeping, grandiloquent; facial expression is impassioned, muscles taut, teeth bared, eyes flaring. The vocal register, especially Johanson's, is deep, thrilling. Perhaps again recalling Twain's satire, the "theatrical" character of the actors' physical performance is emphasized by what we might call its semiotic independence from the script or from acting conventions of psychologically expressive character. The prompt box center stage actually is inhabited by a prompter, who actually prompts the performance (she also exits onto the stage twice, dancing around in a chicken costume). But, rather than hissing forgotten lines, the prompter sits before a Kafkaesque ledger, which has the script on the left, and on the facing right page several columns of notation: ILLUSTRATION, for grand "Shakespearean" gestures; EMOTION, which lists the psychological register of the action; and BEHAVIOR, small, somewhat out-of-character acts.

At the opening of "Anne's" second monologue, the prompter has a range of ILLUSTRATION to choose from ("R. arm higher, L. arm back, hand at hip," or "R. hand way UP, L. hand way UP. Drop both"), as well as EMOTION ("Ecstatic," "Serious," "Lovely," "Dancing," "Towering") and BEHAVIOR ("Smooth eyebrow," "Adjust bra strap"). During each performance, the prompter directs a new combination of gestures to the actors: they know more or less when they will be prompted, but not what gesture or "emotion" they will perform.[16] Perhaps the most fascinating performance is hidden from the audience, as the prompter signals Gridley and Johanson both by miming the gestures (raising her arms, smoothing her eyebrows) and by making the facial expressions (ecstatic, serious) that the actors will then imitate.

The traces of Shakespearean narrative and poetry evanesce from the speakers' memories, but the signs of "Shakespearean" theatre are overwhelmingly, absurdly present on stage. While the diction is contemporary American, the appropriate accent of Shakespeare performance is exaggerated, rather British inflected. The high style of an earlier era tends at once to magnify the "theatrical" character of the performance—recalling a moment in American theatre when declamation was closely associated with social improvement—and to ironize it, as well as its incoherent, stammering, clearly "American" script.[17] The accents of this *Romeo and Juliet* are not so much blemished by what Edgar Allen Poe called "an occasional Anglicism of accent" as they are—hilariously—the invention of the stage: "balcony" becomes "bal-cOny" (rhymes with "phoney"); interrogatives are heavily aspirated ("Hwhy," "Hwhen"; these are marked in the ledger in yellow highlighter, and a note at the end marked "TASKS" reminds both prompter and actors "WH'S"); words like "HHHonest" are given an almost Cockney haitch.[18] Consonants are stressed in surprising ways ("sword" becomes "sWWord"; "dead" is almost always "dea-duh"). When in doubt, diphthong: "doomed" becomes "dee-yoomed"; "moon" is "mewn," and so on. Some sounds are clearly at home only on the stage: "morgue" becomes "MOR-gwah," "poison" and "potion" become "POI-see-on" and "PO-see-on." Perhaps inevitably, an "actor" is always an "ac-TOWR." Shakespeare's *Romeo and Juliet* lives in the book, in lines shamefacedly misrecalled from high school, as "information" sadly displaced in memory by popular films. It requires elaborate modern translation for fearful readers, and, while it provides a useful vehicle for performance, it is mysteriously denatured by film and rendered ineffably ludicrous by the outsized discourse native to its stage.

Although the language of this *Romeo and Juliet* is contemporary, its performance métier is assertively obsolete, locating Shakespeare in a traditional, theatrical past; and yet, as Richard Schoch observes of Shakespeare burlesque more generally, such "parody in fact preserves the continuity of literary traditions."[19] For Kelly Copper, who conceived and directed *Romeo and Juliet* with Pavol Liška, the experience of touring other productions abroad and being told by European audiences that the company's idiom seemed very "American" prompted an interest in the history of American acting. The competition between Edwin Forrest and William Charles Macready that ignited the Astor Place Riots in 1849 inspired the performance style of *Romeo and Juliet*, and an interest in the scenography of American traveling theatres informed the scenic design, a foreshortened wooden stage, six footlights, a stained and tattered beige backcloth surrounded by more sumptuous blue drapery.[20]

Characterizing how the "cultural work that actors do often nominates them as caretakers of memory," Joseph Roach describes the contradiction "at the heart of many American self-conceptions, between nostalgia and progress," a contradiction extended and reciprocated here, as *Romeo and Juliet* invokes the nostalgia for the democratic impulse of nineteenth-century touring Shakespeare that haunts the modern American theatrical imaginary.[21] Produced by a traveling company (the Nature Theater more often performs in Europe than in the United States) who pack up the show in a bag, *Romeo and Juliet* decisively occupies the intersection of a network of Shakespearean representations—in literature, theatre, history, pedagogy—and so evokes the wider cultural field of the "return of the author." Indeed, as school-inflected, Twainesque, Shakespearean Americana, it oddly reciprocates the most visible effort to restore the fantasy of nineteenth-century democratic Shakespeare to American arts and pedagogy, the National Endowment for the Arts *Shakespeare in American Communities* project, which sponsors both touring Shakespeare productions and an extensive pedagogical apparatus. For all that this project may have been designed to preserve the NEA from financial and ideological assault, it clearly functions as an instrument of ideological retrenchment, as Roger Kimball suggested in 2004, lauding Chairman Dana Gioia for turning the NEA away from "Robert Mapplethorpe, photographs of crucifixes floating in urine, and performance artists prancing about naked, smeared with chocolate, and skirling about the evils of patriarchy." *Shakespeare in American Communities* expresses a distinct vision of the appropriate purposes of the NEA: to "cut out the cutting edge and put back the art."[22] Not surprisingly, perhaps, this sense of the proper mission—of subsidy, of the arts—is sustained by a sense of the proper function of performance as well. As Kimball puts it, Gioia "has instituted an important new program to bring Shakespeare to communities across America. And by Shakespeare I mean Shakespeare, not some PoMo rendition that portrays Hamlet in drag or sets *A Midsummer Night's Dream* in a concentration camp."[23]

Shakespeare in American Communities asserts an unexperimental, anti-elitist Shakespeare as the sign and instrument of normative American culture. Identified as a more populist theatre, distracting facts of the nineteenth-century democratic Shakespeare tradition are simply cast in the shade of a bright and urgent nostalgia; Charlotte Cushman's famously erotic Romeo of the 1840s (played opposite her sister as Juliet) and her later celebrity as a "Hamlet in drag" come to mind. Like all acts of surrogation, the NEA revival of lost "traditions" performs a politicized forgetting, in order to denounce a history in which Shakespeare's "work gradually came to be seen as part of high culture rather than popular culture," a mandarin literature to which "everyday people could hardly relate."[24] To restore this everyday Shakespeare, *Shakespeare in American Communities* aims to "revitalize the longstanding American theatrical tradition of touring."[25] Using a familiar trope of American political rhetoric (identifying economic with political structures, the market with democracy), the project revalues business practice (touring, both then and now) as a vehicle of cultural democratization and improvement, which has been mysteriously displaced by suspect, specialized performance forms that do not cater to the broader republic: "Specialized theaters evolved that catered to distinct interests such as avant-garde theater, theater of the absurd, musical theater, and others."[26] As Amanda Giguere notes, the nineteenth-century stage provides the focus for a "collective desire to return to simpler times, with no terrorism, no fear of attack, and no moral ambiguity."[27]

The past, Robert Frost knew, is made simple by the loss of detail.[28] Setting aside misinformation, the *Teacher's Guide* represents Shakespeare as the founding father of the republic of American theatre, asserting the undocumented, perhaps undocumentable claim that "When the English colonists sailed for the New World, they brought only their most precious and essential possessions, including the works of William Shakespeare."[29] Yet by 1750, after a half-century of colonial theatre, Shakespeare was numbered among both original American works and popular British hits—Farquhar's *The Recruiting Officer*, Otway's *The Orphan*, Addison's *Cato*, among others—which, like Shakespeare, may also have been associated with "royalist" rather than patriot taste.[30] Like their British counterparts, great American actors of the nineteenth century, including Edwin Forrest (1806–72), were as well known for their non-Shakespearean as for their Shakespearean roles (Forrest played blackface comedy before his celebrated Othello, and starred in the "aboriginal" drama he commissioned, John Augustus Stone's *Metamora*). Ira Aldridge (1807–67), the "African Roscius," played Rolla in Sheridan's *Pizzaro* before undertaking a brilliant career performing Othello, Lear, and other Shakespearean roles in commercial and court theatres from London to St. Petersburg to Lodz, Poland, where he is buried, a racial exile from playing Shakespeare in the American communities of his day. The *Teacher's Guide* features a photograph of Paul Robeson as Othello, remarking that "Shakespeare's plays were performed by well-known film actors in the twentieth century," but takes no note of Robeson's own history of racial and political struggle in the United States, of his blacklisting as a "well-known film actor," or indeed of the fact that his first performance as Othello opposite a white actress took place in London (with Peggy Ashcroft, 1930); the American community waited until the 1943–4 season to see Robeson play Othello to Uta Hagen's Desdemona.[31] As Ayanna Thompson notes, while the "new generation" learning Shakespeare in school is depicted in the *Shakespeare in American Communities* teaching materials "as something that is not suburban and white, the NEA mentions ethnicity, and specifically refers to Native American populations, but eschews engagement with explicit dialogues about race."[32] Indeed, the NEA's revisionist cultural politics are clearest at the few moments when the nineteenth-century stage is addressed, at least by literary proxy. Predictably enough, the sign that "Shakespeare was so integrated into American culture by the nineteenth century" is Twain's famous scene, in which "Twain had his young hero Huckleberry Finn travel along the Mississippi River by raft with a pair of rogues who tried to pass themselves off as Shakespearean actors to earn money in riverbank towns."[33] Despite Twain's double-barreled satire (the actors and their audiences are both impostors here), the *Teacher's Guide* takes this incident to epitomize the loss of an "oratorical mode of entertainment and education that was prevalent throughout the nineteenth century," a loss that now makes Shakespeare's "words alien to a people who once so effortlessly understood their power," if not—to judge by the Duke, the Dauphin, their audiences—their meaning.³⁴

Shakespeare in American Communities restores a theatrical tradition buffed clean of inconvenient detail; the nineteenth-century stage, typically rewriting and restructuring the plays to suit its own practices and a host of burlesque, artistic, racist, and nationalist purposes, routinely violated the sacred "words" of Shakespearean drama.³⁵ The materiality of the nineteenth-century stage, even the details of theatrical touring, is not that important to *Shakespeare in American Communities*, because theatre, finally, is significant only as a vehicle for the assertion of literary value and the cultural norms said to be enshrined there. Despite its emphasis on stage performance, the "educational materials... used by more than 20 million students to enhance their understanding and appreciation for the language and theatricality of Shakespeare's plays" provide no guidance—indeed, provide no mention—of how the "more than one million high school students" who "have now seen a professional production of Shakespeare" should engage with it critically. Performance is not an object of study, Shakespeare is. Performance is merely the means to "bringing the best of live theater to new audiences."³⁶

When performance does appear in these materials, its purpose is to immerse students "in great thoughts and great language," typically through the practice of "Modernizing Monologues," and rewriting the sonnets as prose love letters, a practice that traces its own gesture of nostalgia, replicating the nineteenth-century tradition of decontextualizing passages for moral and rhetorical instruction, oratory as a means of identifying a spiritualized literature with evangelically troped notions of national identity.³⁷ Snippets of Shakespeare isolated for moral and oratorical instruction: the fantasy of nineteenth-century theatre sustains the restoration of nineteenth-century pedagogy. When students do perform, performance is articulated as a competitive program of textual delivery, a recitation contest in which students listen to passages recited by well-known actors on CD, study them, and perform them; teachers have a grading chart taking in volume, speed, voice inflection, posture, and presence, evidence of understanding, pronunciation, and eye contact. "Two winners from each school will be sent an official award document from the National Endowment for the Arts, signed by Chairman Dana Gioia."³⁸ Alternatively students are invited to perform a "Scene outside the Globe," improvising social interactions from a one-paragraph biography of various real and imagined figures—Queen Elizabeth I, the Earl of Essex, Sir Francis Drake, Boy Apprentice Actor, Wet Nurse—in order to "demonstrate their understanding" of "the social structure of Elizabethan England" learned from the essay of about 1,300 words provided in the *Teacher's Guide*.[39]

In the conjunction of nostalgic performance surrogation, textual modernizing, and an anxious regard for the potential loss of Shakespeare's words, the *Shakespeare in American Communities Project* and the Nature Theater of Oklahoma *Romeo and Juliet* occupy a common cultural terrain.[40] Unlike the polemically anti-elitist rhetoric of the NEA, the touring NTO refuses an organic linkage between the popular and the populist, framing a surprisingly nuanced inquiry into Shakespearean performance as a means of cultural reproduction. Foregrounding the aleatory work of its own performance rhetoric on the text of memory, a rhetoric critically deploying tropes invoked by the *American Communities* project—modernized language, the grand tradition of American acting—the Nature Theater of Oklahoma *Romeo and Juliet* locates performance less as a means of transmission than of instigation, engaging Richard Schechner's sense that performance "is behavior itself," and what it restores is performance.[41]

Fittingly, then, the ethical, rhetorical, historical, and personal challenges of performing Shakespeare in the contemporary theatre take the stage in the final scene. *Romeo and Juliet* closes with the two actors giving yet another "in their own words" performance to reframe the dynamics of contemporary Shakespeare. Although the actors continue to hear the dialogue through their earbuds, their movement and gestures are now their own: there are no instructions in the ledger to prompt them. The scene opens with a relatively frank discussion of the often distant relation between love and sex, and the extent to which people sometimes sacrifice themselves to impersonate what someone else might find attractive, desirable: "That's kinda what actors do, right?" as "Bobby" puts it (106). "Bobby's" anxiety evokes a complex dis/identification between what the actors do here and the remembered experiences of the earlier monologues. After all, actors' introjection of Shakespearean language is useless (however much it might contribute to their understanding of Shakespeare) unless it can be incorporated into an act, the action that sustains the peculiar relations of theatre. Even more so than in the competitive classroom, where reciting the text can be calibrated for a grade, performance appears to be a losing proposition. In the theatre, performance is not a competition with classmates; it is a competition with an ineffable, evanescent presence—it is "a competition with Shakespeare" (112).

As the reciprocal enthusiasm for the "return of the author" from the grip of performance and the liberation of "postdramatic" theatre from the clutches of the literary drama imply, competition is the substance of contemporary Shakespeare performance, which struggles to wrest the drama from its literary moorings into living behavior. Wrapping his arms around "Anne" from behind, fondling her, kissing and licking her ear, "Bobby" asks,

> What does OUR scene have?
> (*pause*)
> That could compete with—Shakespeare's.

Everything and nothing: the seduction of the body seems to stand apart from the discussion, as "Anne," more or less ignoring him, points out that contemporary actors are "PROBABLY—a little OLDER? Than—most Shakespearean actors were," and so able "to bring something different?—to the performance? (*pause*) Than the actors of Shakespeare's time would have brought to it?" What we have, of course, is not only women on stage ("For ONE thing, they were all MALE!"), but an alienated perspective, "a MODERN SENSIBILITY" that distantiates the drama: "we can get the JOY!—of—trying to figure out—why this play still works today! Or why it CAN still work today!"—or, to put a finer point on it, whether what works today is "it" at all: Shakespeare's *Romeo and Juliet* or its charismatic, inalienable, uncanny double (112–13).[42] It is the task of making *the play* work today that differentiates us from Shakespeare: "What is it about the WORDS—that Shakespeare chose to use?—the language that he used?—that makes the play so compelling?" and, evidently, so resistant, to memory and to the stage (113)?

It is difficult to know how to take this question, especially as it is voiced—ShakesPE-AH, LANG-wadge—in this production, which opens a melancholy gap between writing and performing, and seems to long for an impossible fidelity that would transcend the accent of theatre altogether. The Nature Theater of Oklahoma *Romeo and Juliet* indeed stages a performance "about the WORDS," but shows that words—the substance of written literature—are inevitably transformed into something else (action, behavior, performance) by the vagaries of memory, the manifest conventions of the stage, the vulnerable yet dynamic activity of actors and audiences. Using words to frame behavior is the performative challenge, to undertake a legible embodiment in which doing things with words can gain the complex provisional force of action on stage. To recall Kenneth Burke for a moment, theatre necessarily redoubles the *ratios* of dramatic action, sustaining the purposes, agents, and agencies of the drama with its own. "Bobby's" purposes—like those of any actor—can never be fully aligned with Shakespeare's, or Romeo's, a point perhaps implied by his answer to "Anne's" question, "What is it about the WORDS?" of the play: "I don't know. I haven't read it."

> BOBBY: It's not time yet. That's what I know.
> ANNE: Alright...
> BOBBY: I shouldn't read it yet.
> ANNE: Alright...
> BOBBY: 'Cause then talkin' to you would be pointless! (113)

"Bobby," perhaps, wants to keep his eventual performance in the play fresh, alive, but in this moment *Romeo and Juliet* is the instrument of his continued conversation with "Anne," a version, perhaps, of the extended double sonnet that joins Romeo and Juliet, hand to hand and lip to lip—itself much remembered, in principle at least, by the play's informants—that structures their mutual performance at the Capulet ball. "What is there to keep me here?—The dialogue," as Beckett's Hamm might put it.[43] In theatre, the script is the means of present action. Hans-Thies Lehmann notes a "fundamental *shift from work to event*" in the transition from dramatic to postdramatic theatre, but while "Anne" longs for a theatre of the literary work, "Bobby" represents the scripted drama as an instrument of the occasion, part of an event that necessarily redefines the literary work for its own seductive purposes.[44]

Blackout. Applause rises, the house lights come back on, and Anne Gridley and Robert Johansen and the Prompter/Chicken take their bows. The play is over, the audience begins to stir from its seats and head for the exits. And then blackout again. Over the PA system, we hear a highly edited version of the balcony scene from "But soft!..." through "Sleep dwell upon thine eyes": it is Gridley and Johanson, in a delicate, nuanced performance, low-key, intense, contemporary American Shakespeare. In contrast to the play we have witnessed on stage, where the theatrical body and its resources are always out of scale to the apparent expression of the script, here "Shakespeare" speaks directly to us out of the darkness, in our own idiom, unmarked by troublesome bodies, their movements and gestures, the actor's failing memory and stagey rhetoric.[45] The actors no longer act, they "recite in the dark" (113). There have been other voices, mediated "into" the actors, so to speak, via their visible earbuds, and "out" of them too, as words signally held apart from their incarnation as acting by the stagey theatricality of posture, gesture, movement, and intonation. Closing with a voice-over, this *Romeo and Juliet* perhaps implies that Shakespeare performance today leaves no place for actors to inhabit. And while we still inhabit the theatre, our relation to the now invisible actors is no longer theatrical—we have been transformed from agents of the scene into its objects, consumers of performed LANG-wadge. The voices sustain, ground, clarify, enrich the script; it is a lovely, moving, troubling moment, one that perhaps reinforces a familiar sadness, the forlorn sense that Shakespeare is so purely identified with "the WORDS" that Shakespearean play can transpire for us only in words. And yet, the reading also foregrounds its own style in a performance in which *style* has been very much at stake, the extent to which even (mere) reading, recitation, depends for its effectiveness on conventions of emphasis and delivery, volume, speed, inflection, and so on. The actors may finally speak in *our* Shakespearean voice, but that voice too, for all its native intimacy, is now marked, located in the history of Shakespearean representation, a history that, as Kidnie observes, has tended to make the "text seem fixed, outside of history, to the same extent that performance, pulling in the opposite direction, comes to seem provisional, irremediably contaminated by, or lost to, history."[46] *Romeo and Juliet* is, finally, exiled from the stage.

For Kelly Copper, "the audience is left sort of alone to themselves in the dark with this language to make whatever connection to it they can make at that point in the evening."[47] Surrogating the populist, oratorical, American performance derided by Twain and celebrated by the NEA, *Romeo and Juliet* finally summons another nineteenth-century avatar. Sitting in the dark, listening to *Romeo and Juliet*, it is hard not to recall Charles Lamb's famous essay on *King Lear*. For Lamb, *Lear* decisively marked an insuperable division between the sublime performance of reading Shakespeare, and the disheartening performance of Shakespeare in the theatre: "On the stage we see nothing but corporal infirmities and weakness, the impotence of rage; while we read it, we see not Lear, but we are Lear,—we are in his mind."[48] Or, in this case, Shakespeare is in ours. This final scene "interpreting" Shakespeare's words perhaps provides a consummation devoutly wished: the return of the author. And yet, like the typically unstable relation between writing and performance, scripted language and stage action, this final scene of textual delivery, recitation, seems to unsettle a sense that writing can and should determine its use on stage, not least by avoiding one of the theatre's defining resources: the physical embodiment of actors. Perhaps dramatic theatre is always about the loss of drama, at least in high print culture: "Authenticity, in other words, always already present in the text, inevitably eludes performance; performance is measured in relation to the text in degrees of *in*fidelity and *in*authenticity."[49] Actors may be "caretakers of memory," and here they surrogate and so memorialize a remembered mode of performance, all the while urging the disimbrication of acting from subordination to writing.[50] While the notion that the "literary dramatist" needs to be restored to academic critique and education is urgent in that literature, on the stage, it seems that the author has hardly wandered off.

De-dramatizing *Romeo and Juliet*, the Nature Theater suspends an organic narrative channeled through naturalized performance conventions that assert a coherent ideological closure between "the text," the fictive whole worlded on the stage, and our own passive consumption of it. And yet, this *Romeo and Juliet* is preoccupied with Lamb's question: is there a Shakespeare beyond the book? For the Nature Theater "characters," Shakespeare is a testament both to loss and to desire: *Romeo and Juliet* is, for them, a kind of stigma; the vitality of performance is illicit, mere "theater purposes," and the lapsing memory of the stabilizing text elusive, embarrassing. For the actors, theatre is a site of competition, at once the instrument of their extraordinarily affecting energy and discipline, and a monument to the tawdry, the tired—terrible, not terrific. And yet, however evacuated by convention, the generative practice of this performance instantiates theatre as an instrument for making something new, something that takes Shakespeare into its own project of self-invention, something that will happen in this way only once, here and now, with us. Perhaps performance can only bring us farther away from Shakespeare, if by "Shakespeare" we mean the experience we might achieve by reading, from texts. That Shakespeare can only arrive in the theatre by undoing theatre, by replacing the stage of an always-provisional embodiment with the darkened cavern of a readerly consciousness. The Nature Theater of Oklahoma *Romeo and Juliet* suggests that the "interpretive" theatre of the master's voice is powerful, seductive; but however much it may claim to return the author to us, it is finally not theatre at all.

Notes

1. Margaret Jane Kidnie, "Where Is Hamlet? Text, Performance, and Adaptation," *A Companion to Shakespeare and Performance*, ed. Barbara Hodgdon and W. B. Worthen (Oxford: Blackwell, 2005), p. 115. Mark Twain, *Adventures of Huckleberry Finn*, ed. Victor Fischer and Lin Salamo, with Harriet Elinor Smith and Walter Blair (Berkeley: University of California Press, 2010), pp. 178–9.
2. On the "return of the author in Shakespeare studies," see Lukas Erne, *Shakespeare as Literary Dramatist* (Cambridge: Cambridge University Press, 2003), and Patrick Cheney, "Introduction," *Shakespeare Studies*, 36 (2008): 19; Michael Bristol, *Shakespeare's America, America's Shakespeare* (London: Routledge, 1990), p. 97. I have discussed this movement in "Intoxicating Rhythms; or, Shakespeare, Literary Drama, and Performance (Studies)," *Shakespeare Quarterly*, 62 (2011): 309–39.
3. Rachel Anderson-Rabern, "The Naure Theater of Oklahoma's Aesthetics of Fun," *TDR: The Drama Review—The Journal of Performance Studies*, 54.4 (Winter 2010, T-208): 94. On "de-dramatizing" and "scenic écriture," see Hans-Thies Lehmann, *Postdramatic Theatre*, trans. Karen Jürs-Munby (London: Routledge, 2006), p. 74.

4. According to Kelly Copper, the eight monologues represent eight different interview subjects, though one of the monologues is devised from material taken at two separate interviews. The final scene between Anne and Bobby was the result of one of the participants calling Pavol Liška back with some additional thoughts about love after the initial phone interview about *Romeo and Juliet*. The interview subject here was Anne Gridley's mother (Copper, email to author 6 July 2010). My thanks to Kelly Copper and to the Nature Theater of Oklahoma for providing me with a recording filmed at The Kitchen in New York on 27 December 2009 (I saw this production several days later, in early January 2010), for answering several of my questions about the production and the process of its devising, and for providing me with an advance version of the text published as "Nature Theater of Oklahoma's *Romeo and Juliet*," *Theater*, 40.2 (2010): 75–113. I am also grateful to Kelly Copper and Pavol Liška for taking the time to let me see the performance ledger, and for answering many questions about the genesis and production of *Romeo and Juliet* and about their more current work.
5. "Nature Theater of Oklahoma's *Romeo and Juliet*," 78, 89, 94. In transcribing the conversations, Kelly Copper is especially careful to note coughs and to transcribe as accurately as possible the various nonverbal sounds the interview subjects use—the various kinds of "um," "ah," and so on (email, 6 July 2010). Page references to the play are to this edition and are included in the text.
6. Lawrence W. Levine, *Highbrow/Lowbrow: The Emergence of Cultural Hierarchy in America* (Cambridge, MA: Harvard University Press, 1988), p. 35.
7. Karinne Keithley, "Uncreative Writing: Nature Theater of Oklahoma's *Romeo and Juliet*," *Theater*, 40.2 (2010), 70. On the function of Shakespeare in American secondary education, see Denise Albanese, *Extramural Shakespeare* (Basingstoke: Palgrave Macmillan, 2010), pp. 69, 67.
8. Albanese, *Extramural Shakespeare*, p. 70.
9. Adams is quoted in Bristol, *Shakespeare's America*, p. 79.
10. National Endowment for the Arts, *Shakespeare in American Communities: Teacher's Guide* (Washington, D.C.: National Endowment for the Arts, n.d.), p. 17. This volume is part of the Teacher's Toolkit available free from the *Shakespeare in American Communities* website; it contains the *Teacher's Guide*, the *Why Shakespeare?* VHS, the *Recitation Contest*, and other materials.
11. Thomas Cartelli, "Doing It Slant: Reconceiving Shakespeare in the Shakespeare Aftermath," *Shakespeare Studies*, 38 (2010): 33. See, for instance, the cover of *No Fear Shakespeare: Romeo & Juliet* (New York: Spark Publishing, 2003).
12. Cartelli, "Doing It Slant," p. 27.
13. Albanese, *Extramural Shakespeare*, pp. 3, 1.
14. I have discussed the "performative force" of writing in theatrical performance in *Shakespeare and the Force of Modern Performance* (Cambridge: Cambridge University Press, 2003), pp. 1–27.

15. Some reviews misidentify this as a "mock-Elizabethan style" and generalize it to "the traditional manner of bad Shakespearean acting the world over" (Christopher Isherwood, "Just the Gist of a Star-Cross'd Tale, *New York Times*, 21 December 2009), "high-falutin' pronunciations," "fruity voices and grandiose gestures" (Alexis Soloski, "Verona meets Verizon in The Kitchen's *Romeo & Juliet*," *Village Voice*, 22 December 2009).
16. Kelly Copper, email to author, 6 July 2010.
17. Joseph Roach, "The Emergence of the American Actor," *The Cambridge History of American Theatre, Volume I: Beginnings to 1870*, ed. Don B. Wilmeth and Christopher Bigsby (Cambridge: Cambridge University Press, 1998), p. 351.
18. Poe is quoted by Roach, ibid., p. 342. The performance ledger notes a number of TASKS: HYPER-ARTICULATION, SOUTHERN ACCENT, BRITISH ACCENT, BEGINNINGS OF WORDS, ENDS OF WORDS, AMERICAN R'S, which suggest the performance's constant focus on the quality and detail of the speaking. The "southern accent" derives, according to Kelly Copper, from Robert Johanson's Virginia background.
19. Richard W. Schoch, *Not Shakespeare: Bardolatry and Burlesque in the Nineteenth Century* (Cambridge: Cambridge University Press, 2002), p. 19.
20. Kelly Copper, email to the author, 6 July 2010; Keithley, "Uncreative," p. 68. Keithley notes that "Most of the performance parameters for *Romeo and Juliet* emerged from the mid-nineteenth-century traveling Shakespearean theater," using what Kelly Copper describes to her as "acting techniques employed (or imagined to be employed) by great Shakespearean actors"; "Uncreative," p. 70. Copper also notes being inspired by curtains from a collection posted at Curtains Without Borders; email to the author, 6 July 2010.
21. Roach, "Emergence," pp. 338, 339.
22. Roger Kimball, "Farewell Mapplethorpe, Hello Shakespeare: The NEA, the W. Way," *National Review Online*, 29 January 2004. As Todd Landon Barnes notes, after the election of George W. Bush in 2000, the budget of the NEA "rebounded 28 percent (a nearly 27 million dollar increase)," in which nearly "all this new funding was reserved for Gioia's 'favorite' program: *Shakespeare in American Communities*"; "George W. Bush's 'Three Shakespeares': *Macbeth, Macbush,* and the Theatre of War," *Shakespeare Bulletin*, 26.3 (2008): 6. He also notes the "*million*-dollar" contribution by the Department of Defense (3). On his side, Gioia's recourse to Shakespeare, and the successor *American Masterpieces*, might be regarded as having spared the NEA.
23. Kimball, "Farewell." Kimball's PoMo, abbreviating "postmodern," perhaps also expresses a distaste for a wider range of contemporary performance, such as the 1990s group Pomo Afro Homos.
24. *Shakespeare in American Communities: Teacher's Guide*, p. 14.
25. National Endowment for the Arts, *Shakespeare in American Communities* brochure, p. 3. The brochure is available as a pdf file at http://www.nea.gov/pub/SIAC4.pdf, accessed 22 March 2013.

26. *Shakespeare in American Communities: Teacher's Guide*, p. 14.
27. Amanda Giguere, *Shakespeare in American Communities: Conservative Politics, Appropriation, and the NEA* (Saarbrücken: VDM Verlag Dr. Müller, 2010), p. 60.
28. Robert Frost, "Directive," *Poems*, ed. Louis Untermeyer (New York: St. Martin's Press, 1971), pp. 266–8.
29. *Shakespeare in American Communities: Teacher's Guide*, p. 13. "The earliest known staging of his [Shakespeare's] plays in the colonies" was not in 1750, as the *Teacher's Guide* informs us, but in 1730; see Don B. Wilmeth and Jonathan Curley, "Timeline: Beginnings to 1870," *The Cambridge History of American Theatre, Volume I: Beginnings to 1870*, ed. Don B. Wilmeth and Christopher Bigsby (Cambridge: Cambridge University Press, 1998), p. 33.
30. On the repertoire of early American theatre, see Wilmeth and Curley, "Timeline," *passim*. Todd Landon Barnes cites James G. Macmanaway to suggest the unlikelihood that "many copies of Shakespeare were to be found" among the books of the colonists; "Immanent Shakespeareing: Politics, Performance, Pedagogy," PhD dissertation, University of California, Berkeley, 2010, p. 131. He also notes the extent to which the performance of British drama, including Shakespeare, in the years leading up to the Revolution, was regarded as "suited to extravagant royalist tastes," suggesting that the tensions between patriots and royalists that led to the closing of the theatres during the Revolution merely resurfaced during the Astor Place Riot.
31. See *Shakespeare in American Communities: Teacher's Guide*, p. 14.
32. Ayanna Thompson, *Passing Strange: Shakespeare, Race, and Contemporary America* (Oxford: Oxford University Press, 2011), p. 133.
33. *Shakespeare in American Communities: Teacher's Guide*, p. 14.
34. Ibid., p. 1.
35. See, for example, Levine's discussion of Charles Matthews's travesty of the "Nigger's (or Negroe's) theatre" during his visit to New York in 1822 (*Highbrow/Lowbrow*, p. 14), and Roach, "Emergence."
36. "Chairman's Message," in *Shakespeare in American Communities* brochure, p. 1.
37. See *Shakespeare in American Communities: Teacher's Guide*, pp. 17–18. On decontextualization, see Giguere, *Shakespeare in American Communities*, pp. 59, 62; on the nationalist implications of oratorical training, see Barnes, "Immanent," p. 136.
38. National Endowment for the Arts, *Shakespeare in American Communities: Recitation Contest* (Washington, D.C.: National Endowment for the Arts, n.d.), p. 5.
39. *Shakespeare in American Communities: Teacher's Guide*, p. 20.
40. On "surrogation," see Joseph Roach, *Cities of the Dead: Circum-Atlantic Performance* (New York: Columbia University Press, 1996), *passim*.
41. Richard Schechner, "Collective Reflexivity: Restoration of Behavior," *A Crack in the Mirror: Reflexive Perspectives in Anthropology*, ed. Jay Ruby (Philadelphia: University of Pennsylvania Press, 1982), p. 51.

42. For an engaging account of this kind of uncanniness, see Joseph Roach, *It* (Ann Arbor: University of Michigan Press, 2007).
43. Samuel Beckett, *Endgame*, in *Complete Dramatic Works* (London: Faber, 1983), pp. 120–21.
44. Lehmann, *Postdramatic Theatre*, p. 61.
45. Kelly Copper reports that the final moments of the performance are in effect to mirror "what we were doing when we began—taking ordinary language and theatricalizing turns into taking theatrical language and rendering it private, intimate, etc." Indeed, the "actors have had nights where the Shakespeare really gets to them and they are in tears as well as the audience, so it does have an emotional charge, but they're not on emotional display" (Copper, email to the author, 21 February 2011).
46. Kidnie, "Where Is Hamlet?," p. 105.
47. Kelly Copper, email to the author, 21 February 2011.
48. Charles Lamb, "On the Tragedies of Shakespeare, Considered with Reference to their Fitness for Stage Representation," *Works in Prose and Verse*, by Charles and Mary Lamb, ed. Thomas Hutchinson (London: Henry Frowde for Oxford University Press, n.d. [1908]), p. 136.
49. Kidnie, "Where Is Hamlet?," p. 104.
50. Roach, "Emergence," p. 338.

8
Reification, Mourning, and the Aesthetic in *Antony and Cleopatra* and *The Winter's Tale*

Hugh Grady

Theodor Adorno once famously opined that philosophy continues to exist because the moment for its abolition was missed.[1] In an ironic parallel, the same might be said of Marxist literary and cultural theory. It continues because the moment for its abolition was missed, when the old mole of history decided to assert itself instead of subsiding into the hibernation predicted in the famous post-1989 edict of Francis Fukuyama: the end of history.[2] Instead of the steady-state, stable capitalist societies envisioned by Fukuyama, we have witnessed the near-collapse of the global capitalist financial infrastructure with resulting social and political turmoil, including the revival of anti-immigrant and anti-Keynesian forces, and the imposition of austerity and no-end-in-sight high unemployment in both Europe and the United States. This is on top of a slightly older resistance to capitalist globalization manifested in the various religious fundamentalisms and other political movements of our time. And even more recently and unexpectedly, something like both 1848 and 1989 seems to have occurred again in the Middle East. As a result, post-modernist culture begins to have and will hereafter develop different features than it did in the 1990s, and Shakespeare accordingly, in a seemingly endless process of permanent renewal, shows and will show new features as well.

In earlier discussions of post-modernist art—relevant here because the contemporary aesthetic environment always has profound impact on the way a literary classic like Shakespeare is constructed by contemporary critics—fears were often expressed that the contemporary production of a media-saturated society, with the commodified images of media culture constituting larger and larger segments of the lifeworld of post-modern citizens, absorbed and commodified art in a way that threatened its crucial modern distance from the society on which it reflected and which it could critique. Nevertheless, contemporary art, including productions of and writings about Shakespeare, by and large resisted this, precisely by inserting the plays into the contemporary world (or its simulacrums) so that, thus recontextualized, they emerged as reflections on twentieth- and twenty-first-century power, capital, and hatred out of control, like Darko Treenjak's brilliant 2011 production of *The Merchant of Venice* in New York.

Today, after the tenth anniversary of the terrorist attack on the World Trade Center in New York, we can see coming into clearer perspective a demarcation within our post-modern period. In the wake of this attack, modernity seems less menacing, precisely because it is clearly under threat in a way that seemed impossible in the 1990s, and, if we are lucky, may seem impossible again in the not too distant future. However, pre-modern belief structures have reasserted their influence not only in the Islamic world, but all too palpably in the United States, where only a minority of adults accepts the theory of biological evolution, and where the racism many thought swept away by the election of Barack Obama has reemerged precisely in the ferocious and largely irrational attacks on him and his centrist policies from a rejuvenated and empowered Right. In this context, modernity seems well worth defending, along with one of its essential categories, a differentiated, secular concept and practice of the aesthetic. In the first wave of political, Marxist-influenced criticism of the Shakespeare studies of the 1980s and 1990s—represented by post-modernist theory, Cultural Materialism, New Historicism, and important segments of feminism—the aesthetic was seen as part of the problem, as a merely formalist, implicitly apolitical mode of analysis. Yet today, we can see emerging a new aestheticism, taking the necessity for art as a reflection on and critique of empirical society. In this development the aesthetic—the category produced by modernity as a built-in critical and utopian mechanism, constantly endangered but constantly renewed—is relevant again. That is, as I argued in my 2009 monograph *Shakespeare and Impure Aesthetics*, art and the aesthetic can and should be spoken of positively in contemporary critical culture; and, contrary to an influential thesis of Carl Schmitt's, the modern aesthetic can be seen to have come into existence in Shakespeare's era, rather than only in the late eighteenth and early nineteenth centuries.[3] Now, in the context of this collection of essays dedicated to exploring the implications of the present cultural moment on our readings of Shakespeare, to observing and encouraging a return to theory within Shakespeare studies, and to exploring and celebrating the functions of the aesthetic in a changing post-modern world, I want to continue those arguments and apply them to two Shakespearean plays unaddressed in my earlier work, both readings focusing on their aesthetic content in an expanded way. Of course, today there are many different kinds and applications of Marxism, but I will be drawing from the critical theory associated with Theodor Adorno and Walter Benjamin. In the process, I want to illustrate how aesthetic practice and the concept of the aesthetic itself perform important, meaning-providing functions within modernized society—in both its early modern and its post-modern varieties. Thus, in this chapter I am reverting to a well-established Marxist critical assumption—reasserted in the recent upsurge of critical Presentism promoted by Terence Hawkes, myself, and many others—that our interpretations of Shakespeare pursue a double hermeneutic, a dialectical give-and-take between our own historical moment and that of the play's moment of origin; and, in the case of so central a cultural icon as Shakespeare, of course, to many relevant contexts in the long critical history in between. I want to trace out the thematic and aesthetic interactions within two related plays from Shakespeare's relatively late works—*Antony and Cleopatra* and *The Winter's Tale*—in the dynamic relations between power in an early modern reified world and a critical, utopian concept of the aesthetic in critical interaction with and commentary on that world. Such an analysis becomes possible in our own time, as the concepts behind it borrow from an intellectual tradition of social and aesthetic philosophy developed over the centuries since the composition of these plays 400 years ago. And yet it is an analysis, like many historicist ones, that throws light on the political, social, and intellectual world in which Shakespeare was embedded and from which he produced his plays—as well as on our own.

Politics in *Antony and Cleopatra*

Antony and Cleopatra emerges out of the series of Shakespeare's late tragedies as something of a surprise and something that looks forward (as I will discuss in greater detail below) to the very latest tragicomedies, *The Tempest* and, most relevantly here, *The Winter's Tale*. While it shares many qualities with the other tragedies—larger-than-life, publicly defined, legendary characters immersed in epochal political struggles complete with identity crises resolved in spectacular suicides—the feeling of the ending is like nothing in the previous Jacobean tragedies and borrows something from earlier masterpieces *Romeo and Juliet* and even *1 and 2 Henry IV*.

Like all the plays based on Plutarch, this one is set in a thoroughly political world following the logic of Machiavellian power. In previous works I described this power as "reified," borrowing from the usage of Karl Marx and his twentieth-century developer Georg Lukács. The term evokes the subjectless, machine-like operations of power systems following rules with an autonomous, independent logic of their own, not under anyone's personal control. Marx used the term once—the German is *Verdinglichung*—in a posthumously published work, vol. 3 of *Capital*, to evoke one of the most salient qualities of the capitalist system he had described through several related concepts: its status as a socially generated system that nevertheless operates according to its own logic, out of the control of individual actors—or, indeed, of society as a whole.[4] Lukács, influenced by the first generation of German sociologists like Simmel and Weber, extended the term not only to the economy as a reified system, but to include the law and state bureaucracy.[5] Jan Kott in fact cited this usage of Lukács' when he attempted to describe something very similar to it in Shakespeare's histories and tragedies as the Grand Mechanism, the endless cycle of one tyrant succeeding another, that he saw in Shakespeare.[6] My own usage of the term, however, tries to be more historically specific than Kott's and attempts to avoid his tendency to essentialize the Mechanism. At the same time, it owes something to the work of Michel Foucault, who never evoked either Lukács or Kott, but who did, at least in his interviews and lectures if not always in his books, see room for the democratization of power and the work of counter-discourses.[7] And as my use of the term Machiavellian as another way to look at systemic power in Shakespeare suggests, the concept also owes something to historical and political processes described so trenchantly by Machiavelli in his *Il Principe* and *I Discursi*.[8]

In its treatment of power, *Antony and Cleopatra* harks back to the 1599 *Julius Caesar*—the first play Shakespeare developed out of material in Plutarch, and a play that, like those of the Henriad that were written in the immediate years before it, takes a dispassionate, analytic approach to political power struggles.[9] It can, as I just indicated, also be termed a Machiavellian approach in the sense of designating an objective treatment of politics as a system of reified power following its own logic. While the Folio editors placed the play among the tragedies, in many ways it is more like Shakespeare's history plays, but set in the Roman world rather than in medieval England. Critics have never been able to agree on which side the play inducts its audience to identify with, and I take this as a marker of its dispassionate, analytic approach to political power as such. To be sure, as a drama the play inducts us into multiple, shifting sympathies—here with Caesar and Antony, there with Brutus and Cassius, momentarily for the brutally assassinated Caesar, and so on. However, these disparate moments never crystallize into anything like the "good" and "bad" camps of, say, *King Lear*. As I have argued elsewhere, the most stable epiphany the play offers is an analysis of power as empty, mechanical, deadly, and destructive, different in feeling but not conceptually unlike some of Marlowe's jaundiced tragedies; something like Walter Benjamin's German baroque *Trauerspiele*, in fact. And by the end of *Antony and Cleopatra*, we can easily make a similar judgment concerning that later and richer play's treatment of power politics.

In its opening, however, the later play famously presents Antony as a truant to chivalry—or to Roman honor, and thus to the power system in which honor has meaning. "Take but good note, and you shall see in him / The triple pillar of the world transformed / Into a strumpet's fool. Behold and see" (1.1.11–13), the minor character Philo instructs the audience. As any number of critics have seen, however, this first perspective—affirmative of political power and based on masculine, "Roman" values of military valor and political responsibility—is soon challenged by a second, slowly developing one, located in the court of Cleopatra—the play's famous "Egyptian" values, erotic, pleasure-valuing, feminine, and Orientalist. As the play progresses, the apparently valorized Roman values are slowly revealed to be a façade covering a value-free system of power. Antony, struck by a "Roman thought" and determined to break his strong Egyptian fetters, reenters the Roman world and its value system—and reveals it to be one of treachery and violence. Back in

Rome, he deals with the threat of Pompey, renews his alliance with Octavius Caesar through a political marriage to his sister Octavia, and seems to regain his ability to combine an aristocratic image as charismatic leader with a cunning political acumen. However, the fragility of this combination is revealed in an otherwise plot-delaying scene developed out of Plutarch, when Pompey's man Menas proposes to Pompey a treacherous scheme to murder the three triumvirs while they are being feasted on Pompey's barge (2.7.58–77). Pompey refuses to countenance the plan, though he tells Menas that he would have been happy had it been carried out without his knowledge:

> Ah, this thou shouldst have done
> And not spoke on't. In me 'tis villainy,
> In thee 't had been good service. Thou must know
> 'Tis not my profit that does lead mine honour;
> Mine honour, it. Repent that e'er thy tongue
> Hath so betrayed thine act. Being done unknown,
> I should have found it afterwards well done,
> But must condemn it now. Desist and drink.[10]

For his part, Menas is disgusted with the lack of resolution of his master and vows to leave him; much as Enobarbus will later leave Antony. This incident reveals something of the tension of an endeavor combining aristocratic *noblesse* with Machiavellian brutality, and this is a contradiction in which Antony is deeply implicated. Of course, Machiavelli himself was highly aware of the importance of a prince's ability to dazzle his followers and evoke their admiration. Nevertheless, he is clear that these are appearances to be courted by the prince that should never interfere with political strategy. But we see Antony in his conflict with young Octavius constantly making the wrong choices, as Shakespeare pointedly underlines. For example, there is Antony's fantasy, recalling that other victim of the same condition, Sir Harry Hotspur from *1 Henry IV*, of a one-on-one combat with his enemy to settle the issues between them—a fantasy archly dismissed by Octavius. And there is his reasoning on why, against military advice, he decides to wage a naval battle against the superior navy of his adversary; "For that he dares us to't" (3.7.29) is Antony's only explanation. The advisor Comidius contrasts this approach with Octavius Caesar's, after Enobarbus reminds us that "So hath my lord dared him to single fight" (3.7.30):

> Ay, and to wage this battle at Pharsalia,
> Where Caesar fought with Pompey. But these offers
> Which serve not for his vantage, he shakes off,
> And so should you. (3.7.31–4)

At the purely political level, this play enacts the victory of impersonal power over aristocratic charisma when the colorless, instrumental Caesar thoroughly defeats the charismatic Antony. In Wyndham Lewis's terms, a modernist fox has defeated a feudalistic lion. However, to mark this is only to underline the extent to which this play veers in its ending away from the political, Machiavellian world and ends in an attempt to rise above it to another realm entirely. It will be the work of the rest of this section to try to give a name to that realm—without negating the reality of the political.

The Aesthetic in *Antony and Cleopatra*

Cleopatra herself is perhaps the best way into this realm, though she is by no means exempted from the theme of power. Still, she is also the most original and challenging aspect of the play, as in turn she is satirized, vilified, eroticized, idealized, and immortalized in a dazzling sequence of scenes and perspectives that more than justify Enobarbus's famous praise of her infinite variety. Up until her spectacular suicide at the play's ending, however—arguably even in that—she also is a very political animal, a part of the system of power that is one of the play's most pervasive motifs. Her feelings for Antony, while strong and sexual, are inextricably bound up with her political interest in maintaining the kind of dominance over him that we witness in the play's opening scenes. Indeed, her earlier dalliances with Pompey and Julius Caesar, and her later toying with the offers of Octavius, demonstrate not only a weakness for the attractions of powerful Roman men, but a well-honed strategy of manipulating them through her sexuality. This interpretation is certainly fervently believed by Antony's enemies in Rome: "He hath given his empire / Up to a whore; who now are levying / The kings o'the'earth for war" (3.6.66–7), Octavius explains to Octavia.

At the same time, the play seems to evoke gender stereotypes in the painful events around the naval battle between Antony's forces and Octavius's. Cleopatra, who insisted against Enobarbus's better judgment that "as the president of my kingdom I will / Appear there for a man" (3.7.17–18), loses heart at the beginning of the battle, retreats, and is followed by a distracted Antony, setting off the chain of events that ultimately leads to her and Antony's humiliation and defeat.

The play displays a tissue of thematic cross-currents, including, to be sure, the famous symbolic and erotic ones of G. Wilson Knight's classic analyses,[11] but pointedly containing as well many he missed. Above all, somewhere in the interstices of the play is the kind of materialist reduction that was provided for us in Iago's vision of the events of *Othello* and by the play as a whole in the nihilistic satire *Troilus and Cressida*; that is, the stripping away of what this conception holds are the mere outer, deceptive trappings of love and honor, the revelation of these ideals as deceptive coverings of noble appearances over primal, and base, lust, power hunger, and ego assertion. It is as if at the lowest points in the play's presentation of its two eponymous characters, an X-ray flashes to reveal the deathly skull and bones beneath the flesh. In Cleopatra's ignominious retreat to an enclave, and in Antony's fervent desire to kill her in revenge, the play seems to have taken us to some moment of essentialist revelation.

Of course, the play doesn't end there, in the style of the dark revelations at the conclusion of *Troilus and Cressida*. Instead, it takes what first readers almost always find a wholly unexpected turn and moves to one of the most idealizing tragic endings ever written—if indeed tragic is the right word for it. The play turns from a deflating mode to an exalting one, from darkness to heroic death and idealizing mourning, and from history to a utopian aesthetic founded on both *eros* and *thanatos*.

In his extraordinary work on the history of death in the Western world, Philippe Ariès had linked *Romeo and Juliet* to the tradition of *Liebestod* or love-death as a baroque moment, predominately occurring from the fifteenth to the seventeenth century, in which death was coupled with sex as two "natural" qualities of humanity that act as bulwarks against humanity's ability to conquer nature. For Ariès, they are upwellings of a nature within us that manifests as a deep passion resistant to reason and human technological progress.[12]

I discussed this diagnosis of *Romeo and Juliet* in my *Shakespeare and Impure Aesthetics*, finding the analysis to be a generally strong one, but misplaced as a diagnosis of the ending of that earlier love tragedy, which seemed to me to feature instead a utopian, harmonious interaction between nature and human society more characteristic of the earlier medieval than the Baroque period.[13] However, I think that *Antony and Cleopatra* is a Shakespearean play much closer to Ariès's conception of baroque *Liebestod* than the earlier play. In *Antony and Cleopatra*, death blasts the characters out of an untenable, all too human world that proved to provide, even through the pleasures of imperial world domination, less ecstasy and passion than the extraordinarily idealized and heightened eroticism of these two legends. In the death of Cleopatra, the joy of the worm famously unites and intensifies *eros* and *thanatos* and enables a triumphant apotheosis rather than a proper tragedy.

There is of course mourning as well as exaltation—and especially in Cleopatra's lyric mourning of her lover. For her, Antony's death deprives the world of all meaning and finally accomplishes something of the melting, the dissolving of the world in love, that the play's imagery had evoked on several occasions:

> The crown o' the earth doth melt. My lord!
> O, withered is the garland of the war.
> The soldier's pole is fall'n. Young boys and girls
> Are level now with men. The odds is gone,
> And there is nothing left remarkable
> Beneath the visiting moon. (4.16.65–70)

Wallace Stevens, in his celebrated lyric "Sunday Morning," famously wrote that "Death is the mother of beauty."[14] The last dramatic movement of *Antony and Cleopatra*, from the death of Antony to the play's very end, is a remarkable case in point. Several theorists have argued that all art bears the imprint of mourning, that it is an attempt to reassemble a meaningful world out of the chaos and desperation of loss—perhaps, as Kleinian psychoanalyst Anna Siegel thought, including (or starting with) the loss of the sense of unity with the mother that every human experiences.[15] And clearly, mimetic death and mourning are among Shakespeare's most powerful aesthetic resources, perhaps even more pervasive in his oeuvre than desire itself. Mourning idealizes the object of its loss and bathes its images in an aura of beauty, just as Cleopatra does for Antony, blotting out the embarrassing, even shameful details of his botched suicide and his far from perfect death. However, she more than makes up for these lacks in the masterfully staged suicide of her own, replete with baroque frissons merging the deadly, the erotic, and the maternal in the figure of the joyful and biting worms she applies to her breasts. The play ends in the oxymoron of tragic triumph, of sex and death over power and ego—and of legend over history proper.

Several critics have thought that this complex of themes is also a triumph of the aesthetic, and I agree, though it is a relatively understated evocation of this anachronistic term compared to other of Shakespeare's works. The relation of this complex is fairly clear within Adorno's concept of the aesthetic, which he sees as a category of modernity emerging in a series of differentiations from pre-modern religious and other symbolic systems. To oversimplify somewhat for the moment, Adorno sees the art of modernity as a secular consolation and holding place for the sense of sacredness, unity with nature, and a sense of intrinsic meaningfulness lost as traditional cultures advanced and succumbed to various stages of modernization and secularization. He saw art as moving beyond superstition—and in that sense as a decisive part of Enlightenment and modernity— but also as preserving pre-modern, eroticized perceptions of nature and of human nature and as a buttress against and consolation for the inevitability of death.[16] As we have seen, all of these motifs are present in *Antony and Cleopatra*. Unlike *Romeo and Juliet*, with the concluding image of two golden statues to be erected as representations of the vanished lovers, or even *Timon of Athens*, with Timon's environmental artwork of a gravesite, this play leaves us no tangible symbol for this aestheticization; except, perhaps, that of the legend of the two lovers themselves, in the way Cleopatra describes to her keeper Dolabella:

> I dreamt there was an Emperor Antony...
> His legs bestrid the ocean; his reared arm
> Crested the world. His voice was propertied
> As all the tunèd spheres. (5.2.75–83)

And of course, there is this play itself, which does metatheatrically if reductively evoke itself in Cleopatra's famous remark, "and I shall see / Some squeaking Cleopatra boy my greatness / I' th' posture of a whore" (5.2.215–17). In the end, Cleopatra embraces death like a lover and goes on to triumph.

Thus, this play, like that other love tragedy *Romeo and Juliet*, enacts a precarious balance between those two ultimates of the human condition, desire and death, and it does so by using both of the emotions associated with these themes in self-conscious aesthetic patterns of great beauty. Each asserts a symbolic triumph over death by desire, precisely in the imaginary space created in each play's aesthetic sphere. The reality of death asserts itself, certainly, at another level and with famously powerful effect. There is both a symbolic triumph of desire over death crystallized within dramatic and poetic art, and a mourning and a recognition of death's inevitability and the cruelty of chance.[17] And as I noted at the beginning of this chapter, this pattern not only looks back to *Romeo and Juliet* (and to the other plays of 1595–1600), but seems clearly transitional to the late tragicomedies as well. To see how the dialectic formed by the interactions of reification, mourning, and the aesthetics works in these plays, I want to turn next to *The Winter's Tale*.

Tragicomic Aesthetics

Like the three other extant late tragicomedies, *The Winter's Tale* departs from the tragic convention of an ending with the death of the hero and thus departs from tragedy's specific strategy of mimetic death and mourning as aesthetic resources. However, death is very definitely part of the tragicomedy—and of this play specifically—and it too uses mimetic mourning to help idealize and create beauty. However, the "happy" ending allows for the triumph of aesthetic imagination over cold reality to be more directly expressed, creative of a different complex of emotions at the conclusion.[18] Here in particular, the play becomes meta-aesthetic in its celebrated device of a statue (or apparent statue) coming to life to resolve the many loose ends of the plot and create a bittersweet conclusion, symbolically asserting the victory of *eros* and reproduction over *thanatos* and individual death, mourning, and underlining the reality of death, but in the process symbolically overcoming it.

As in *Antony and Cleopatra* (and so many other of Shakespeare's plays), the plot begins in a political milieu, albeit one in which the reified power underlying and producing absolute monarchy is not represented as a system so much as alluded to almost allegorically in the figure of the tyrant Leontes. In *The Winter's Tale*, power is a much less important theme than in *Antony and Cleopatra*, but it is not wholly absent—it merely takes a highly personal, psychological form. In this play the events of the first, tragic half unfold in details more domestic than political, reminiscent in that way more of *Othello* than of *Antony and Cleopatra*. Yet, as Jean Howard wrote, the mixture is in fact quite appropriate if we understand the play's politics to be very largely sexual politics, indicting the tyranny of a patriarchy whose disastrous effects, on their subject as well as tyranny's objects, are pointedly noted in the bleak atmosphere and unredemptive deaths, and the degradation of the reproductive female body at the end of Act 3.[19] Thereafter, however, we are in a different kind of dramatic world than Shakespeare had produced heretofore; or at least, before the imperfect experiments in this new genre written in temporal proximity to this play, *Pericles* and *Cymbeline*. And the change has to do with his deployment of aesthetic and meta-aesthetic effects in a new and characteristic way.

The deaths that bring us to the conclusion of the play's first half—all connected to Leontes' Lear-like moral blindness and unchecked monarchical power—are far bleaker in affect than the triumphal ones of *Antony and Cleopatra*. We seem to be in a world dominated by the royal abuse of power and disastrous patriarchal jealousy and possessiveness. Momentarily, we are in the tragic universes of *Othello* and *King Lear*—or even *Oedipus Tyrranos*.

What follows, however, from the very end of Act 3, with the apparent intervention of a benevolent but also punishing Providence intruding on the "pagan" cosmology of the play, is a combination of "things dying and things new born" (3.3.104–5). In the second half of the play, we enter a stylized pastoral realm of harmony with nature and an ideologically aristocratic fantasy of a hidden princess whose nobility shines through her humble surroundings—itself undercut by a counter-discourse ennobling the rural characters and their natural lives, their sexuality, and, in the appealing figure of Autolycus, even their merry swindling. Sexuality and reproduction, rather than death, come to fore, especially in the celebrated lyric pastoral of Perdita's distribution of allegorical flowers, a comic-pastoral inversion of Ophelia's tragic and mad floral gifts.

And the dialogue shifts to telling variations on the ancient *topos* of art versus nature—art, to be sure, not in its post-Enlightenment sense of aesthetic symbolic productions, but more in the sense of its classical and early modern meaning as a skill, a set of humanly devised techniques that enable cultural productions and the transformation of nature—though all of the practices later termed "the fine arts" were and are also arts in this sense as well. The discussion ends with a capping and paradoxical resolution: "the art itself is nature..."

The play also, of course, veers from the relative realism of its opening to a much more stylized and "artificial" form of a fairytale plot ("like an old tale still" (5.5.56), the Third Gentleman explains of one more unlikely plot twist), manifesting an unlikely, Providence-revealing human world. The tragedy of the exposure of the infant Perdita becomes the occasion for the healing of the rift between Polixenes and Leontes through the marriage of their children—but unknown to each other as such (a device so convenient to the peculiar aesthetic effect of the tragicomic ending that Shakespeare had recourse to it again in *The Tempest*). The tragic death of the innocent and virtuous Hermione is simply canceled through an unexpected twist that the audience might take as miraculous; at least until closer attention to the text reveals, at the end, that it is simply a highly unlikely but naturalistic stratagem of the sainted Paulina. Perdita's adoptive family is rewarded with a carnivalesque inversion into gentility, and the unmarried Camillo finds a wife in the widow Paulina. All families are reconstituted, all wrong is made well, and a utopian, Providential conclusion is constructed without irony or much of any undercutting—except that of the ravages of time and the bittersweet memory of the death and suffering now being recompensed, however tardily.

Many of these unlikely, but highly emotional plot devices are narrated rather than staged, in order to end the play with one singular dramatic effect: the statue apparently coming to life. In this, more directly than in *Antony and Cleopatra*, a highly idealized version of the utopian aesthetic is allegorized in an ending that is highly meta-aesthetic and charged both with mourning, idealization, and something else beyond—a sense of wish fulfillment, of dreams come true constituting a secular, aesthetic version of the idea of a religious afterlife of reward for suffering.

Many readers and critics have been puzzled by the incorporation within the text of the name of the supposed sculptor of the statue (which turns out not to have been a statue), Guilio Romano. Some have suspected an elaborate in-joke, since Romano was the artist of some highly erotic book illustrations that circulated in Shakespeare's London. If so, the text itself provides us with no knowing wink or dig in the side. Romano is simply termed "that rare Italian master... who, had he himself eternity and could put breath into his work, would beguile nature of her custom, so perfectly is he her ape" (5.2.88–90). This idea of the artist's mission is reminiscent of some of the dialogue along similar lines in the opening scene of *Timon of Athens*, when the Poet and the Painter discuss an allegorical painting and comment on its skill and evocativeness. In the light of what we learn at the very end, however—that the statue at first appears to be a kind of Pygmalion, yet then is revealed to have been not an artifice come to life, but nature itself in the form of the living, breathing, and now aged Hermione—we are left to puzzle over the meaning of a celebration of artistic skill and art as a mimesis of nature that gives way to an idea of nature *tout court*. "The art itself is nature" (4.4.97), we remember. Nature itself has wrought that suspension of natural law that is the miraculous; only instead of a miracle, a feigned feigning, a mimesis of nature that skips mimesis in favor of the real thing, is enacted. Nevertheless, something about the aesthetic is affirmed in this complicated set of substitutions. Reversing the dictum of the sheep-shearing scene, nature itself turns out to be art rather than vice versa; that is, this all takes place in the fictional, aesthetic space of the stage, the sense of happiness and dreams come true not magic, but artificially wrought after all.

Even though the playtext asserts the subordination of human artifice to nature, the aesthetic nature of that text reverses the terms and affirms artifice—and art in something of the modern sense as well. As Adorno saw, it is a new category created in the differentiations of modernity, holding the place of the miraculous and the sacred: a vision projected within an artfully crafted work of poetic drama. In deconstructing the binary pair art and nature, the play affirms an idea of a symbolic practice that departs from realism by representing to us the fulfillment of natural and social longings—for love, for forgiveness and acceptance, for redemption—while it calls attention to the existing world's lack of those very qualities.

In leaving the world, the aesthetic underlines the difference between it and our desires, leaves us bitter and sweet, and shows

Shakespeare to have mastered the logic of much later aesthetic theory. In this play as in a few other moments of his works, he emerges as a voice of the idea of the modern aesthetic well *avant la lettre*, a practice then as now resisting easy accommodation to a reified world of power, commodification, and ideology. This is one important way in which Shakespeare continues to speak to the urgency of the present moment some 400 years after his texts began their long journey through time and space, a small beginning leading, as Terence Hawkes has put it in the Foreword to this volume, to a big splash indeed. He was an Icarus who flew as close to the sun as perhaps anyone, and we are still learning from and co-creating his meaning.

Notes

1. Theodor Adorno, *Negative Dialectics*, trans. E. B. Ashton (New York: Continuum, 1983), p. 3.
2. Francis Fukuyama, *The End of History and the Last Man* (New York: Maxwell Macmillan International, 1992).
3. Schmitt's linking of the aesthetic and Enlightenment liberalism—using, it should be noted, a somewhat truncated notion of the aesthetic—occurs at several points in Schmitt's writings, but is centrally discussed within a 1929 essay, Carl Schmitt, "The Age of Neutralizations and Depoliticizations," trans. Matthias Konzett and John P. McCormick, *Telos*, 96 (1993): 130–42. In perhaps covert form, it is an issue in his recently translated 1956 discussion of *Hamlet*; Carl Schmitt, *Hamlet or Hecuba: The Intrusion of Time into the Play*, trans. David Pan and Jennifer Fust (New York: Telos Press, 2009). For an excellent, clarifying analysis of how this notion fits into Schmitt's right-wing critique of nineteenth-century liberalism—and one that is also critical of Schmitt's chronology of the aesthetic—see Victoria Kahn, "Hamlet or Hecuba: Carl Schmitt's Decision," *Representations*, 83 (Summer 2003): 76–96. For a related argument along these lines in addition to Kahn, see Christopher Pye, "Against Schmitt: Law, Aesthetics, and Absolutism in Shakespeare's *Winter's Tale*," *South Atlantic Quarterly*, 108.1 (2009): 197–217.
4. Karl Marx, *Capital: A Critique of Political Economy*, vol. 3, ed. Frederick Engels (New York: International, 1967), p. 830; a translation that, however, does not use the term "reification" in its rendering of the German *Verdinglichung*, but the phrase "the conversion of social relations into things." On Marx's usage and the subsequent usage in the later Marxist tradition, see "reification," *A Dictionary of Marxist Thought*, ed. Tom Bottomore (Cambridge, MA: Harvard University Press, 1983).
5. Georg Lukács, *History and Class Consciousness: Studies in Marxist Dialectics*, trans. Rodney Livingstone (Cambridge, MA: MIT Press, 1971).

6. Jan Kott, *Shakespeare Our Contemporary* (London: Methuen, 1967). For a cogent analysis of Kott's borrowings from Lukács on reification, see Madalina Nicolaescu, "Kott in the East," in *Great Shakespeareans: Volume 13: Empson, Wilson Knight, Barber, and Kott*, ed. Hugh Grady (London: Continuum, 2012), pp. 131–53.
7. I developed the connection of Foucault to Lukács' notion of reification and related theories in Hugh Grady, *Shakespeare's Universal Wolf: Studies in Early Modern Reification* (Oxford: Clarendon Press, 1996), pp. 47–51.
8. Hugh Grady, *Shakespeare, Machiavelli, and Montaigne: Power and Subjectivity from "Richard II" to "Hamlet"* (Oxford: Oxford University Press, 2002).
9. Hugh Grady, "The End of Shakespeare's Machiavellian Moment: *Julius Caesar*, Shakespeare's Historiography, and Dramatic Form," in *Shakespeare and Renaissance Literary Theories: Anglo-Italian Transactions*, ed. Michele Marrapodi (Surrey: Ashgate, 2011), pp. 119–36.
10. William Shakespeare, *Antony and Cleopatra*, *The Norton Shakespeare*, 2nd edn., ed. Steven Greenblatt et al. (New York: Norton, 2008), 2.7, pp. 70–77. All subsequent quotations from Shakespeare are from the same edition and are given parenthetically in the text.
11. G. Wilson Knight, *The Imperial Theme: Further Interpretations of Shakespeare's Tragedies* (New York: Barnes and Noble, 1931), pp. 199–262.
12. Philippe Ariès, *Western Attitudes toward Death: From the Middle Ages to the Present*, trans. Patricia M. Ranum (Baltimore, MD: Johns Hopkins University Press, 1974), pp. 56–8.
13. Hugh Grady, *Shakespeare and Impure Aesthetics*, Cambridge: Cambridge University Press, 2009), pp. 193–224.
14. Wallace Stevens, "Sunday Morning," in Richard Ellman and Robert O'Clair, eds., *Modern Poems: A Norton Introduction*, 2nd edn. (New York: Norton: 1989), pp. 150–53; V: 3–13.
15. Hanna Segal, "A Psychoanalytic Approach to Aesthetics," in her *The Work of Hanna Segal: A Kleinian Approach to Clinical Practice* (New York: Jason Aronson, 1981), pp. 185–206.
16. Theodor Adorno, *Aesthetic Theory*, ed. Gretel Adorno and Rolf Tiedemann, trans. Robert Hullot-Kentor (Minneapolis: University of Minnesota Press, 1997); for a summary of these themes, see Grady, *Shakespeare and Impure Aesthetics*, pp. 22–35.
17. I made several of these points about the parallels of these two plays in Grady, *Shakespeare's Impure Aesthetics*, p. 203.
18. Ernst Bloch, "Happy End, Seen Through & Yet Still Defended," in his *The Principle of Hope*, vol. 1, trans. Neville Plaice et al. (Oxford: Blackwell, 1986), pp. 441–7. My thanks to Kiernan Ryan for his help in locating this citation.
19. Jean Howard, Introduction to *Antony and Cleopatra*, *The Norton Shakespeare*, p. 2876.

9
The Hour is Unknown: *Julius Caesar*, et cetera

Mark Robson

> And are etceteras nothings? —*2 Henry 4* (2.4.181)

I

There is a line in Shakespeare's *Julius Caesar* that I have found funny–both amusing and peculiar, that is–for a long time now. *Julius Caesar* was the first Shakespeare play I read at school, so the humor I found in it was one that appealed to a certain teenage cynicism. The line appears in a passage in which Shakespeare chooses very deliberately to depart from his source in North's translation of Plutarch's *Lives of the Romans*, giving us a line that, as Hamlet might have put it, puzzles the will. In the so-called Orchard scene, having been given a paper that has been found by his servant, Brutus begins to read it aloud:

Brutus, thou sleep'st. Awake and see thyself!
Shall Rome, et cetera. Speak, strike, redress! (2.1.4–5)[1]

Brutus continues, suggesting that he must piece out what this "et cetera" means. However, there is an ambiguity perhaps in his phrasing: "Thus must I piece it out." This could be a musing ("so, now I have to work out what this means"). But it seems more likely that the "Thus" is more emphatic ("it has to mean *this*"), since Brutus tells us he has already received several other letters that said more or less the same thing. The meaning of *et cetera* in this instance is already known.

Even if Brutus seems to know what the line means, this is still distinctly odd. Arthur Humphreys, the editor of the Oxford Shakespeare edition, notes of this line, with perhaps a touch of exasperation: "Why Shakespeare preferred this cryptic hint to the undisguised instigations in Plutarch is not clear." The most recent Cambridge editor of the play gives no note at all for the line.[2] When I was 14 I knew exactly what *et cetera* meant: boredom. Either Shakespeare or Brutus could not be bothered either to write or to read whatever came between "Shall Rome" and "Speak." Read in this way, modern British and US usage might replace *et cetera* with *blah blah blah*. "Shall Rome" then becomes the opening of a speech that is too familiar in its sentiment or expression to be worth spelling out, tired, trivial, trite. In other words, it is all too obvious what should follow, and that is precisely what makes it uninteresting.

There are other possibilities, perhaps. For example, this curious line may have originated as the mark of a forgetting, a lapse in which someone (Shakespeare? A scribe? The editors of the Folio?) marked the beginning of a speech with every intention of coming back to it and filling in the intervening lines, with "Speak" marking the end of the passage to be inserted. And then whoever it was forgot to come back and replace the *et cetera* with the "real" lines, forgetting also then to tidy up Brutus' piecing out. *Et cetera* might then be read as an accidental evil. Yet, maybe the fact that *et cetera* scans makes it more likely that it would have been missed, or maybe it simply makes it more mysterious, as if *et cetera* were not an accident at all but the speech as it was "intended" to be.

What is worth pausing over is the fact that what is used as the filler should be *et cetera* at all. As the OED tells us, the Latin origin brings together *et* "and" and "the rest," from *cēterus*, "the other." The first definition is:

> 1. As phrase: And the rest, and so forth, and so on (cf. Gr. καὶ τὰ λοιπά, Ger. *und so weiter*), indicating that the statement refers not only to the things enumerated, but to others which may be inferred from analogy. Occasionally used when the conclusion of a quotation, a current formula of politeness, or the like, is omitted as being well known to the reader....

What *et cetera* most commonly marks, then, is precisely the already known, even as it points toward that which is not present, or that which is present but only in the form of analogy. (The German *so weiter* carries a stronger sense of distance, of spacing, of further and farther, of continuing on as traveling.) *Et cetera* thus does something odd: it makes us aware of what is not included, of the rest, of the other, it heightens a sense that there has been an omission, but in prompting this awareness it stresses not difference but similitude, likeness, agreement, and the analogue. In logic, analogy is the process of reasoning from parallel cases or from the assumption that if some attributes of things are similar, then other attributes will be, too (*OED*, "analogy," 7b). *Et cetera* thus invites comparison ("there is more to be added here, we are omitting something"), but only to forestall it ("whatever might be added is not substantially different from what is already here, so it can safely be omitted"). (It is tempting to relate this *et cetera* to "Et tu Brute?")

Et cetera, then, in all its splendid inconsequentiality, opens on to a series of questions with greater import for the reading of this play, and of Shakespeare more widely.

II

Much, perhaps the majority, of Shakespeare criticism is open to description as a series of meditations on "Shakespeare and..." There are innumerable comparisons of Shakespeare and his contemporaries, as well as with a dazzling parade of other writers, both earlier and later.[3] There are thematic or topical versions of the same critical pattern (most of the titles in the Oxford Shakespeare Topics series take precisely this format, for example). At its simplest, the project of historicisms old and new is one of asserting a relation between some aspect of Shakespeare's texts and something thought to be proper to the period in which they originated, and many such projects remain at that level of complexity. Transhistorical or comparative studies set for themselves the task of setting Shakespeare at some other point or elsewhere. The word "and" does not need to appear as itself for the same logic to be at work: "Shakespeare in...," "Shakespeare for...," "Shakespeare without...," and so on, are all variants that make the same claim for relation between Shakespeare and something other. Shakespeare's own texts raise the problematic that all such critical modes must face; namely, how to know that something is not being "belied" with "false compare"?

Yet, defining this something other that may act as grist for the comparative mill is also not such an obvious task, in part because

"Shakespeare" has come to stand in for so many things: there is Shakespeare the historical human being (but then there are biographical difficulties and debates), Shakespeare the writer (but also the authorship controversy), Shakespeare the cultural icon (with positive and negative assessments of that role), Shakespeare as shorthand for a body of texts (which much textual scholarship is devoted to complicating), *et cetera*. Divided by forms of difference that appear from "within" Shakespeare as much as between Shakespeare and some putative "outside," "Shakespeare and..." doubles such questions of identity and identification. The very openness of such chains of association and dissociation, of such concatenations, to future determinations (and indeterminacies) is marked by a certain logic of the *et cetera*.

In the analysis of the *et cetera* that comes about by virtue of a response to a series of essays that appear under the name of "Deconstruction and...," Jacques Derrida wonders about all the *and*s, beginning with those marked—that is, more or less explicit—but then quickly adding:

> But there are so many others, between all the words, more clearly between some than between others, and sometimes even within [*au-dedans*] certain words. *Etcetera*, for example.... And each writer, and each poet, and each orator, and each speaking subject, even each proposition can put to work a different "and," different as to its modality, as to its number, and sometimes to say the same "thing," at least to say what realists in a hurry would call the same "thing," where we should have to distinguish at least between thing, object, sense and meaning [*sens et signification*], etc. And do so precisely [*justement*] by appropriate reductions.[4]

To "end" that list on the *and* with the openness of another *et cetera*, and then to follow that by opening the next sentence with an "and," is to mark the problem in an exemplary fashion. Derrida similarly stresses the hovering between difference and sameness, the unknown and the (too) known, that marks *et cetera*'s iterations.

And what is also peculiar in Derrida's taking on of the *et cetera* is its relation to theatre, and especially to Shakespeare's plays. As Derrida notes in a footnote to "Et cetera," this problematic of the "and" already presents itself in his essay "Aphorism Countertime."[5] In that earlier essay, Derrida reads the specificity of the conjunction Romeo *and* Juliet, remarking in particular the staging of that concatenation of proper names. Without such naming of the context for an "and" by the use of proper names, it is always potentially empty. The difficulty, as Derrida suggests, lies in the theatricality of the *and* itself:

> Romeo *and* Juliet, the conjunction of two desires that are aphoristic but held together [*tenu ensemble*], maintained in the dislocated now [*maintenus dans le maintenant disloqué*] of a love or a promise. A promise in their name, but across and beyond their given name, the promise of *another name*, its request rather: "O be some other name..." (II. ii. 42). The *and* of this conjunction, the theater of this "and," has often been presented, represented as the scene of a fortuitous contretemps, of aleatory anachrony.[6]

It is the power of the "and" that holds and holds open a co-presence–fundamentally theatrical in appearance–with that which is present held in a spatio-temporal here *and* now (*tenu... maintenus... maintenant*), always already structured by *différance*. In the context of our discussion here, what is perhaps most intriguing is the relationship between this theatricality of the "and" and the dislocation of the "now." In the reading of *Romeo and Juliet* that Derrida stages in "Aphorism Countertime," the countertime of the contretemps hinges on the simultaneity of the *and*; that is, it depends on the ability of time to be something other than singular. It is this that opens up the possibility of a consciousness of anachrony, in which anachronism is not something to be avoided.[7] After Derrida, then, anachronism is not what it used to be.

III

The urgency of "now" is felt in several of Shakespeare's plays, but perhaps never so pressingly as in *Julius Caesar*. The word "now" appears over 60 times in this play, which is not in itself so unusual, according to concordances. Some of those uses are relatively light in meaning (inceptions such "Now, Cinna...," "How now...," "What now...," and so on), but most seem designed to mark awareness of the moment, to draw attention to a point in time; that is, to remark on the present as in need of attention.[8] The urgency comes from the political situation, a moment of war and its aftermath, conspiracy and battle, in which the initiative is to be seized moment by moment and in which speed (of judgment, of decision, of action, and so on) is demanded.

(But when is "now"? As Hamlet defines as he wonders, defining wonderfully, "If it be now, 'tis not to come. If it be not to come, it will be now. If it be not now, yet it will come" [5.2.165]. It is not obvious that this entirely clarifies the issue.)[9]

Is it an irony, then, that this is also the play that contains the most famous instance of Shakespearean anachronism? Indeed, I remember distinctly learning the word anachronism at school as we read through this play. The key anachronistic element is the striking clock, of course, and this has often been thought of as a lapse, a slip in Shakespeare's attention, or else as a sign that early modern historiographers are not concerned with accuracy as modern historians would understand it. However, there is a way of thinking about this anachronism as an integral part of the play's structure. As Marjorie Garber has proposed:

> The presence of a modern clock in Caesar's Rome abruptly reminds the audience of the double time period in which the play is set. Not only a history of the classical past, it is also a story of the present day. The supposed anachronism of the striking clock abruptly jars the audience from any complacency it may be feeling about the difference between "then" and "now."[10]

Read in this way, appreciation of anachronism becomes a vital critical tool, and it is encouraging that it is becoming more readily accepted within contemporary Shakespeare criticism.[11]

Such pointing to the urgency of the moment begins in the first scene. Wounded by the holiday antics of the workers, Marullus recalls the name of Pompey, and recalls as well their celebrations "many a time and oft," and then falls to the distinct rhetorical patterning that will become so much a feature of the play:

> And do you now put on your best attire?
> And do you now cull out a holiday?
> And do you now strew flowers in his way
> That comes in triumph over Pompey's blood?
> Be gone! (1.1.48–52)

The anaphoric stress on "And... now" makes clear the need for comparison, for the framing of that now against past and future times in order to put it in perspective, while also endowing that with which the comparison is made with a certain fixity, since it is the repeated anchor for a series of actions "now." Marullus speaks in order to connect passion to persuasion, to make his anger at what he perceives as the ingratitude of the workers take on a force that will have effects; namely, the reinterpretation of the return of Caesar by reference to a past that is figured as unassailable in its quality.

The play opens, then, with this moment of dissensus. At stake is a clash between different views of the world that inhabit the same space and time, but where dissensus is marked as a difference in relation to time and to the now. To reinforce the point, Flavius then gives instructions that the "images" of Caesar be "disrobed," despite Marullus' reminder that it is the feast of Lupercal. Two things may be immediately noted: first, that the images in question may not themselves be removed; second, that they are open to a series of competing recontextualizations and reinterpretations, political, religious, or otherwise. There seems to be no distinction in Flavius' mind between interpreting the world and changing it; or rather, what he recognizes is the inextricability of the aesthetic and the political at the level of perception (*aisthesis*). While this might be read in quasi-Benjaminian terms as an aestheticization of politics, in which the image becomes another manifestation of the victory parades of the powerful such that there is a perceptible dialectic of civilization and barbarism at work in and through the images and objects displayed, it might also be thought along lines closer to those offered by Jacques Rancière's conception of the politics of aesthetics as the partition of the sensible.[12]

Rancière's understanding of the relation between the aesthetic and the political as both partaking of a logic of partition in which people, objects, practices, discourses, and modes of speaking are given a place within a social structure—and are thereby accounted for or taken into account (or designated as of no account)—means that for him no aestheticization of politics is either necessary or possible, just as politics need not be "added" to aesthetics since it was always already "there." No artwork appears, for Rancière, without being accompanied both by a certain understanding of "art" and its functions, and by a certain form of collective and individual life that is bound up with the presuppositions and positions relating to those art practices.[13] However, rather than rendering a social structure monolithic, it is precisely at the level of perception and of the "sensible" that forms of dissensus and disagreement become possible and necessary, and open up the regimes of art and the image to transformation. It is precisely such arguments over the meaning of an image or object–and thus the structures that make them meaningful or tell others what these things mean–that constitute politics. To offer a redescription of the world is potentially to change it, and one of the purposes of an attention to history and the history of art becomes the recognition of moments at which other possibilities become visible, making apparent both that the past might have been other than it appears to have been and that there is no historical necessity dictating the shape of the future. In Rancière's recent work, this is frequently conceptualized as competing temporalities occupying a "single" moment.

IV

To go all too quickly and telegraphically, early modern studies has become divided between those who wish to testify to the timeless qualities of Shakespeare's works (certain modes of humanism), those who view it as firmly embedded in the moment of its production and reproduction (historicisms old and new), and those who wish to stress its ability to free itself of those origins and to function in current and future contexts (Presentism, post-humanism, deconstruction, *et cetera*).[14] There are, of course, points of intersection between these groupings, and certain thematic issues stemming from the plays also unite them. As Hugh Grady proposes, for example, "the many claims for the timelessness of artworks–a timelessness that will always turn out to depend on the 'now' in which the artwork is constituted–have their moment of truth in this fascination of art with these elemental human ultimates [sex and death]."[15] As Grady goes on to suggest through a reading of *Romeo and Juliet*, Shakespeare's sense of the aesthetic is precisely articulated in terms of a relation between the tragedy of individual death and the pleasure of artistic immortality. This "impure" aesthetic–in which artworks are in a complex relation, both positive and negative, to a world in which desires are repressed and disappointed, only to find expression in the aesthetic experience that acts as their place-holder–allows Grady to remain attentive to "the play's strong assertion of the reality of *other possibilities*... its status as *other* than reality, its creation of a counterfactual space in which we can vicariously experience and clarify our desires and needs."[16]

In *Julius Caesar*, it is the fascination with death rather than sex that dominates, and in particular the relationship between death and time.[17] While it is common to think about death in relation to finitude, mortality, the threat of loss, and so on, in *Julius Caesar* temporal awareness is also what prompts death, primarily through murder and suicide. This is most obviously conveyed as a relation between time and death in which the emphasis is placed on a tension or trembling between predictability and unpredictability. As Casca puts it in a phrase that inscribes death at the heart of a life apprehended as apprehension: "Why, he that cuts off twenty years of life / Cuts off so many years of fearing death" (3.1.101–2). The frequent invocation of omens, portents, dreams, soothsaying, and so on marks a desire to master the future that is repeatedly frustrated. The oscillation between the known and the unknown—for characters and for the audience—takes on a particular political charge in the context of the play's staging of debates over sovereignty, legitimacy, and the mechanics of power (violence, war, rhetoric, and so on). As Hannu Poutiainen has recently argued, the murder of Caesar fulfills an apotropaic function, warding off a future evil that has already marked the present, and read in this way that death becomes an attempt to predict and control the future.[18] This is only one possibility suggested by the play, and other modes of future-oriented thinking might include:

1. Prophecy, soothsaying, portents, augury, dreams, and divinations.
2. Invocation of Fate, fortune, destiny, or the gods.
3. Desiring and wishing. At 3.3.259, for example, Antony speaks of Octavius' appearance in the city as being the answer to his wish.
4. Language: a) Rhetorical speeches, including set-piece attempts to persuade and thus to prompt a certain course of events; b) written texts that have a similar purpose, including the notes left in Brutus' house and garden, but also the warning of Artemidorus and Caesar's will; c) oaths, promises, curses, and other performative utterances.

5. Suicide and other forms of death.
6. Imagination and fear.
7. Honor, reputation, and the future in the minds of others.
8. The ghost.
9. Et cetera.

What I want to suggest is that the numerous strategies that characters and the play offer for controlling—or failing to control—the future may be folded back onto a consideration of the structural and formal openness of Shakespearean drama.

As I have remarked elsewhere, there is within Shakespeare's texts an aesthetics of strangeness; that is, an estranging of the aesthetic. This is often hinged around an interpenetration of the "content" of the texts—in which, for example, characters remark on something as strange—and a process of formal estrangement, in which the presentation of that content is itself strange, odd, unsettling, uncanny, and this structure often manifests itself as a concern with the unknown, and more especially with a troubling of the borders between the known and the unknown.

In *Julius Caesar*, the sense of a division between a former moment marked by the relative status of Caesar and the public's attitude toward him and the "now" of the play's action is repeated in the second scene, when we are introduced to Brutus. What we are given to know of Brutus in this initial scene is tied to questions of the knowability of the present. As Cassius remarks:

> Brutus, I do observe you now of late;
> I have not from your eyes that gentleness
> And show of love as I was wont to have.
> You bear too stubborn and too strange a hand
> Over your friend that loves you. (1.2.32–6)

It is hard not to stumble over that locution "now of late." The present-tense "do" suggests a present observation, but it is a present now that the "of late" dilates to force the comparison of past and present: "now of late" is not quite "now." For Cassius, this perceived alteration in Brutus makes him strange. Brutus responds by proposing that the difference that Cassius perceives is not one that is best thought of as indicative of a temporal relation to the world, but instead as marking a war taking place within him, what we might think of as a moment of internal dissensus.

For Cassius, this explanation is evidence of Brutus' misperception. Cassius asks Brutus if he can see his own face:

> BRUTUS
> >   No, Cassius; for the eye sees not itself
> >   But by reflection, by some other things.
> CASSIUS
> >   'Tis just;
> >   And it is very much lamented, Brutus,
> >   That you have no such mirrors as will turn
> >   Your hidden worthiness into your eye,
> >   That you might see your shadow. I have heard
> >   Where many of the best respect in Rome–
> >   Except immortal Caesar–speaking of Brutus,
> >   And groaning underneath this age's yoke,
> >   Have wished that noble Brutus had his eyes.
> BRUTUS
> >   Into what dangers would you lead me, Cassius,
> >   That you would have me seek into myself
> >   For that which is not in me?
> CASSIUS
> >   Therefore, good Brutus, be prepared to hear.
> >   And since you know you cannot see yourself
> >   So well as by reflection, I your glass,
> >   Will modestly discover to yourself
> >   That of yourself which you yet know not of.
> >   (1.2.52–70)

The argument is effectively the same as that which has been made about the status of the present time. Perception is always a matter of relation, and the thing in itself can only be perceived by its difference from or similarity to "some other things." There is some ambiguity here, since it is not wholly clear whether Brutus is suggesting that the eye sees itself as an object by reflection, as if in a mirror, or whether he is, rather, using "eye" to stand in for the act of seeing, and thus to indicate visual perception as a capacity of the eye that the eye cannot itself see. Again, a difference is opened between, on the one hand, knowledge of the thing and its qualities, in which it is the status of the object that is at stake, and, on the other, that faculty by which things are known, in which it is the faculty itself that comes into question. This might be expressed as the difference between seeing the truth and seeing truly, but this difference is always haunted by the suspicion that you cannot have one without the other and that the space between the two is impossible to sustain. How could one see the truth without seeing truly? How could true sight exist without being able to say that what one sees is the truth of the object seen? And which notion of truth is at work in either case, *adequatio* (correspondence of perception and object) or *aletheia* (unveiling or, more literally, unforgetting, with all of its quasi-platonic resonances of recognizing a truth already known)?

This leads us into a problem in terms of what to make of Cassius' speech. The concluding suggestion that many wish that "Brutus had his eyes" makes apparent the aesthetic stakes of this political moment, and vice versa; that is, the significance of perception (in a strong sense, as *aisthesis*) to this or any other form of politics. In his note to this line, Humphreys offers two alternatives for characterizing this wish: that Brutus would see things as they stand, or that he would see things as an anti-Caesarian does. The first might be a claim to be beyond ideology, and thus that only those subjected to Caesar fail to see the true nature of the world. The second might be a claim that there is only ideology–thinking of that term here strictly in terms of the image and of sight–but that, while competing ideologies exist, one perspective is superior or at least preferable to any other. Cassius certainly appears to offer himself in the role of the one who can demystify, the one supposed to know, adopting a position that is all too conventionally at once theological, philosophical, and political: it is Cassius who can reveal the hidden, but this hidden is thought of as a shadow (the quasi-platonism is obvious). Cassius wishes to stand in the place of the "other thing" necessary for reflection, but not as a passive object; Cassius divides the identity of Brutus into what he knows of himself and what is known of him by others. Cassius then goes on to vouchsafe this opinion by appealing to what Brutus already knows of him, of his character. So there is a further fold to this matter of perception: Brutus is able to see the truth of Cassius' identity, and thus he must accept Cassius' version of his own. Cassius becomes the mirroring other thing.

Shakespeare likes nothing better than to tell his characters–and by extension the audience–that what he, she, or they can see is not what it appears to be. So while the passage on the eye's inability to see itself may in this instance be prompted by a reading of Sir John Davies's 1599 *Nosce Teipsum*, as is often noted, the idea is one that seems to have had a more than local resonance. From the injunction to "look awry" in *Richard II* to Othello's desire for "ocular proof," and, further, to the synaesthetic complications of looking with ears and hearing with eyes in *King Lear* and the sonnets, these plays present signs and wonders while repeatedly telling us not to suspend our disbelief.[19]

V

There is a suggestion that the openness of things, images, objects, practices, and so on to reinterpretation may not be entirely comforting in its effects. As Cicero proposes, this susceptibility to hermeneutic violence is related to the sense of the age's strangeness. Accepting that there have been numerous seemingly supernatural sightings and odd events, Cicero wonders nonetheless what interpretive work remains to be done:

> Indeed it is a strange-disposèd time.
> But men may construe things after their fashion,
> Clean from the purpose of the things themselves. (1.3.33–5)

Even if it may be conceded that the time is inclined to strangeness, the meaning of the portents is not simply manifest. The problem here lies in the relation between construal and purpose: while construal is evidently a form of construction, a making that always seems poetic or fictional, this comes into conflict with what Cicero sees as an originary form of construction that he calls purpose; that is, with a sense of architectonic intention. That this may be a matter of "fashion" only highlights this element of invention (fashion deriving from the Latin *facĕre*, to make). Things seem to possess purpose such that it is possible for that purpose to be discerned beyond the interpretation given according to fashion, but the very point of strangeness is that it comes to interrupt the frameworks by which it would be judged. As the *OED* tells us, the Latin root of "strange" in *extrāneus* makes it a marker of foreignness or alienness, of the external, of the outside. The senses that it takes on of rarity, unfamiliarity, of singularity and the unknown, stem from the fact that it refers to that which does not belong, and thus for which there is no experience by which it may be thought. The strange marks the difference between something that is in a place but not "of" it and that which is effectively unremarkable, or unmarked.[20]

The strange is not a question of essence but of interpretation, then. What this means is that while it is possible for two people to admit that something is strange, what they then make of this strangeness is contingent. This is not a *sensus communis*, even if what is perceived is shared, but rather the opening to dissensus and disagreement: a space widens within *common sense*, such that what is sensed is common, but the sense that is made of it is not. As Cassius points out, the effects of the wondrously odd may be a kind of denaturing or a revelation of the one who perceives, a making visible of the subject then as much as the object:

> You are dull, Casca, and those sparks of life
> That should be in a Roman you do want,
> Or else you use not. You look pale, and gaze,
> And put on fear, and cast yourself in wonder,
> To see the strange impatience of the heavens.
> But if you would consider the true cause
> Why all these fires, why all these gliding ghosts,
> Why birds and beasts, from quality and kind,
> Why old men, fools, and children calculate,
> Why all these things change from their ordinance,
> Their natures and preformèd faculties,
> To monstrous quality, why, you shall find
> That heaven hath infused them with these spirits
> To make them instruments of fear and warning
> Unto some monstrous state.
> Now could I, Casca, name to thee a man
> Most like this dreadful night,
> That thunders, lightens, opens graves, and roars
> As doth the lion in the Capitol–
> A man no mightier than thyself or me
> In personal action, yet prodigious grown
> And fearful, as these strange eruptions are. (1.3.57–78)

Cassius begins by doubting the "Roman" qualities of Casca: does he not possess them or simply not use them? The effect of strangeness is to produce fear and wonder, but Cassius attributes this to an inability to work out the true cause (what has just been discussed as the "purpose") of the strange events. Cassius then slips into rhetorical mode, attempting to persuade with the force of a repeated (and again anaphoric) "Why?" There is a slide from one use of "monstrous" and of "fear" to the next, and in the intervening lines there is a change in tense that allows for a change in signification. These portents are a vision of the future, they are prodigies of the prodigious Caesar, a future already inscribed in the present but not inevitably so. The strangeness of the times means that the future refuses to remain safely at a distance, but keeps bleeding into the present moment, casting a shadow over events, bestriding them like a colossus.

Caesar certainly possesses the Roman qualities that Cassius values more firmly than Casca. Caesar expresses the same sense of the relation between death, life, and fear to which Casca gives voice, but gives it a distinct inflection by projecting it on to others:

> Cowards die many times before their deaths;
> The valiant never taste of death but once.
> Of all the wonders that I yet have heard,
> It seems to me most strange that men should fear,
> Seeing that death, a necessary end,
> Will come when it will come. (2.2.32–7)

The problem for many of the characters lies precisely in this idea that death will come when it will come, however beautifully the single syllables round out that resolution as the last line ends as it begins. That "will" seems a little imprecise, and what it opens up is the chance to see that there are two distinct ways of thinking about the future. One is to see it as predictable; that is, to see the future as a definite product of features already apparent and readable in the present. Even if we are able to recognize certain contingencies or accidents that may interfere with our prediction, we are still happy to rely on the pattern of this predictability. This is the kind of thinking that we see in Casca's reply to Brutus' invitation to dine with him the next evening: "Ay, if I be alive, and your mind hold, and your dinner worth the eating" (1.2.288–9). It is also the logic used by Cassius to persuade others of the necessity of Caesar's death.

However, there is also a more troubling because more open sense of the future. This can be seen in phrases such as "you go to do you know not what" (3.2.228, see also 2.1.334). This opening to the accident and to the contretemps is not something that unhinges the drama, but is instead what motivates it by exposing it to the unknown and the unpredictable, even if it remains structurally necessary that this future may be monstrous (as Derrida always stressed). The effect is disquieting, especially for those who would reduce political action to a form of instrumentality, and Brutus expresses it in the following way:

> O that a man might know
> The end of this day's business ere it come!
> But it sufficeth that the day will end,
> And then the end is known. (5.1.123–6)

VI

There is a mode of death that runs counter to such intimations of mortality or fear of finitude, and it is one that might also be thought of in terms of a relation to time, and more particularly as a claim on the future. Suicide is used by Shakespeare with startling frequency across his work, and in *Julius Caesar* it presents itself in a culminating sequence that is never far from the play's meditation on strangeness.[21] The play offers at least five examples of suicide as action or topic of contemplation, most obviously in the cases of Brutus, Cassius, Titinius, and Portia (the other is Brutus' reflection on Cato). Suicide, here as elsewhere, is frequently prompted by a sense that the future is known, and those who desire death see it as an escape, whether from pain, punishment, dishonor, grief, or some other foreseen eventuality (Othello, Antony, Cleopatra, Gloucester, Lucrece, Romeo, Juliet, et cetera, are the obvious examples).

One of the most curious versions of this logic comes in the death of Portia in *Julius Caesar*. The play marks the death explicitly as strange:

MESSALA
  Had you your letters from your wife, my lord?

> BRUTUS
> No, Messala.
> MESSALA
> Nor nothing in your letters writ of her?
> BRUTUS
> Nothing, Messala.
> MESSALA
> That, methinks, is strange.
> BRUTUS
> Why ask you? Hear you aught of her in yours?
> MESSALA
> No, my lord.
> BRUTUS
> Now, as you are a Roman, tell me true.
> MESSALA
> Then like a Roman bear the truth I tell,
> For certain she is dead, and by strange manner.
> BRUTUS
> Why, farewell, Portia. We must die, Messala.
> With meditating that she must die once,
> I have the patience to endure it now. (4.2.231–42)

Messala finds two things that demand he use the word "strange" here: the "manner" of Portia's death and the fact that Brutus is seemingly not aware of it. Earlier in the same scene, we have seen that Brutus already knew of Portia's death (and this repetition of the news, as well as the flatness and rapidity of Brutus' reaction to the second telling, has led some to speculate that there are signs of revision in the text here). To swallow fire, as Portia reportedly does, is indeed a strange way to die, but Shakespeare is doing no more than follow his sources. As Humphreys, following Kittredge, notes, however, this has frequently been thought improbable, and that unbelievable aspect is largely to do with the explanation for the death, given by Brutus as "impatience." Suicide is a mode of dying that has always been peculiarly resistant to interpretation, no doubt because it so obviously demands interpretation by those who live on.[22]

Brutus' own death has been predicted in the encounter with the Ghost of Caesar, and the Ghost is another character who claims to know the future. Here Shakespeare would have found another incidence of strangeness in North's version, which tells us that Brutus "saw a wonderful strange and monstrous shape of a body coming towards him, and never said a word."[23] "Strange" and "monstrous" resonate with the other portents, and this might lead us to think that just as they anticipated the death of Caesar, so this anticipates another death that must be read as a form of repetition. Poutiainen offers an intriguing suggestion:

> The apotropaic murder of Caesar begets the suicide of Brutus; the murder gives birth to a self-murder that is supposed to annul and settle the first murder. Thus the suicide of Brutus is not–or, at least, not uniquely–the tragic end of a fallen hero. On the contrary: it is, by force of an autoimmune after-effect, *an autoapotropaic act against the first apotropaic act*. The first apotropaic generates an *antiapotropaic*, which, as *autoapotropaic*, may annul its origin only by repeating it and hence *cannot* annul it.[24]

The structure here is familiar: difference and sameness meet, fatally, in the attempt to assert one over the other. The desire to make the future different is only possible by an act that cannot do other than repeat and thus revive precisely the structure it is attempting to end. In the case of Brutus, the desire to leave this world must encounter the problem of the Ghost: life and death, past, present, and future, now and another moment cannot be held apart or simply opposed, no matter with what violence.

VII

"What is't o'clock?" The question is so crucial to the play that it is asked twice (2.2.114 and 2.4.23). It is this concern for knowing when "now" is that opens the way to anachronism, both "in" the play and in the theatre. In the Orchard scene with which we began, Brutus begins by confessing that he has no idea how near it is to day. Soon he will say that he cannot remember whether or not tomorrow is the Ides of March.

This might be read as designed to produce a certain impression of Brutus' character, but it may also have an emblematic weight: the play's reproducibility will always mean that it is open to iterations that cannot be programmed and that cannot have been part of any originating purpose. And yet, Shakespeare's texts always demonstrate that curiously doubled awareness of death and survival, of both their finite incarnations and their ability to "live" beyond them. In *Julius Caesar*, this can be seen in the neatly meta-theatrical moment in which the events of the conspiracy are foreseen as open to repetition:

> How many ages hence
> Shall this our lofty scene be acted over
> In states unborn and accents yet unknown! (3.1.111–13)

Shakespeare's scene is a repetition, a reworking of sources (in Plutarch and others) that will prompt its own revisions and restagings. And the figure for this structure is both spatial and temporal, the unborn and the unknown. Humphreys offers two notable glosses for this speech. One comes from Samuel Daniel's 1599 *Musophilus*, in which he ponders the future of English poetry, wondering "to what strange shores / This gain of our best glory shall be sent." The other comes from M. W. MacCullum's *Shakespeare's Roman Plays and their Background* (1910): "What a strange effect these words are apt to produce...! ... We experience a kind of vertigo, in which we cannot distinguish the real and the illusory, and yet are conscious of both in their highest potence." In considering the strange shores to which poetry may travel, Shakespeare produces an effect that is itself strange, uncanny, marked by and marking the aesthetic's other possibilities, yet unknown.

Another name for this unknown might be "et cetera." The precise "content" of this phrase cannot be known. Or else it was always already known. It hovers between the unreadable and the too-well-known-to-require-reading, and is thus at once an opening to a form of dissensual history, a contretemps, in which the past reveals its potential to be and to have been something other than that which is "known" about it, and also, at the same time, an opening to a future that must possess the capacity to present aspects that are both predictable and unforeseeable, knowable and unknowable. Yet, the troubling aspects of that sentence come in the least-freighted words: "at once," "at the same time," all the difficulty lies there. When and where, for Shakespeare, might this time be located? The appearance or apparition of "et cetera" in *Julius Caesar* might, then, be taken to emblematize the structure of Shakespeare's textual legacies. There is more to this than a matter of literary and theatrical interpretation: in such strange-disposèd times as our own, in which past and future are ritually invoked to justify action in the present, often action of the most brutal and violent kind ("Speak, strike, redress!"), and often accompanied by a coercive, consensual understanding of those past and future moments, that knowledge used in turn to identify and identify with and against others, real and imagined, projected and desired, the force of those textual legacies to interrupt that consensual violence has never been stranger–and never been more urgent– than "now."

Notes

1. All quotations from the play will be taken from *Julius Caesar*, ed. Arthur Humphreys (Oxford: Oxford University Press, 1984).
2. William Shakespeare, *Julius Caesar*, ed. Marvin Spevack (Cambridge: Cambridge University Press, 2004).
3. See Mark Robson, "Jonson and Shakespeare," in *Ben Jonson in Context*, ed. Julie Sanders (Cambridge: Cambridge University Press, 2010), pp. 57–64, which pursues some of these ideas more fully.
4. Jacques Derrida, "Et Cetera... (and so on, und so weiter, and so forth, et ainsi de suite, und so überall, etc.)," in *Jacques Derrida* (Paris: L'Herne, 2004), pp. 21–34; 24; trans. Geoffrey Bennington with same title, in *Deconstructions: A User's Guide*, ed. Nicholas Royle (Basingstoke: Palgrave, 2000), pp. 282–305; 287–88 (trans. sl. mod.).
5. "L'aphorisme à contretemps," in *Psyché: Inventions de l'autre*, 2 vols (Paris: Galilée, 2003), 2: 131–44;"Aphorism Countertime," trans. Nicholas Royle, in *Psyche: Inventions of the Other*, ed. Peggy Kamuf and Elizabeth Rottenberg, 2 vols (Stanford, CA: Stanford University Press, 2008), 2: 127–42.
6. Derrida, "L'aphorisme à contretemps," p. 133; "Aphorism Countertime," p. 130.
7. On the status of anachrony in Shakespeare studies, see my "Shakespeare's Words of the Future: Promising *Richard III*," *Textual Practice*, 19.1 (2005): 13–30. For a broader discussion, see Jeremy Tambling, *On Anachronism* (Manchester: Manchester University Press, 2010).
8. Let me signal from the outset my sympathy with Nicholas Royle's reading of the "to" and "today" in this play in "The Poet: *Julius Caesar* and the Democracy to Come," in *In Memory of Jacques Derrida* (Edinburgh: Edinburgh University Press, 2009), pp. 1–20.
9. On the implications of this use of "now" and especially its negative forms, see Nicholas Royle, "Not Now," in *In Memory of Jacques Derrida*, pp. 21–37.

10. Marjorie Garber, *Shakespeare After All* (New York: Anchor Books, 2005), p. 411.
11. See for example, the discussion in Cary DiPietro and Hugh Grady, "Presentism, Anachronism, and the Case of *Titus Andronicus*," *Shakespeare: A Journal*, 8.1 (2012): 44–73.
12. See, most obviously, Jacques Rancière, *Le Partage du sensible: Esthétique et politique* (Paris: La Fabrique, 2000); *The Politics of Aesthetics: The Distribution of the Sensible*, trans. Gabriel Rockhill (London: Continuum, 2004). See also Mark Robson, "Jacques Rancière's Aesthetic Communities," *Paragraph*, 28.1 (2005): 77–95.
13. Rancière's fullest elaboration of this is to be found in *Aisthesis: Scènes du régime esthétique de l'art* (Paris: Galilée, 2011).
14. For less schematic surveys, see Hugh Grady, "Shakespeare Studies, 2005: A Situated Overview," *Shakespeare: A Journal*, 1.1 (2005): 102–20; and Lucy Munro, "Shakespeare and the Uses of the Past: Critical Approaches and Current Debates," *Shakespeare: A Journal*, 7.1 (2011): 102–25.
15. Hugh Grady, *Shakespeare and Impure Aesthetics* (Cambridge: Cambridge University Press, 2009), p. 33.
16. Grady, *Shakespeare and Impure Aesthetics*, p. 223.
17. This is not to say that it is a play without love. See Hélène Cixous, "What is it o'clock? or The Door (We Never Enter)," trans. Catherine A. F. MacGillivray, in *Stigmata: Escaping Texts* (London: Routledge, 1998), pp. 57–83.
18. Hannu Poutiainen, "Autoapotropaics: *Daimon* and *Psuché* between Plutarch and Shakespeare," *Oxford Literary Review*, 34.1 (2012): 51–70.
19. I have discussed these examples in, respectively, "In the Bitter Letter (A Rendition of *Othello*)," *Oxford Literary Review*, 34.1 (2012): 89–108; "'An empty body, a ghost, a pale incubus': Shakespeare, Lacan and the Future Anterior," *Shakespeare Yearbook*, 19 (2010): 55–74; and *The Sense of Early Modern Writing: Rhetoric, Poetics, Aesthetics* (Manchester: Manchester University Press, 2006), ch. 7.
20. See Robson "In the Bitter Letter," p. 94.
21. For a fuller treatment of early modern attitudes to suicide, see Mark Robson, "General Introduction," *The History of Suicide in England 1650–1850*, 8 vols (London: Pickering and Chatto, 2011), 1: vii–xxvi.
22. This is a major thread in my *Untimely Death: Contemporary Culture in a Time of Suicide* (forthcoming).
23. *Shakespeare's Plutarch. B.Litt. Vol. 1: Containing the Main Sources of Julius Caesar*, trans. Thomas North, ed. C. F. Tucker Brooke (London: Chatto and Windus, 1909), p. 163.
24. Poutiainen, "Autoapotropaics," p. 64.

Index

Note: 'n.' after a page reference refers to a note number on that page.

Adams, Joseph Quincy, 151
Adorno, Theodor, 3, 172, 185
aesthetics, 173–4, 178–86, 182, 184–6, 194, 197, 206
and politics, 199
Africanus, Leo, 28
Agamben, Giorgio, 3, 61
Agas Map of London, 131
anachronism, 10–11, 12, 13, 15, 17–22, 23, 193, 205–6
Arcadia (Sir Philip Sidney), 19, 88
Arendt, Hannah, 61–4, 65–9 (*passim*), 73, 77–8
Ariès, Philippe, 179–80
artisanship, 60–2, 65–6, 69, 78–9
Auden, W. H., xii–xiii

Barton, John, xviii
Benjamin, Walter, 3, 22, 174, 194
and historical allegory, 10, 12–14
Trauerspiel, 10, 22, 176
Blackfriars theatre, 86
Bloch, Ernst, 187 n.18
Breughel, Pieter the Elder, xiii, xxi
Burns, Ken, 143
Butterfield, Herbert, *see The Whig Interpretation of History*

capitalism, 68–9, 103–5, 107, 114, 117, 136
Carr, E. H., xiv
cartography, 30, 85, 87
Clark, Sir George, xiv
Cleopatra (in *Antony and Cleopatra*), 178–9, 180

commons, the (common-field lands, agriculture), 105–6, 109, 110–14, 121–2
enclosure of, 105–6, 110–15 (*passim*), 116, 119–20, 128, 136
court masques, 86
craft(work), *see* artisanship
Croce, Benedetto, xix, 8 n.7
Cultural Materialism, 4, 45

death, 179–82, 196–7, 202–3
Derrida, Jacques, 3, 12, 15–17, 191–2
dwellings, 61, 64, 66, 77–9, 118
see also space, architectural
Discourse on the Commonweal of this Realm of England (Thomas Smith), 110
DIY movement, *see* artisanship
Dryden, John, xv

Eagleton, Terry, 40
early modernity, 62, 84–5, 104–5
ecocriticism, 3, 104, 127–8, 129
see also green economics
ecological issues, 91, 103–9, 113–14, 127–8
in early modern England, 112, 135–6
see also hydraulic fracturing
ecology, 61, 66, 72, 85–6, 91–2
ekphrasis, 20, 22, 86, 88
Elizabeth I, xx, 26, 27, 89, 136
environmentalism, xv, xvii, 86, 91–2, 94, 103–7, 126–7
see also ecocriticism, ecology, green economics
environmental issues, *see* ecological issues

The Faerie Queene (Edmund Spenser), 19, 88, 89, 141
feminist criticism, 3, 52–3
Fernie, Ewan, 7 n.5, 32 n.17, 56 n.4
Fish, Stanley, 40
Florio, John, 89
Foucault, Michel, 175
  see also power
Forrest, Edwin, 158, 160
Freud, Sigmund, xv, 45
Frost, Robert, 159
Fukuyama, Francis, 172
future, the, 196–7

Gajowski, Evelyn, 7 n.5, 32 n.10, 57 n.4
gardening (early modern), 128–31
Gascoigne, George, 19
Geertz, Clifford, 39–40
globalization, 105
Globe theatre, 74, 86, 90, 162
Golding, Arthur, 21
Gore, Al, 2, 126
Grady, Hugh, 3–4, 7 n.5, 39, 56 n.4, 81 n.42, 101 n.26, 195–6
Gramsci, Antonio, 68
Greenblatt, Stephen, 39–40
green economics, 104, 106–7, 111, 113, 114, 117, 120
Greg, W. W., 42, 53

Hagen, Uta, 160
Haklyut, Richard, 28
Hall, Peter, xviii
Hawkes, David, 121
Hawkes, Terence, 3–4, 7 n.5, 33 n.17, 56 n.4, 174
Heidegger, Martin, 64, 66, 75, 85, 95, 97
  see also Phenomenology
Herder, Johann Gottfried, 5
historicism, 3, 4, 5–6, 8 n.7, 24, 35 n.25, 40, 195
  see also New Historicism, Cultural Materialism

history
  and the interpretation of literature, xii–xiv, 5, 8 n.7, 10, 13–14, 22, 23
  according to Derrida, 15–17
  construction of, xii, xiii–xv, xix, xi, 38–9
  see also historicism, neoclassicism, Presentism
Hockney, David, xxi
Howard, Jean, 183
Huckleberry Finn (Mark Twain), 149, 150, 160
hydraulic fracturing (fracking), 91, 127, 142–3

imprese, 51
An Inconvenient Truth (book/film), 2, 126
interpretation, 201–2, 204

Jones, Inigo, 86
Jonson, Ben, 1

King, Martin Luther Jr., 2
Kott, Jan, 175, 187 n.6
Kyd, Thomas, 20
Kyoto Protocol, 126

Lamb, Charles, 166
  see also Tales from Shakespeare
land stewardship, 94, 96–7, 112, 126–7, 128–32, 135
Latimer, Hugh, 110
Lefebvre, Henri, 92–4
Lever, Thomas, 110
Lily's Grammar, 18
Livy, 13
locus, 96
Longus, 20
Lukács, Georg, 175

Machiavelli, Niccolò, 175, 176, 177
Manners, Francis, Sixth Earl of Rutland, 51
maps, *see* cartography

MacCallum, M. W., 206
Macready, William Charles, 158
Marlowe, Christopher, *see Tamburlaine*
Marx, Karl, xv, 114, 175
Marxist criticism, 3, 41, 42, 45, 172, 173
Merleau-Ponty, Maurice, 85
McKerrow, R. B., 53, 54
medieval drama, 84
Middleton, Thomas, *see Your Five Gallants*
Millington, Thomas, 43
modernism, 45
modernity, 9, 24, 84–5
  see also early modernity
modernization, 85
Montaigne, Michel de, 89
More, Thomas, *see Utopia*

National Endowment for the Arts (US), 153, 158–62, 166
Nature Theater of Oklahoma, xix, 149–58, 162–7
neoclassicism, 19, 21
New Bibliography, 42, 45–6, 53, 55
New Criticism, 5, 153
new economics, xvii, 107–8, 109
  New Economics Movement, 104, 108–9
  see also green economics
New Historicism, 3–5, 39
  see also historicism, history and the interpretation of literature
New Textualism, 42, 44, 53, 55
News from Nowhere (William Morris), 105

Obama, Barack, 2, 126, 127
Olivier, Sir Laurence, 153
Orientalism, 12, 23–5
Ovid, 12, 13, 19–21

The Painful Adventures of Pericles Prince of Tyre (George Wilkins), 49, 50

pastoralism, 19–20, 85, 88–9, 91, 94, 95
Pavier, Thomas, 43
Peacham, Henry, 17–18, 20
Peele, George, 27
  The Battle of Alcazar, 27–8, 29–30
Phenomenology, 64–5, 85–6
place
  affective attachments to, 83, 86, 92, 95, 118
  representations of, 86, 90–1
  theories of, 85, 91, 94–5
  see also dwellings, space, *locus* and *platea*
platea, 96
Poe, Edgar Allen, 157
Ponet, John, 110
Pope, Alexander, xv
Postcolonialism, 23
Post-modernism, 42, 45, 53, 172–3
Poutiainen, Hannu, 196
power, 91, 96, 138, 174, 175–6, 178, 183, 196
Presentism, xiv–xxi (*passim*), 4–5, 9–12, 14, 23, 38–9, 41–3, 53, 55, 56–7 n.4, 127–8, 195
  see also Shakespeare's presentism
Profumo, John, xviii–xix
Puttenham, George, 19

Queer Studies, 39

Rancière, Jacques, 194–5
Ranke, Leopold von, 38–9
Rose theatre, 21, 44
Rowse, A. L., xx

Said, Edward, 23–5
Schmitt, Carl, 3, 173–4, 186 n.3
Seneca, 12, 20
Shakespeare, William
  anachronisms, 12, 13, 18, 20, 22
  and allegory, 13, 19, 129, 131
  and editorial practice, 41–3, 49–56 (*passim*)
  see also New Bibliography

Shakespeare, William – *continued*
  and education, 151–3
  and history, xiii–xiv, 2, 191
  and/in the present, xiii, 1–3, 9, 192, 197–8
  and suicide, 203–5
  and timelessness/timeliness, 1–2, 9–10
  Antony and Cleopatra, xvii, 174–82
  As You Like It, 88, 105, 115–16, 117–20
  Hamlet, 15, 44, 48, 54, 55, 153
  1 Henry IV, xx, 138
  Henry V, xx
  Julius Caesar, xvii, 175–6, 188–207
  King Lear, 44, 153, 166
  Macbeth, 72
  Measure for Measure, 48
  A Midsummer Night's Dream, 88
  Othello, 28–9, 44
  Pericles, xvi, 49–53, 60–2, 66–79
  Richard II, xv–xvi, 126, 128–42, 143–4
  Richard Duke of York (3 Henry VI), 43–4, 45–8
  Romeo and Juliet, xix, 45, 52, 54, 55, 149–58, 162–7, 192
  The Taming of the Shrew, 45
  The Tempest, xvi, 76, 84
  Titus Andronicus, 9, 11–15, 17–23, 28–31
  Twelfth Night, 48
  The Wars of the Roses, xviii
    see also Barton, John and Hall, Peter
  The Winter's Tale, xvii, 74, 182–6
Shakespeare in American Communities (NEA), 152, 153, 158–62
Shakespeare's presentism, 13, 19
Sidney, Sir Philip, *see Arcadia*
slavery, 27
Smith, Thomas, *see Discourse on the Commonweal of this Realm of England*

space
  architectural, 61, 63, 65, 75, 76
  as environment, 61, 65, 68–70, 78
  Cartesian, 85
  theatrical, 64, 65, 67–8, 71, 74, 84
  theories of, 65, 92–5
Spenser, Edmund, *see The Faerie Queene*
Strachey, William, 89
Stevens, Wallace, 180
Stukely, Thomas, 27–8

Tamburlaine (Christopher Marlowe), 30
Tales from Shakespeare (Mary and Charles Lamb), 153
terrorism, 12, 22, 23, 24, 31, 37 n.44, 173
transhumanism, 83
Tribble, Evelyn, 65–6, 74
Twain, Mark, xix, 149, 153, 166
  see also *Huckleberry Finn*

usury, 121
Utopia (Thomas More), 89, 105, 114–15

Virgil, 19, 20, 88
virtual reality, 84, 90

West Side Story (film), 153, 154
The Whig Interpretation of History (Herbert Butterfield), 39
Wilkins, George, 66
  see also *The Painful Adventures of Pericles Prince of Tyre*
William Shakespeare's Romeo + Juliet (film), 154
Williams, Carlos Williams, xiii

Your Five Gallants (Thomas Middleton), 51

Printed and bound in the United States of America